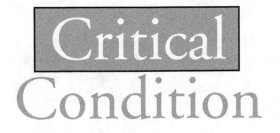

Critical
Condition

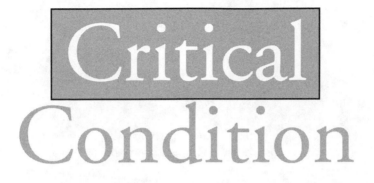

Critical Condition

HOW HEALTH CARE IN AMERICA BECAME BIG BUSINESS— AND BAD MEDICINE

Donald L. Barlett and
James B. Steele

DOUBLEDAY

NEW YORK LONDON TORONTO SYDNEY AUCKLAND

To every American who deserves better health care.

PUBLISHED BY DOUBLEDAY
a division of Random House, Inc.

DOUBLEDAY and the portrayal of an anchor with a dolphin are
registered trademarks of Random House, Inc.

Copyright © 2004 by Donald L. Barlett and James B. Steele

Book design by Chris Welch

Library of Congress Cataloging-in-Publication Data
Barlett, Donald L.
Critical condition : how health care in America became big business—and bad
medicine / by Donald L. Barlett and James B. Steele.—1st ed.
p.   cm.
Includes bibliographical references and index.
1. Medical care, Cost of—United States. 2. Insurance, Health—United States.
3. Medical policy—United States. 4. Medical economics—United States.
5. Medical care—United States.   I. Steele, James B. II. Title.
RA410.53.B37 2004
362.1′0973—dc22   2004055288

ISBN 0-385-50454-3

All Rights Reserved

PRINTED IN THE UNITED STATES OF AMERICA

November 2004

3 5 7 9 10 8 6 4

Contents

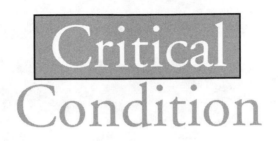

Critical
Condition

The Crisis

You are standing in line at a supermarket to buy a box of Cheerios. You notice that the two customers in front of you are making the same purchase. The cashier rings up the first box at $5.41, just as advertised in the newspaper. But when the second box is scanned, the price registers $6.76. Strange, you think. Even more strange, the customer doesn't seem to notice the difference. Then it's your turn. The cashier scans the box, and the price flashes $29.92. Why would anyone pay more than five times as much as another person for an identical box of cereal? They wouldn't. But when it comes to health care, you don't have any choice. And that's precisely the kind of spread that hospitals use in selling their services. Except you don't know it—it's their secret.

When you hear a politician, an economist, a corporate executive, talk about the wonders of the free market in health care, they neglect to mention that the system is rigged in a way that would not be tolerated in the sale of any other consumer product. In the supermarket, you know precisely what every other customer pays for a box of cereal or can of soup. But in the health care industry, that information is difficult, often impossible, to come by. Health care providers can—and do—charge one customer five times, in some cases even ten times, as much as another.

At least in the supermarket you have a choice of whether to pay the going price. When it comes to the cancer treatment you need to live or the emergency care your sick child requires in the middle of the night, you have no choice.

Welcome to health care in America, a system in which the person you work for, or don't, determines what you pay for medical services. A corporate executive, a clerk for a Fortune 500 company, and a retiree on Medicare generally pay the least. The self-employed, people unable to secure insurance because of preexisting conditions, the working poor, and folks who make too much money to qualify for government-paid Medicaid—but not enough to afford health insurance—are charged top dollar. If they are hospitalized and don't happen to have an extra $10,000, $50,000, or $100,000 tucked away, they can put at least part of the tab on their credit cards, as they are advised to do by health care providers, and pay an additional 17 percent in interest. Or they can have their wages attached. If they manage to scrape together enough money to buy health insurance, the insurance companies will charge them more than anyone else, too.

Over the last few decades, American health care has radically changed. A system that was largely not-for-profit has become a field where the profit motive and market forces affect every decision. Publicly held corporations answerable to stockholders decide which doctor you may see, how much medication you can take, whether you can be evaluated by a specialist, whether you qualify for a test, how long you stay in a hospital, how many therapy sessions—physical or psychiatric—you may attend. Patients wait months for appointments that once could be made in days. Their medical condition is evaluated by clerks with no medical training. Patients who are so sick that they meet the strict criteria for hospitalization are discharged before they are well, despite the protests of their doctors.

And these are the lucky ones—the ones who have health insurance. Beyond them are forty-four million others, their numbers growing, who do not. They are working Americans who can't afford to pay the premiums, or who live in an area where there are no providers, or who are viewed by insurers as high-risk liabilities. These are the people who don't seek help unless they are critically ill, who postpone a test or a surgical procedure until their condition is acute, or who, because they are embarrassed by their inability to pay, put off treatment until it's too late. Of these, 18,000 die every year.

Beyond the forty-four million are tens of millions more who are underinsured. They have marginal coverage. Faced with serious illness or injury, they would be wiped out. And beyond them are tens of millions more who have what they believe is high-quality health insurance, but who in fact would lose their life savings and be forced into bankruptcy if they or a family member came down with a debilitating disease or chronic condition.

American health care has become a lottery. If you work for a large company that provides generous benefits, you win; if you work for a small company or as an independent contractor, you lose. You may be working hard at a job important to society—as a teacher's aide or as an assistant at a daycare center or a nursing home—but that doesn't mean a thing when you get sick. In health care, equal treatment doesn't exist.

Politicians love to say that the United States has the best health care system in the world. In truth, it doesn't come close. Certainly, no one disputes that the nation has many talented, highly trained professionals who work with the latest equipment, who are knowledgeable and capable of delivering first-rate care. But what kind of system shuts out forty-four million Americans? What kind of system excludes people with illnesses beyond their control? What kind of system insures a husband but denies coverage to his wife? What kind of system forces people to choose between risking financial ruin and risking their lives?

Much of the turmoil is a direct result of a national policy to run health care like a business, a misguided notion promoted by Washington over the last two decades that the free market and for-profit health care would restrain costs and bring high-quality care to all. On both counts, the experiment has failed miserably. In the meantime, tens of billions of dollars—money that could have gone into patient care—has been drained from consumers and corporate subscribers and transferred to investors, executives, and others who have a stake in perpetuating this myth.

The result is a chaotic system that has shifted its focus from saving lives to saving dollars, one that discourages preventive medicine and rewards overtesting and overmedicating; a system that allows insurers to reject those most likely to require medical attention and keep only the healthiest; a system where six times as many people die from medical mistakes as from HIV/AIDS; a system that forces doctors to spend as much time negotiating with insurers over referrals and fees as they do treating patients.

America's health care system is totally out of whack. Insurers pay for medication to improve a man's erection and deny coverage for women's birth control pills. Taxpayers subsidize the cost of pharmaceutical research and then pay more than anybody else in the world for the drugs produced through that research. Government imposes needlessly cumbersome regulations on health care facilities, then withholds the resources that would enable them to comply. Wall Street rewards investors who acquire health care properties and then cut staff and services to make the facilities more attractive to the next buyer. American companies that do business in the global marketplace are forced to absorb costs their international competitors don't face. Doctors who make mistake after mistake are seldom sanctioned, driving up the malpractice insurance premiums of all the good doctors. Hospitals charge the highest prices to those least able to pay.

Not surprisingly, in a system so complicated and unwieldy, involving so much money, health care is riddled with fraud and abuse. Nursing homes bill Medicare for "therapy sessions" that consist of seating patients in front of a TV. When hospitals feed patients, they charge it off as "social skills group therapy sessions." Insurers cheat patients and doctors; patients cheat doctors and insurers; doctors cheat insurers and patients; and all cheat federal and state governments.

The entry of for-profit, business-minded companies into health care was supposed to make it more efficient. Instead, it's given us the world's largest, costliest health care bureaucracy, engulfed by red tape and maddening complexity. The average American spends countless hours on the telephone correcting billing mistakes, arranging medical appointments, obtaining test results, or securing referrals—an exercise in frustration that cumulatively costs the economy billions of dollars in lost time. As a result, costs once borne by insurers have been transferred to you. In some areas of the country, waiting times for routine tests such as mammograms stretch into months. Too often, treatment delayed means care denied.

Rather than health care for everyone, the free market has given us huge corporations with multibillion-dollar market caps, presided over by the new corporate royalty, whose names regularly appear among America's highest-paid executives.

Although the system richly rewards some, it fails to protect its most vulnerable citizens. It discourages doctors from practicing in rural areas, where specialists are in such short supply that low-income children must depend on volunteer physician airlifts from big cities to perform tonsillectomies and other routine procedures. At the same time, the system has made it possible for unscrupulous practitioners to victimize elderly patients by performing painful, dangerous procedures that are unnecessary but highly profitable.

It's no secret that health care in America is in crisis. In interviews for this book over the last five years, patients, doctors, nurses, and other professionals expressed deep despair. People who have health insurance worry they will lose it. People who don't have it feel that they are just a hope and a prayer away from disaster. Middle-aged parents who didn't think twice about health care coverage when they were in their twenties wonder how their young adult children will pay for it. Many of the new jobs being created offer only minimal benefits or none at all. Corporate layoffs have converted full-time employees with health coverage into independent contractors with no benefits. Retirees, once promised health care insurance for life by their former employers, worry about what will happen as companies scale back or revoke the coverage at the time they most need it.

The level of anxiety rises and falls from family to family and from region to region because health care delivery varies from house to house and from coast to coast. In some areas, doctors and nurses are reasonably content; elsewhere they are quitting. Some physicians encourage bright young students to enter medicine; others urge them to become lawyers or Wall Street bankers. Some hospitals are succeeding; others are on the brink of bankruptcy. Malpractice costs are a flash point in some states and aren't much of a factor in others. Some patients are at peace with their insurers, while others are engaged in a constant war.

But everywhere there is uneasiness. Almost everyone knows somebody who has experienced the reality of what health care has become—a friend or relative who has no coverage, a young person who can't pay the premiums, a parent whose child needs expensive specialized treatment, or an elderly person who can't afford prescription drugs. "Why should people have to worry about their health care, something this basic?" asks a retired Colorado executive who has lived in Europe and Asia and who has seen the national health care systems of other nations. "No other country permits this. It's a crime."

Equally appalling, the United States spends more on health care than any other nation—15.3 percent of gross domestic product in 2003. That's a greater percentage than Germany, France, Japan, Italy, Canada, and other developed societies spend to cover all their citizens. In those countries with universal coverage, no one has to think twice about seeking care if they become ill. No one loses his home. No one goes bankrupt.

Most Americans sense that access to health care is narrowing, that quality is declining, and that this downward spiral will continue as costs rise and as insurers and corporations shift more of the expense to individuals. In the face of federal neglect, some states are trying to fashion solutions to deal with these mounting problems. But this is a national breakdown that will require a national solution.

As long as Washington remains wedded to the illusion that market-based medicine will cure health care's woes, tens of billions of dollars a year will continue to vanish in waste, inefficiency, fraud, and in profits to companies that make money by denying care.

It doesn't have to be this way. America's health care crisis can be cured, and, unlike almost every other major challenge facing the nation, it can be solved without spending more money. We already invest enough of our national wealth on medical care. The plan should be to treat this crisis as seriously as if it were an epidemic, and to redirect resources where they belong—into taking care of the health needs of every American.

A Second-Rate System

It was billed as a "Garage Sale for Mason." By the time all the donations had come in, no garage could hold them. So the clothes, toys, old appliances, tools, car accessories—everything—were loaded onto a church moving van and carted to an open lot next to the Heartland Furniture store on the south side of town. Volunteers marked every item with white price tags, then spread them out in the lot in row after row for the big event Saturday. Nobody had any idea how many would come, but when the gates opened, people poured in, and for hours neighbors, friends, and passersby flowed through to buy something and to say hello to the six-year-old boy in whose name the event was held.

Mason McIlnay was just completing kindergarten in Salem, Oregon, when doctors discovered that he had neuroblastoma, an aggressive childhood cancer that already had spread to his bone marrow. He had been troubled by pain at night, and at first his doctor thought he might have just pulled a muscle. A CT scan turned up the cancer. Over the next two months, Mason would be in and out of the hospital for surgery, chemotherapy, and treatment of infections and side effects, as he battled a famously virulent cancer. His medical expenses ran into the tens of thousands of dollars.

It was a bill that Mason's parents, Les and Gina McIlnay, could not afford to pay. They had no health insurance. As employees of the family flower shop, with a computer and video business on the side, they felt they just couldn't afford it. "You never consider that something like this would ever happen to you," said Les.

Friends and neighbors of the McIlnays got together to organize a fund-raiser for the family. Everyone pitched in, searching basements, storage bins, and closets to donate something for the "Garage Sale for Mason." That afternoon they raised $14,000. Another fund-raiser at a car show brought in $9,000. The McIlnays were humbled. Les said he had "never seen an event like it." A Cub Scout leader and a volunteer along with Gina at their boys' school, Les was used to helping, not needing help, so the outpouring from the community was all the more remarkable. While the proceeds from the two events certainly eased the couple's financial burden, the McIlnays still had thousands of dollars in medical expenses outstanding.

Every weekend in neighborhoods across America, fund-raisers like this help collect money to pay someone's medical bills. They may be for a teenager who has a serious sports injury, a young mother who isn't covered by her husband's insurance policy, a victim of a catastrophic illness whose insurance has run out—anyone who has been blindsided by the overwhelming expenses of an unexpected major medical problem. These fund-raisers take many forms: auctions, walkathons, concerts, pancake breakfasts, bingo games, pie socials, car washes, barbecues, basketball competitions, church suppers, dances, and hot-air balloon rides.

In Simms, Montana, a colt, assorted livestock, and three tons of hay are auctioned off to assist with the medical expenses of horse trainer Lennard Rains, who was thrown through the windshield of his truck in an accident that paralyzed him from the chest down. In Fond du Lac, Wisconsin, a dance and raffle at the Elks Club raise money for chemotherapy treatments for Kyle Goebel, a seventeen-year-old high school senior who has bone cancer. In Quarryville, Pennsylvania, students and faculty of Solanco High School stage a variety show to benefit Meg Walck, a teacher's wife who is battling a rare cancer. In Estancia, New Mexico, a local band performs during a dinner at the Short Stop Cafe to raise money for six-year-old Kasey Solomon, who needs a heart transplant. In Belvidere, Illinois, police officers host an all-you-can-eat chili supper at the local VFW club for community-service officer Ray Edwards, who was left with medical bills after the death of his wife. In Asbury Park, New Jersey, musicians volunteer their talent for a concert to benefit Bernie Brausewetter, a blues guitarist who suffers from congestive heart failure.

In Minetto, New York, friends and colleagues of graphic artist Dan Distler organize a banquet and silent auction to help him pay his medical bills while he fights lung cancer. In Clifton Heights, Pennsylvania, guests pay $25 a person to attend a buffet featuring a DJ and a raffle, to defray the medical expenses of thirty-year-old Ken Fleischman Jr., who is undergoing chemotherapy to treat lymphoblastic lymphoma. In central Texas, 850 people turn out for a barbecue and auction at the Medina County Fair Hall to help with the medical expenses of sixteen-year-old Josh Schueling, a high school football player who broke his neck while making a tackle and became paralyzed below his chest. In Omaha, Nebraska, members of the community line up to pay five dollars a plate for a spaghetti dinner at the American Legion post to contribute to the cost of fifteen-year-old Jeff Spellman's kidney transplant. In Severna Park, Maryland, members of the Antioch Apostolic Church perform at a gospel songfest to help pay medical expenses for Henry Bundy, a twenty-five-year-old bakery worker who was diagnosed with a brain tumor. Near Tampa, Florida, students and staff at the Wesley Chapel Elementary School present "The True Story of the Three Little Pigs" in the school cafeteria to raise money for Stephanie Granier, a fifth-grader who has non-Hodgkin's lymphoma.

These outpourings represent the very best of America, the volunteer spirit of which the nation is justly proud, when friends, neighbors, families, and caring strangers come together to help someone in need. But what does it say about the richest country on earth that its citizens must depend upon raffles and spaghetti dinners to pay the medical bills—a situation that exists in no other civilized country? What does it say about members of Congress and presidents, Democrats and Republicans all, who are content with a health care system that ignores the needs of tens of millions of Americans while it makes multimillionaires out of those who profit from disease and death? What does it say about lawmakers and presidents who, along with their spouses and families, enjoy the very best that American health care has to offer, while they consign their constituents to a system that drives millions of sick people and their families into bankruptcy and poverty? And finally, what does it say about those lawmakers and presidents who refuse to overhaul a system that spends $1.7 trillion—that's *trillion*—on a health care system that overall is little better than mediocre.

American health care mediocre? Not if you believe the people in Washington. In June 2003, President George W. Bush told seniors in Miami: "We live in a great country that has got the best health care system in the world, and we need to keep it that way." That sounded much like former president Clinton, who, although he wanted to recast portions of the system, said in February 2000: "We do have the best health care system in the world . . . "

This is one of America's most enduring myths, that the United States has "world-class health care." It doesn't. To be sure, it does offer the very best of care to some folks. It does offer world-class high-tech surgery and some space-age medical procedures. But these benefit 2 or 3 percent of the population at most, along with the richest citizens of other countries who come here for the highly specialized treatment. Overall, isolated pockets of excellence aside, the system is second-rate when it comes to meeting basic day-in, day-out medical needs of the population at large.

Many countries around the world take far better care of their people, achieve better results from their health care systems, and do it all with far fewer dollars. In 2001, per capita health care spending in the United States amounted to $4,887. That was 75 percent more than the $2,792 that Canada spent. Yet Canadians can expect to live two and a half years longer than Americans. The Canadian life span at birth: 79.8 years. The American: 77.1 years. U.S. spending was 205 percent greater than Spain's, yet the Spanish can expect to live 2.1 years longer. As for the Japanese, with a life span of 80.9 years, the world's longest, they can expect to live nearly four years longer than Americans. This even though Japan's per capita spending on health care is only 41 percent of U.S. outlays. In sum, Americans pay for a Hummer but get a Ford Escort.

On this scale, the United States does not even rank in the top ten. But the statistics are even grimmer when life span is counted in years of healthy living. A comparatively new yardstick devised by the World Health Organization (WHO), this formula subtracts from traditional life expectancy the number of years spent in poor health, the years when individuals are unable to engage in all the activities their peers do, when they are confined to beds in nursing homes and must be fed by someone else. By this measure, the United States in 2002 ranked a distant 29th among the countries of the world, between Slovenia and Portugal.

At birth, American males can anticipate 67.2 healthy years of life. But the men in Sweden fare better. They get another 4.7 years, even though the country spends less than half per capita what the United States does on health care. Italian women enjoy 74.7 years of healthy living at birth, while for American women it's 3.4 fewer years. The women in San Marino, an enclave in central Italy that bills itself as the world's oldest republic, do even better. They can plan on 75.9 years of healthy living—or 4.6 years longer than American women. Men in Iceland may expect a healthy life for 72.1 years, or 4.9 years longer than American men. This even though Iceland's per capita spending on health care is little more than half that of the United States.

The United States also compares poorly with other industrialized countries in infant mortality, with 6.9 deaths per 1,000 live births in 2000. In Japan, it was 3.2; in Sweden, 3.4; in France, 4.6; in Denmark, 5.3.

And in a more revealing WHO global ranking of health care, the United States placed even farther down the list at No. 37—between Costa Rica and Slovenia, nowhere near the top five countries, France, Italy, San Marino, Andorra, and Malta.

How is this possible, especially since the United States devotes 15.3 percent of its gross domestic product to health care—double that of many countries, triple of some? The WHO survey considered two factors the U.S. government and health care community ignore: Does everyone have access? Is the cost distributed equitably across all of society? WHO reasoned that "a fairly financed health system ensures financial protection for everyone. Health systems can be unfair by either exposing people to large, unexpected costs they must pay on their own or by requiring those least able to pay for care to contribute more, proportionately, than wealthier citizens." On that score, Americans have little competition. "The United States and South Africa are seen as the only prominent examples of industrialized countries that do not have comprehensive social health insurance."

Thereby rests the second most enduring American myth: that all citizens have access to the highest-quality care if they really need it. Again, in isolated instances this is true. Some of Baltimore's inner-city poor get the very best medical care America has to offer at Johns Hopkins, albeit as winners of a kind of sickness lottery. The same is true in

select other cities. But the overwhelming majority of people, especially
the working poor and middle-income families—including those with
insurance—can get that care only if they make draconian sacrifices.
They must be willing to lose everything.

RAMPANT OVERCHARGING

Almost everybody knows that a hospital stay can be hazardous to your
financial health if you don't have insurance. What isn't so well known
is that hospitals charge the highest prices to those who don't have
insurance. In other words, those least able to pay are charged the most.
In a system riddled with inequities, this may be the most egregious.

Hospitals have a so-called official price list for their services. It's the
equivalent of a sticker price on a car. Big health insurers, health maintenance organizations (HMOs), and Medicare negotiate to obtain volume discounts off those rates, so they pay only a fraction of a hospital's
official price. Studies show an uninsured person who is not backed by
the muscle of a pool is billed three, four, five, sometimes as much as
ten times more than an insurance company whose patient has the
exact same treatment.

OU Medical Center in Oklahoma City, Oklahoma, charged an
uninsured patient $85,400 for a craniotomy. A typical insurer would
have paid $15,600 for the same procedure. Medicare would have paid
$13,900. For the unfortunate Oklahoma patient, the bill represented a
447 percent premium over the price an insured patient would have
been charged and 514 percent over Medicare. The OU Medical Center
is part of the country's largest for-profit hospital chain, HCA Inc.

Florida Hospital in Orlando, Florida, charged an uninsured patient
$35,200 for an appendectomy. A typical insurer would have paid the
hospital $7,000 for the same procedure. Medicare would have paid
$6,200. For the uninsured Florida patient, the bill represented a 403

percent premium over the price an insured patient would have been charged, and 468 percent over Medicare. The hospital is part of the Adventist Health System, which is owned and operated by the Seventh-Day Adventist Church.

The Medical Center of Aurora in Aurora, Colorado, charged an uninsured patient $24,100 for cranial and peripheral nerve disorder treatment. The average insurer would have paid $4,600 for the same care. Medicare would have paid $4,100. For the hapless Colorado patient, the bill was a 424 percent premium over the price an insured patient would have been charged and 488 percent over Medicare. The Medical Center of Aurora is an acute-care hospital in the eastern metropolitan Denver area that is part of a joint operation by HCA and HealthONE, the largest health care delivery system in the metropolitan Denver area.

Every type of hospital—for-profit, nonprofit, community, and university—takes advantage of our most vulnerable citizens in this way. The victims are Americans who work at low-paying jobs and fall between the economic cracks, folks who earn a little too much money to qualify for Medicaid or charity, but not enough to afford the stiff premiums for health insurance. Even middle-income families who are insured can find themselves confronting huge bills from an unsympathetic hospital if they have a catastrophic medical expense not covered by their plans. Unlike the very poor, who have few if any assets, many middle-class families have salaries, savings accounts, and homes—assets that hospitals aggressively pursue.

This practice of gouging the uninsured and those with limited coverage would probably have remained a secret to all but hospital insiders had it not been for the work of a crusading activist, Kevin Brendan Forbes.

Half Irish and half Chilean, K.B., as he is known, was raised Hispanic in a working-class family in the Los Angeles suburb of San

Marino. His Irish father was a printer and union organizer. His mother, a Chilean immigrant, was a hospital social worker.

After college in Los Angeles, Forbes dabbled in journalism and taught English as a second language near Watts before gravitating to politics, where he worked in a series of conservative Republican campaigns. He served as Pat Buchanan's press officer in his bid for the Conservative Party nomination for president in 1996. Two years later, he signed on in a similar role for billionaire Steve Forbes (no relation) when he made a run for the White House. In the political arena, K.B. learned to frame issues and attract press coverage, skills that he would later use helping hospital victims, "people who have no voice."

In 2001, Forbes latched on to the issue that would soon make him the bane of hospital corporations and administrators across America. He remembers to this day how it happened:

He and some friends were at a bar in Long Beach talking about the problem of the uninsured. Someone mentioned a sister, a young woman about nineteen, who had recently been in an automobile accident. She had been banged around by the impact and suffered cuts and bruises. As Forbes recalled, the woman had been hospitalized for "one night, two days, something to that effect, and was charged over $23,000. Unbelievable! We were just astounded."

He decided that something had to be done to educate people about the issue. He and a couple of friends first tried to interest Hispanic organizations but got no takers. "So we decided to start our own group."

Initially, Forbes's ad hoc committee garnered some publicity from Spanish-language media in Los Angeles, which produced stories about other Hispanics who faced similarly outsized hospital bills. He spent the next three months burning up the Los Angeles freeways, driving some 8,000 miles to speak to groups, to gather information from patients who had received oversized bills, and to collect data comparing hospital bills of uninsured patients with those submitted for the same procedures on insured patients. In June 2001, Forbes issued his first report documenting that southern California hospitals were billing self-paying uninsured Latinos almost five times the amount they were charging HMOs. Forbes concluded that the hospitals charge huge fees "so that they can offer superficial discounts and arrange long-term payment plans while making a profit on the most vulnerable: the uninsured Latino."

The report generated another round of publicity, and leads began to pour in about similar practices elsewhere. Before long, Forbes's ad hoc committee evolved into Consejo de Latinos Unidos (Council of United Latinos), a public charity, though it was still a shoestring operation, working out of donated office space in East Los Angeles with Forbes its only full-time employee. Hispanics still comprised most of the cases, but its base began to broaden.

Investigations spread to San Antonio, Orlando, Philadelphia, St. Louis, New Orleans, Fort Myers, Denver, Chicago, Miami, and Oklahoma City. To develop a profile in each city, Forbes first visited the local courthouse, where he never failed to find cases, sometimes in the hundreds, of hospitals suing their patients and trying to seize their wages or homes. "Then we go door knocking," he said, to interview onetime patients and obtain copies of their medical bills. The pattern that had been so evident in Los Angeles—that working people bore the brunt of the overpricing—continued to hold.

In Chicago, Carlos Colon, a Home Depot clerk, had surgery at Our Lady of Resurrection Medical Center to remove what he thought was a cyst in his neck. A typical insurer would have paid $6,900; Medicare, $6,100. Colon was charged $74,396 for a one-week stay at the hospital, a 978 percent premium over the price the hospital would have billed for an insured patient. When Colon, who was supporting a family on less than $2,000 a month, could not pay a bill that was more than three times his annual earnings, the Catholic hospital sued and garnished his wages. Forbes estimated that it will take the young man, who must fork over $300 a month, at least twenty-five years to pay off the debt with interest. In Altamonte Springs, Florida, Lucia Floriana, an uninsured housekeeper, rushed to Florida Hospital one day because she feared she was "going to have a stroke or a heart attack." She was charged $10,542 for two days and was subsequently sued when she couldn't pay.

Forbes discovered to his astonishment that hospitals even inflated medical charges of their own employees and sued them when they couldn't pay. Isidro Valverde had delivered bed linens for years at Queen of Angels Medical Center in Los Angeles when his wife, Julia, was treated there for breast cancer in November 2000. She died in February 2001. Fourteen months later, Valverde received a bill for $7,000 covering his late wife's hospitalization. He had insurance, had paid a $500 deductible, and had taken each hospital bill to the business office for payment. For reasons that were never clear, a claim was rejected, signaling a nonpayment on the hospital's records. This put Valverde squarely in the hospital's litigation bull's-eye, and he was sued.

After a hospital visit, uninsured patients are stunned by the size of their bills. They have little warning it's going to be that large. When they were sick, they weren't focused on money; they were just trying to get well. Before the initial shock wears off, hospitals often follow up by offering a "discount" for the treatment. For example, if a patient pays in full within a specified period, such as sixty or ninety days, the hospital may offer to "discount" the bill by knocking $20,000 off a $60,000 total. The discounts are meaningless for most patients because the amount owed is still so far beyond their means, sometimes more than a year's salary. Hospitals then suggest that the patient use credit cards to pay the bill.

Some hospitals have full-time collection departments. Tenet Corporation has its own division called Syndicated Office Systems (SOS).

HCA farms out much of the work to the nation's largest debt collector, NCO Group Inc., a publicly held company based in the suburbs of Philadelphia. NCO collects all kinds of personal debts, including gambling debts, but has found the collection of hospital bills one of its most promising sectors. Michael Barrist, NCO's chief executive officer, told Wall Street analysts in 2003 that all the hospital chains were seeing a "huge" increase in delinquency and bad-debt write-off, which was good news for his company: "It's a common phenomenon which again we will benefit from in our traditional collection business and have been benefiting from."

NCO appears to have a special incentive to extract money from HCA patients. The company has what it calls a "long-term collection contract with a large client to provide collections services." NCO earns a "bonus" if collections exceed amounts it has guaranteed the client. Conversely, NCO is "required to pay the client if collections do not reach the guaranteed level."

With such a powerful inducement, NCO agents are masters at squeezing working families who are struggling with huge hospital bills. Early in 2004, the Jorge Silva family of Denver came face-to-face with the NCO collection machine. Two years earlier, Silva's wife, Alondra, had given birth to a baby girl at Presbyterian/St. Luke's Medical Center. Kaitey Deluna-Silva came into the world with defective bronchial tubes and required surgery to save her life. She was in the hospital for weeks. Presbyterian billed the family $213,802. Silva, a worker for a gravel company, wanted to make payments, but the hospital bill was more than six times what he earned in a year. Presbyterian/St. Luke's agreed to write off $85,521. On February 4, 2004, NCO proposed a "settlement":

> In an effort to assist you in resolving your account with Presbyterian/St. Luke's Med Center, we have been authorized to extend you an offer to settle your account as follows:

Pay the settlement amount of $128,281.26 by Mar 17, 2004.
This settlement has been calculated as follows:
Outstanding Account Balance: $213,802.10
Adjustment: $85,520.84
Settlement Amount: $128,281.26
If you choose to accept this offer to settle your account, please
return your payment with the stub below . . .
In the event you elect not to accept this offer our normal collec-
tion efforts will continue . . . If you would like to pay by credit card
or if you have any questions regarding this offer please call the num-
ber listed above. Thank you for your attention to this matter and we
sincerely hope you will take advantage of this offer.

That letter shows why health care providers and those members of
Congress who support the existing system are living in a fantasy world.
Let's suppose the Silvas could find a credit-card company willing to
accept a charge of $128,281, with a preferred-customer interest rate of
17 percent, and give the couple forty years to pay it off. Interest payments alone would add up to $648,872—or five times the proposed
discounted settlement. Combined interest and principal payments
would top out at $777,153. The Silvas would be indentured servants
for the rest of their lives. With annual credit-card payments of $21,833,
there would be just enough money left for food and a ghetto apart-
ment. But nothing else. No electricity. No heat. No telephone. No car.
No medicine. No movies. Nothing—for the next forty years.

The pressure that collection agents exert is intense. Patients and
their family members talk of receiving as many as four or five telephone calls a day at their jobs threatening them with legal action if
they don't pay promptly. They talk of intimidating letters that warn a
lien will be placed on the family home. They talk of visits from collection agents who force them to sign agreements they can't fulfill because

of their limited means. Even when they make payments, bill collectors harass them to pay more. Ultimately, many find their wages are garnished, or they are forced to file for bankruptcy. Some lose their homes.

It happened to Jack and Donna Brown, a Florida couple. Like many other food service workers, neither Jack, a cook, nor Donna, a waitress, had insurance when she entered Lee Memorial Hospital in Fort Myers for colon surgery. Later, complications forced her to be readmitted, and eventually her hospital charges came in at $57,000. That was more than the couple could afford to pay on their limited incomes. After the hospital sued them, the couple filed for bankruptcy and sold a home they were building. "We tried paying our medical bills," Jack Brown told Forbes. "I worked very hard. We lost a home because of this lawsuit."

While Forbes has uncovered scandalous pricing schemes in many types of hospitals—religious as well as nonsectarian—among the worst offenders, he says, are those affiliated with hospital giant HCA. The Nashville-based company typically charges individuals many times more than insurance companies pay for the same services, then relentlessly badgers patients by threatening them with liens or seizures and forcing them to turn over substantial portions of their wages. The HCA cases, Forbes says, are "the most appalling stories the Consejo has ever documented."

Betty Cosgrave, a retired seamstress in Sanford, Florida, went to HCA's Central Florida Regional Medical Center in pain from an apparent gallstone attack. Ultrasound confirmed the presence of gallstones, but after the hospital learned that she did not have insurance, she was sent home. Nevertheless, she got a $2,400 bill for her eight-hour visit. Although she was living on a meager fixed income, she agreed to pay $20 a month. Then the bill collectors started harassing her to increase her payments, which she was unable to do. "They would tell me that if I did not pay them the money they were going to take me to court," she told Forbes.

An Oklahoma City auto mechanic, Russell Cox, sought treatment as an outpatient for a broken ankle at HCA's OU Medical Center and was charged $14,217, a figure easily ten times greater than an insured outpatient would have been charged. HCA offered a "discount" if Cox would pay $1,099.40 a month for six months. When he was unable to do so, the hospital sued him.

Why do hospitals charge the uninsured more? They claim they don't. In the twisted logic of hospital financing, they say the uninsured just don't get group rates like everyone else. A hospital association official told the *Miami Herald*: "They [the uninsured] don't pay higher rates. It's that they don't get discounts. That's the whole concept of group purchasing. You negotiate a deal. Individuals don't get the deal. This is not rocket science, and it's not new to economics." It also just happens to be good business. Extracting cash from the uninsured has become a major source of revenue. Forbes calculated that HCA alone overcharged the uninsured by $2.1 billion in 2002. The financial incentive has driven the trend steadily up during the last decade. Hospitals say it isn't all their fault, that under the U.S. system, where some people have coverage and others don't, hospitals sometimes get stuck with the bill. Hospitals provide "$22 billion in care each year for which no one pays," says the American Hospital Association. The lack of universal health coverage leaves hospitals, insurers, and other members of the system fighting among themselves over the money that is there.

As long as the practice remains out of sight, hospitals will keep exploiting the uninsured. But when it has been exposed to public view, some individual institutions change course. For years, the prestigious Yale–New Haven Hospital, regularly ranked by *U.S. News & World Report* as one of the nation's best, attached wages, imposed liens, and repossessed homes of working families. After the policy became public in 2003, an embarrassed Yale backed away and said that henceforth it wouldn't impose liens and would go easier on those who owed money.

The hospital announced a new payment schedule giving the uninsured lower rates and, ever so quietly, withdrew most of the liens and closed some 3,200 delinquent accounts.

There have been some victories on behalf of the uninsured, but for K. B. Forbes there is still a long way to go. In the meantime, there are rewards. "I sleep real well at night," he said. "Not like these hospital executives."

WITHOUT A SAFETY NET

Everyone knows the basic statistics: Forty-four million Americans have no health insurance. That's equal to the combined populations of Massachusetts, Alabama, Oregon, Iowa, Connecticut, Mississippi, Vermont, Arkansas, West Virginia, Montana, Louisiana, Indiana, Maine, and Nebraska. Fourteen states in all—every man, woman, and child off the health care books. No other industrialized country would tolerate this. And the number of the uninsured keeps right on growing, along with the population.

In the late 1940s and early 1950s, President Harry S. Truman advocated a universal health care system to cover everyone. The medical establishment—principally the American Medical Association (AMA)—opposed it with such intensity that the idea went nowhere. The AMA's position drew strong support from those groups who saw the Red Menace everywhere. It was the Cold War era, and any proposal for government involvement on such a large scale was thought surely to be part of a Communist plot, although oddly no one seemed to pin the label on the nation's mandatory and publicly financed education system. Truman's successor, President Dwight D. Eisenhower, also opposed universal coverage for much the same reason, even though he personally had received government-paid health care for most of his life through the military and the Veterans Administration. Nonetheless, President

Eisenhower recognized the dilemma. "We know that the American people will not long be denied access to adequate medical facilities. And they should not be," Eisenhower said in 1954. "We cannot rest content knowing that modern health services are beyond the financial or physical reach of many millions of our fellow citizens. We must correct these defects."

But not too hurriedly. It wasn't until 1965 that President Lyndon B. Johnson pushed through legislation creating the two largest federal programs to deal with some of the uninsured: Medicare to cover everyone over the age of sixty-five and Medicaid for all those individuals and families living in poverty. Medicare was financed entirely by the federal government, with a payroll tax applied equally on all employers and employees. Medicaid's costs were shared by the federal government, out of general tax revenue, and the states.

For the first time, millions of Americans were protected by basic health insurance. The pressure was off, and the rest of the uninsured disappeared from view. It wasn't until 1980 that the country began to notice them again, in a study by the National Center for Health Services Research. Even the government agency was taken aback. "One surprise of this study was the large number of persons who reported being uninsured—26.6 million persons or about 12.6 percent of the civilian population," the center reported.

Still, Congress ignored the issue. By 1987, according to the Census Bureau, the ranks of the uninsured had swelled to "at least thirty-one million people and perhaps as many as thirty-seven million." Although the numbers bounced up and down through the years, the long-term trend moved in one direction only. By 2003, the uninsured population had grown to forty-four million.

Who are these people? For the most part, according to the Kaiser Commission on Medicaid and the Uninsured, they are between the ages of eighteen and sixty-five and come from low-income working families. Two-thirds have incomes below $30,000, which makes them too "wealthy" to qualify for Medicaid and much too poor to buy their own insurance. "Nearly 70 percent come from families where at least one person works full time and another 12 percent from families with part-time employment."

In addition to the forty-four million without insurance, there are tens of millions of people who are underinsured. They have insurance, but it does not come close to covering the costs they may incur if they become sick. It's sort of like having homeowner's insurance only to discover after your house burns down that it will pay to rebuild just one-fourth of it.

The exact number of Americans who are uninsured or inadequately insured is unknown, but it certainly exceeds 100 million. Yet perhaps the most misleading statistic of all is the number of Americans who do have health insurance. America's Health Insurance Plans, the industry trade association, puts the figure at 200 million. But this statistic is nearly meaningless, because it includes thousands of insurance plans with mammoth disparities in coverage. They range from the blue-chip plan that covers members of Congress and takes care of all their medical needs to high-deductible policies for working families who must shell out thousands of dollars a year in medical expenses before their policies pay one cent.

Health insurers have written all sorts of restrictions into their policies—loopholes, caps, exclusions—to minimize their exposure. They may write you a policy but decline to cover any expenses for a preexisting illness, the kind of protection people need most. If you lose your job or must drop out of school because of illness, you may lose your health insurance. While a government plan called COBRA allows workers whose jobs are terminated to buy an individual policy at the group rate of their former employers, in what often turns out to be the cruelest congressional hoax of all, even that rate is far more than the average worker can afford. If you are able to keep your policy during a major illness, you may find that it has a low cap that is exhausted in a matter of days of hospitalization. Moreover, according to The Commonwealth Fund, health insurers are implementing across-the-board plans to restrict coverage: "In addition to paying more for their care, many privately insured adults also report that their plans are cutting back or placing new limits on covered benefits."

Increasingly, the health-insurance industry is designed to shut out those who are perceived to be liabilities—or even potential liabilities. Corinne Cooper, professor emeritus of law at the University of Missouri–Kansas City, went into business for herself in Arizona after her academic career and struggled to obtain health coverage as the owner of a small business. She asks, "Is insurance only to protect the people who don't need it?"

Even those who have top-of-the-line health coverage find out belatedly that it's not enough when a major illness strikes.

A TEACHER LEARNS A LESSON

For most of her life, Lynn Oldham was in excellent health. An English teacher at Manasquan High School, a seaside community on the New Jersey coast sixty miles south of the tip of Manhattan, Oldham played tennis and sailed the area's scenic waterways that have long made that region off the Atlantic Coast a mecca for summer visitors. Like many school districts, Manasquan had a generous sick-day policy, but Oldham rarely made use of it.

Shortly before the start of the 2002 school year, when she was fifty-one, Oldham discovered a lump in her breast and her physician recommended that it be removed. Surgery was scheduled at Monmouth Medical Center in Long Branch. In October, Oldham took a few days off from teaching her ninth- and eleventh-grade English classes for the surgery. After the operation, her doctor gave her good news: The cancer had not spread. Although the prognosis was favorable, physicians recommended that she undergo chemotherapy and radiation as a precaution. Oldham wasn't worried: "I felt great, and I expected the chemotherapy to go very easily."

Her first treatment, on October 31, came off without incident. A week later, when she and her husband, Michael Granucci, were about to take a walk on the beach, something they often did, she didn't feel up to it. Her stomach hurt. That evening, the pain intensified, and in the middle of the night she woke Mike to tell him she was in agony. When she telephoned her oncologist, she was told to go immediately to the emergency room.

At Monmouth Medical Center, doctors determined that Oldham's intestine was paralyzed, a rare but not unheard-of side effect from chemotherapy. Her bowel had become blocked and had perforated. The rupture triggered an infection that was rampaging through her body, shutting down her organs. That weekend, while she was in the hospital, she suffered a heart attack and a stroke that paralyzed her left side. Her kidneys and lungs began to fail. Doctors hooked her up to a respirator and advised her husband to gather their family to say good-bye. The couple's four children and twenty other family members and friends rushed to the hospital. By then she was unconscious. Doctors scheduled bowel surgery for Sunday, emphasizing that it was highly risky.

Against the odds, she survived. She was in a coma for a month after the surgery, fed through a feeding tube, and even after she regained consciousness her condition remained grave for two months. She stayed in the hospital for rehabilitative therapy, the feeding tube still in place, for three more months.

During the six months she was in the hospital, Oldham focused her energy on getting better. In those days, she didn't think much about what her medical bills would be. Besides, she had health insurance. Blue Cross of New Jersey was the school's carrier, and she had supplementary coverage through another Blue Cross policy offered by her husband's company. "I thought I was in excellent shape for insurance," she would recall later.

But her coverage had a catch-22 aspect. It was in force only as long as she was on the school district's payroll. Yet the severity of her illness meant that she faced additional surgery and rehabilitation that would prevent her from returning to work anytime soon.

Initially, she dealt with this by using her sick days. During eleven years at Manasquan, she had accumulated several months of sick leave because she was seldom ill. A colleague, Pete Pappas, who taught phys-ed at Manasquan, came up with a novel way to extend the insurance. He circulated a letter to the teachers, administrators, staff, and custodians at the high school asking them to donate one of their sick days to Oldham. She needed eighty-nine days to get through the rest of the school year; 120 persons each donated a day. Pappas raffled off the extra days to redistribute them to the donors.

Oldham came home in May in a wheelchair, unable to walk or to use her left hand. Her vision was impaired. She knew she would not be able to teach that fall, and when her sick leave ran out, she began paying $750 a month for a temporary COBRA policy to continue her coverage. With this new insurance hurdle, Oldham's colleagues swung into action again, planning a fund-raiser to help pay her COBRA coverage and the family's mounting out-of-pocket medical expenses. "At first I said no," she recalled. "I wasn't used to taking. But then friends came to me and said, 'You can't turn down something that people want to do to be kind.'" The fund-raiser was a dinner and raffle at a popular Manasquan bar that raised more than $20,000. Oldham was "bowled over by the support" by the "incredibly generous" people who had come forward to help her.

In the beginning, Blue Cross of New Jersey appeared to be routinely paying the bills. But about ten months after she became ill, that changed. "Then they started questioning everything and assigned me to a caseworker who called and said she was assigned because my case was 'so involved'—in other words, so expensive," she said. "She was starting to question my need for therapy, for home care, for everything. And when you're ill, that's the last thing you need."

Oldham knew a little about how complex and misleading medical bills could be. Her first husband, an FBI agent, had died of cancer in 1993. Six weeks after his death, she received a bill for $50,000 from a hospital collection agency. It was eventually reduced to $2,700, but even that experience did not prepare her for the barrage of bills that were to come during her illness. Consulting physicians and surgeons, dissatisfied with the payments they received from Oldham's insurers, sought payment from her directly for the balance. Monmouth Medical Center sent a bill for thousands of dollars for services and surgical supplies that apparently were not covered by her insurance. Soon collection agencies sent bills, too, many of which were not itemized and contained no clue as to the basis of their claims.

The chore of battling Blue Cross and the bill collectors fell to her husband, Michael, a plant manager who waged what Oldham called a "paper war." He wrote letters to the bill collectors, sought reimbursements from insurers, and pressed for itemized statements of charges. And always there were the phone calls. "One question with one bill can take forty-five minutes," Oldham says. "So often, when you finally do get a human being on the phone, it's a young clerk or a receptionist who has no idea how to answer you, and then they pass you on to someone else. It's endless."

One upsetting letter from the hospital warned that her account was about to be turned over to a collection agency because her "insurance provider wasn't meeting its contractual obligations." The hospital requested that Oldham contact the insurer to determine the problem and get back to the hospital's billing department.

"You have to fight every single bill," she said. "And not everyone is capable of doing that when they're emotionally disabled by grief or illness, or when they haven't even finished a course of treatment and aren't at the top of their game." She estimates that her husband has spent hundreds of hours trying to settle billing questions. "I have that advantage," Oldham says. "But it demands a highly educated and professional person to take these people on. It demands letter-writing skills. What about the people who can't do that?"

Even so, Oldham and her husband still have thousands of dollars in expenses. Because of the baffling nature of the bills they receive, they have no idea how much they might ultimately have to pay. Oldham no longer panics but is still unnerved by a call from a collection agency. "I'm a person who always paid my bills on time," she said.

After eighteen months of persistent effort, Oldham regained her ability to walk unassisted. But she still has major impairments. She has lost half the vision in her left eye as well as peripheral vision in her right. Her left hand doesn't work. "I can't drive, I can't type, I can't move the way I'd like to," she admits. Nevertheless, she knows she is lucky to be alive. "When I walk into my doctor's office," she says, "they call me the miracle girl."

She hopes to return to her teaching job, but if she can't there will be yet another insurance challenge. She will not be eligible to renew her COBRA policy indefinitely. Still, whatever happens, Oldham considers herself more fortunate than those who face medical catastrophes with no insurance or without the help of an advocate like her husband.

"It's a terrible thing for an impoverished person, an elderly person, for people who have never been faced with a major illness," she said. "What scares me is the thought of a little widow who gets a bill and might take $50,000 of her life's savings and turn it over to a medical center because she doesn't know how to question it. My advice is 'Don't pay a thing until you've questioned it.'"

SPENDING MORE FOR LESS

The Dartmouth Atlas of Health Care, a project of the Center for the Evaluative Clinical Sciences at Dartmouth Medical School that tracks the distribution and use of medical resources, offers this blunt assessment of the current state of American medicine: "Spending continues to increase without evidence that what we are doing results in better outcomes or better patient satisfaction."

Between 1980 and 2002, per capita health care spending in the United States shot up from $1,067 to $5,440—an increase of 410 percent. During that same period, disposable personal income per capita climbed at half that pace, going from $8,848 to $26,974. As a measure of how medical expenses keep claiming an ever-larger share of people's money, health care outlays were 12.1 percent of disposable income in 1980. By 2002, that figure had reached 20.2 percent.

Until the late 1990s, Americans with insurance through their employers were insulated from rising costs. For years, corporate America had picked up the full insurance tab for both its workers and retirees. As health care costs became a larger portion of corporate expenses, companies pushed some of the costs off on workers. The process began, as such potentially jarring trends often do, slowly. Companies paid 90 percent of the insurance cost, workers the other 10 percent. The plans became less generous in what they covered. Then the employee's share edged up to 20 percent or above. About the same time, companies began dumping their retiree plans, either slashing or terminating the health care coverage they once had promised for life. With some exceptions, only public employees and some union workers still receive fully paid health care as a fringe benefit.

The next stage in the evolving crisis will exact the heaviest toll of all. Many, if not most, companies plan to freeze their contribution at a fixed dollar level. Let's take a family policy in 2003, which cost an average $9,100. If the All-American Widget Company pays 75 percent—or $6,825—that will be it. If the policy goes up $1,000, the company will still pay $6,825. Employees will shoulder the entire increase, boosting their share of the bill from 25 percent to 32 percent. Total out-of-pocket expenditure: $3,275. In the era of modest wage increases, this means many workers will see their entire raise go to health care, and perhaps even part of their existing pay. Co-pays for visits to doctors' offices and deductibles will continue rising. Also, a new three-tier pricing system for prescription drugs has become the norm. In its annual survey of corporate health care policies, Mercer, the human resource consulting firm, found that co-pays in 2003 averaged $10 for generic drugs, $21 for brand names on a plan formulary, and $37 for those drugs not included on the formulary. Those numbers will continue upward.

Barring an unforeseen burst in job creation, the ranks of the underinsured and uninsured will continue to swell. As companies prune their payrolls and replace full-time employees with part-time workers and independent contractors, those people will be forced to fend for themselves in the health care insurance market. Because they have no buying leverage, they will be hit with the highest bills of all.

An unmarried self-employed person in Philadelphia, Pennsylvania, for example, paid $4,660 in 2004 for a limited health care plan offered by Independence Blue Cross and Pennsylvania Blue Shield, which control three-fourths of the southeast Pennsylvania market. That's up 71 percent from 1998—or five times more than the inflation rate. During that time, the nonprofit Blues squirreled away $2 billion in extra "profit."

So exactly what is propelling the runaway costs that make medical care unaffordable to ever-growing numbers of Americans? Let us count the culprits. Many people overuse the system. They check into ERs when there's no emergency, they visit their doctor without a serious medical reason to do so, they demand medication, especially antibiotics, that they don't need. Doctors, fearful of malpractice lawsuits, accede all too willingly to their patients' entreaties. They order needless lab work, X-rays, CT scans, and MRIs and write prescriptions as fast as they can. Too many hospitals insist on having all the latest technology. Too many want to have a surgical unit that performs as many complex procedures as possible—from heart valve operations to kidney transplants. The news media—especially television—churn out daily stories urging their viewers and readers to undergo assorted tests, from colonoscopies to full-body scans, without ever mentioning the cost in dollars or the real savings in lives across the entire population.

But the driving force behind these and all other factors is one that politicians refuse to recognize: Washington's blind obsession with market-based health care, the notion that competition is always good and can never have a bad result.

To be sure, the market approach is unbeatable in most segments of the economy. Competition among multiple producers that turn out goods and services leads to innovation, better products, and lower prices. The concept works flawlessly when the commodity is cars, furniture, cereal, doughnuts, computers, clothing, gasoline, or any other consumer item.

The glaring exception to the theory is health care. The very core principle of the market system, that companies will compete by selling more products to everyone, is actually the last thing the health care system needs. The goal should be to sell less, not more—that is, fewer doctor visits, fewer diagnostic tests, fewer hospitalizations, fewer consultations with specialists, and fewer prescription drugs.

But when was the last time you saw a newspaper headline or television newscast lauding Microsoft because it sold fewer software programs? Or that stock in General Motors soared because it sold fewer cars? Or that the Dow Jones Industrial Average surged on word that General Electric's revenue would go down—not up?

Nevertheless, that's exactly what an efficient health care system needs to provide a longer and better quality of life for everyone. This was the theory on which managed care through competition was sold. It didn't work.

WATCHDOG FOR THE DRUG COMPANIES

Nowhere are the market's shortcomings clearer than where costs are spiraling the most—prescription drugs. In 1980, drug expenditures totaled $12 billion, according to the Centers for Disease Control and Prevention (CDC). By 2002, that figure had climbed 1,250 percent to $162 billion. That was eight times more than the increase in spending on national defense; nine times more than the growth in outlays for veteran services and benefits. In 1980, spending on drugs accounted for a scant 4.9 percent of total health care outlays. By 2002, it had doubled to 10.4 percent. It now is on its way to 15 percent.

Only part of the increase is due to inflation. The rest is because pharmaceutical companies are selling more drugs to more people for longer periods of time, another indicator of a dysfunctional model. The comedian Chris Rock drove this point home in one of his humorous sketches in the 1990s:

"They got AIDS out there. You think they gonna cure AIDS? No . . . They ain't gonna cure AIDS. They ain't never curing AIDS. Ain't no money in curing it. The money's in the medicine. That's how you get paid. Sick people . . . coming back and back . . ."

Rock made his point quite eloquently by focusing on AIDS. But AIDS patients then and now make up a tiny slice of the U.S. drug market. Now there are conditions where the potential for consumers is counted in the tens of millions. Pharmaceutical companies offer multiple drugs for elevated cholesterol, which millions of patients are urged to take for years, if not a lifetime. Same with high blood pressure— more millions of patients, more millions of prescriptions for years. Also sexual dysfunction. Likewise depression. Always, the drug prescribed is the newest and most expensive on the market. And always, it works best if taken for years.

Whatever their purpose, prescription drugs in the United States cost from 30 percent to 60 percent more than the exact same medications sold anywhere else in the industrialized world. That's because governments elsewhere do not consider drugs to be just another consumer item, like cars and clothing, but rather products vital to the health of their people. Although the process differs, each country has a mechanism to restrain the sticker price of prescription drugs to levels considered fair and reasonable, and still allow pharmaceutical companies a profit. France, for example, permits companies to sell their drugs at any price. However, according to a congressional study, if pharmaceutical companies want "the national health care system to reimburse patients for the cost of the drugs, the companies must agree to a lower, negotiated price."

Congress, on the other hand, allows pharmaceutical companies to charge whatever they want, which ends up making the medication too costly for millions of Americans. Congress even prohibits Medicare, the largest buyer of prescription drugs, from negotiating a price, thereby sticking taxpayers with the inflated tab. This would be like permitting Boeing to put whatever price tag it wanted on the latest jet fighter it was selling to the Air Force.

The premium prices Americans pay have made the pharmaceutical companies the country's most profitable industry. In 2002, New York–based Pfizer Inc., the world's largest drug company, reported a return on sales of 28.4 percent. That was two and a half times better than the 10.7 percent return of General Electric Company, perennially ranked as America's best-managed business. It was nearly nine times better than the 3.3 percent return of Wal-Mart Stores, the country's largest and best-run retailer. And it was nearly thirty-two times better than the 0.9 percent of General Motors Corporation, America's largest car manufacturer. Of course, because most Americans receive their health insurance—and prescription drug plans—through their employers, corporate America was simply transferring its earnings to the pharmaceutical industry. As for all the millions of individuals who had to pay for their own drugs, or the government agencies that purchased them for the poor, they were on their own.

After several years of double-digit increases in prices during the 1990s, resourceful older Americans living on fixed incomes took the matter into their own hands by traveling to Canada and Mexico, where they could purchase the same medications for half or less their cost in the United States. Through word of mouth, their numbers grew. Eventually, senior citizens organized bus pilgrimages, especially to Canadian cities along the U.S. border. In 1998, stories that described the practice started popping up in newspapers. A typical article, which appeared in the Portland, Maine, *Press Herald*, summed up the distress:

> Filling their prescriptions in Canada could save participants hundreds of dollars on their medications. The trip also is intended to highlight the plight of the elderly in the United States, where drug companies overcharge them, critics say.
>
> "There are people who worked in the mills and worked hard all their lives who now cannot afford medication," said Bob Goldman, president of the Maine Council of Senior Citizens, which is sponsoring the trip. "That is the great tragedy of this issue."

For older folks, a doctor's prescription was a double whammy. In addition to having little disposable income to pay for expensive drugs, seniors also were among those who were charged inflated prices.

Patients covered by private insurance could buy medicine at a discount, but seniors and all others who had no insurance and walked into a pharmacy were billed at a higher price than anyone else. For example, preferred customers paid $43 for Zocor, Merck's cholesterol-lowering drug, while seniors and others without insurance were charged $105.

As more stories surfaced in newspapers and magazines, and eventually spread to radio and television, the number of people joining drug-buying expeditions to Canada increased dramatically, alarming the drug industry and the U.S. Food and Drug Administration (FDA). Both conveyed the impression that Canadian drugs were unsafe. FDA officials were quoted over and over as saying such purchases were illegal, sometimes hinting that American buyers might face federal prosecution. As FDA Commissioner Jane Henney put it in July 1999:

"Either the active ingredient is different or some of the other materials in that drug are different, and that could have consequences for one's health. So we have primarily legal concerns here, but also some public health concerns as well."

Or as William K. Hubbard, associate commissioner for policy and planning, described the danger: "Drugs in the United States are treated very strictly in terms of safety and quality. These drugs that come from Canada do not have the same safety profile." In fact, there is no evidence that Americans have been harmed by drugs purchased in Canada, and the FDA itself admits it knows of no such cases. Drugs sold in Canada are identical to medications on sale in U.S. pharmacies. More than anything, the FDA's dire warnings have served to help the drug industry maintain its huge profits.

This is not to suggest that millions of Americans jumping on buses, trains, and planes and heading for Canada is the solution to bloated drug prices in the United States. But neither are so-called Medicare discount cards financed with taxpayer dollars, along with multibillion-dollar handouts to insurers and drug companies to create the illusion that a market-driven system is functioning. That so many Americans choose to travel to Canada or Mexico only underscores the depth of the public's anger over prices and the federal government's refusal to do anything.

The issue promises to become even more contentious. After Congress blocked efforts to legalize drug purchases from Canada in 2003, more than a dozen cash-strapped state and local governments announced plans to go it alone and buy the lower-priced Canadian drugs for Medicaid patients, their own employees, and prisoners. Among the defiant: California, Wisconsin, Minnesota, Vermont, New Hampshire, and Oregon.

The FDA countered with warnings of lawsuits and angry attacks on state and local officials pursuing the Canadian strategy. As always, the agency insisted it was concerned only with protecting American consumers. ABC-TV News told viewers: "The FDA has warned that getting drugs from Canada is illegal and insists that it cannot guarantee the safety of those drugs."

In the face of the FDA's threats, some states backed down. Some went ahead. Local governments, like the City of Springfield, Massachusetts, continued doing what they had been doing before the practice became controversial: saving several million dollars a year by filling prescriptions north of the border.

Minnesota governor Tim Pawlenty, a Republican, ignored Washington's threats and mounted the most aggressive campaign. The state's Department of Human Services established a Web site (www.MinnesotaRxConnect.com) "designed to make it easy for Minnesotans to learn about buying prescription medicine from Canada, compare available pricing and to determine whether buying from Canada is appropriate for them." Minnesota officials also visited each of the Canadian pharmacies listed on the Web site, assured they were licensed by the province where they were located, "and reviewed the safety standards required by Canadian authorities and the safety procedures used by the pharmacies in filling mail order prescriptions."

After the user-friendly "order your medicine from Canada" Web site was up and running, Pawlenty announced the second phase of his low-cost-drug initiative: The state's 120,000 employees and their dependents who use the Web site "would be able to obtain their medicines with no out-of-pocket expense." Said the governor: "For state employees, we're able to provide more than forty-five prescription drugs at no cost to them. By enabling state employees to have their prescriptions filled by Canadian pharmacies, we have the potential for significant savings for the State of Minnesota and our employees."

The drug companies, for their part, took out insurance in case the FDA scare tactics failed. They threatened to shut off supplies to Canadian pharmacies if sales to Americans continued. If necessary, the industry was prepared to deprive sick Canadians of their medicine to keep prices higher in the States. In a "Dear Pharmacy Owner/Pharmacist" letter to every Canadian pharmacy, Pfizer Inc., whose inventory includes a half-dozen drugs that bring in more than one billion dollars a year each, asserted its "commitment to safeguarding the integrity of the pharmaceutical supply system and protecting the supply of Pfizer medicines for Canadians . . ." Then came a warning:

> We also reaffirm that Pfizer products purchased by you may only be sold in Canada . . . You may not at any time, either directly or indirectly, export out of Canada any Pfizer products . . . Should Pfizer have reason to believe that you are in breach of its terms of sale, pending completion of any investigations it chooses to carry out, Pfizer reserves the right, in its sole discretion, to suspend or refuse further sales to you . . .

While the industry's intent to preserve its pricing policies at any cost was obvious, was the FDA really concerned about protecting Americans from unsafe drugs? Or was it, too, upholding the economic interests of the drug companies? Lastly, was the FDA really more diligent in protect-ing American consumers than health authorities in Canada? Hardly. In truth, most drugs sold in the United States are manufactured in whole or in part outside the country. The Pfizer plant in Ireland that makes the best-selling cholesterol-lowering drug Lipitor ships one box to the United States, another to Canada. Same drug. Same strength. But judge the FDA's zealous claims about its commitment to drug safety for yourself.

In July 2001, Health Canada, the FDA's Canadian counterpart, issued a warning about the antidepressant nefazodone, marketed under the trade name Serzone by the Bristol-Myers Squibb Company. Health Canada said the drug was causing liver damage that "resulted in hospi-talization, liver transplantation, or death." It took the FDA another six months to come to the same conclusion and issue an order requiring a similar warning when the drug was prescribed in the United States. It stated in part: "Cases of life-threatening hepatic failure have been reported in patients treated with SERZONE . . . Patients should be advised to be alert for signs and symptoms of liver dysfunction (jaun-dice, anorexia, gastrointestinal complaints, malaise, etc.) and to report them to their doctor immediately if they occur. SERZONE should be discontinued if clinical signs or symptoms suggest liver failure . . . "

The FDA delay allowed Bristol-Myers to achieve record sales of $334 million for Serzone in 2001. That was up from $318 million a year earlier, and up from $185 million in 1997. But in 2002, the num-bers started going in the other direction. Sales plummeted by 34 per-cent to $221 million, primarily, according to the company, "as a result of a labeling change indicating a serious side effect of the product."

In the fall of 2003, Health Canada again led the way. After meetings with regulators, Bristol-Myers agreed to pull Serzone from the Cana-dian market. The reason: Now there were fifty-one reports of Cana-dian patients who suffered liver damage while taking the drug. Two patients had to undergo liver transplants. One died.

Back in the States, Public Citizen Health Research Group, a leading consumer organization headed by Dr. Sidney M. Wolfe, continued to press the case against Serzone by filing a supplement to its original petition to ban the drug. "We found almost as many deaths from liver failure reported in the last fourteen months we examined as in the seven previous years (nine vs. eleven)," Public Citizen said.

The FDA would not be stampeded. The agency so obsessed with products coming out of Canadian pharmacies was more tolerant of a domestic drug company. It allowed Bristol-Myers to keep Serzone on the U.S. market—far and away its most lucrative—and the company agreed to advise doctors and other health care professionals of the new concerns. In a warning letter dated October 2, 2003, Bristol-Myers said that in some cases liver damage occurred "as early as a few weeks" after patients began taking the drug, and in other instances after up to three years of continuous use. The company acknowledged that "to date, no risk factor to predict patients who will develop irreversible liver failure with nefazodone has been identified. Also no clinical strategy, such as routine liver function tests, could be identified to reduce the risk of liver failure." Translation: There was no way of knowing whose liver would fail after taking the drug to ease anxieties and depression.

Canada was not alone in its concern. Turkey also banned the sale of Serzone. So, too, did Spain. Sensing a trend, Bristol-Myers yanked it voluntarily across Europe, citing poor sales as the reason. As for the FDA, it continued to insist that U.S. consumers were adequately protected by a warning label advising them—if they read the fine print—that some would require a liver transplant and some would die. Perhaps most remarkable, patients were risking transplants and death for a drug whose benefits were at best questionable. In clinical trials, people who took placebos—in effect, sugar pills—reported about the same improvement as those who took Serzone.

In any case, with sales falling and the number of lawsuits by consumers claiming they were harmed by the drug rising, Bristol-Myers quietly removed Serzone from the U.S. market in June 2004.

Does it make any difference if Canadian authorities issue drug warnings before the FDA? It certainly did in the case of the drug Cordarone. Just ask Kenneth Krutz of Chicago, who in 1988 retired after more than four decades from his job as a plant superintendent at Acra Electric Corporation, a manufacturer of custom heating elements in Schiller Park, Illinois. In the years that followed, Krutz and his wife traveled and spent their newfound leisure time with their five children, eleven grandchildren, and two great-grandchildren. Active all his life, he continued to work on home-renovation projects, fish, and build miniature airplanes.

In February 1997, the seventy-three-year-old Krutz was in generally good health, except for an irregular heartbeat treated with medication. That month, his cardiologist started him on Cordarone. Within weeks, Krutz began to lose vision in both eyes. By June, he was legally blind. That same month, Wyeth-Ayerst Laboratories, Cordarone's maker, sent a letter to health care professionals advising of an expanded warning label:

> LOSS OF VISION. Cases of optic neuropathy and/or optic neuritis, usually resulting in visual impairment, have been reported in patients treated with amiodarone [Cordarone's chemical name]. In some cases, visual impairment has progressed to permanent blindness. Optic neuropathy and/or neuritis may occur at any time following initiation of therapy.

For Krutz, the warning came too late. If he had lived in Canada, things might have turned out differently. Years earlier, Wyeth's parent, American Home Products, had issued a similar warning on Cordarone sold in that country. Wyeth's decision not to issue the same warning to Americans at an earlier time "was driven, at least in part, by financial concerns related to its ability to market the product," according to a court opinion. The court found that Wyeth "deliberately placed misleading information on its packaging in order to preserve sales."

Despite the Canadian action, the FDA did nothing to require a similar warning for the U.S. market. Instead, it merely directed Wyeth to stop promoting Cordarone for general usage, which was far beyond what it had originally been approved for in 1985—"a drug of last resort" to be given only to seriously ill patients. Wyeth's belated letter to physicians informing them that some patients who took Cordarone were going blind was sent four months after a Multnomah County, Oregon, jury awarded $21.9 million in compensatory and punitive damages to Douglas Axen, a former social studies teacher who also lost his eyesight after taking the drug. Wyeth appealed the jury verdict but lost all the way to the U.S. Supreme Court. Krutz also sued, and Wyeth settled for $10 million before going to trial, although the company continued to maintain that its drug did not cause the blindness.

At least Krutz and Axen lived. Other patients who received the drug suffered serious lung damage, another one of its side effects. Some died.

Putting aside the question of whether the FDA or Health Canada is the more rigorous regulator, the fact is that the Internet has transformed drug buying, and all the FDA's efforts to scare Americans about the dangers of purchasing drugs from Canada ignore the reality of the marketplace. Americans can sit at home in front of their computers and order all the latest prescription drugs—including narcotics that can be resold on the street. Some Internet sites offer electronic consultations with doctors standing by, mouse in hand. Others ship the drugs, no questions asked. Some sites are legitimate. Some are not, selling adulterated or fake products.

Offshore Pharmacy, located somewhere in cyberspace, offers prescription drugs for any condition, from Prozac and Xanax for depression to Celebrex and Vicodin for pain relief, as well as everyone's early favorite for improved bedroom performance, Viagra. The Web site emphasizes that "we believe ordering medication should be as simple as ordering anything else on the Internet. Private, secure, and easy . . . Choose your medication, point, click, order and you're done. Your medication is on its way. No prescription required, no long lengthy forms to fill out." How is it possible to have prescription drugs shipped to your home without first obtaining a prescription? Offshore Pharmacy explained:

"As you know, the Internet has changed the way we live. A lot of the new services that were never in existence a few years ago, are now commonplace. Online medical purchase is among the 'new' services that have been created as a result of the Internet. Although they are a relatively new idea in health care, they are becoming widely accepted as a convenient way to improve patient access to medical care. Instead of a traditional physical exam by the physician, the patient is allowed to decide for himself depending on the symptoms what's right for him." As for one of the advantages: "Your personal privacy and sense of comfort are a priority to us. Our medications are primarily the drugs people may have trouble ordering in real life. Drugs like Viagra and Cialis may cause many people undue embarrassment in talking about or purchasing. Being able to purchase online and have the drugs shipped right to your home can eliminate that embarrassment."

EMERGENCY IN THE ER

The profit motive that sparked an explosion in cyberpharmacies also has radically changed the way hospitals do business. Insurers, HMOs, and investors have put so much pressure on hospitals to cut costs and reduce staff that sometimes they have to shut their doors.

Imagine sitting in your living room and feeling a sharp pain in your chest. You have trouble catching your breath. You call 911. Within minutes an ambulance arrives. EMS personnel carefully lift you onto a gurney, load you into the ambulance, and head for the nearest hospital, with siren blaring and lights flashing. Just as you are almost there, the driver is radioed to keep going; the hospital doesn't have a bed. The driver races on to the next hospital. But it has the same problem: no beds. The ambulance drives on as precious minutes tick by until it finds a hospital that agrees to accept you. Far-fetched? It happens every day in America.

It's called ambulance diversion, and it's declared when all the beds in a hospital's emergency room are occupied. It can last a few minutes or a few hours. When there's no room in the ER, the hospital informs local EMS workers that incoming ambulances will not be allowed to deliver any but the most critically ill patients because the hospital is on "divert" status. The ambulance then must proceed to the next-closest hospital. Most laymen have never heard the phrase, but in the hospital world it's become as familiar as the terms ER and ICU.

Joseph Gardner was a divertee. A twenty-seven-year-old tester for Andover Controls, a maker of sophisticated energy- and temperature-control systems in Andover, Massachusetts, Gardner felt ill while he was at work on the afternoon of April 19, 2001, and began having difficulty breathing after he got home. He unbuttoned his shirt and went to the front door, gasping for air. His mother and sister became alarmed and called 911 at 5:10 P.M.

An ambulance quickly arrived and paramedics helped Gardner onto a stretcher. His sister, Michelle, assumed he would be rushed to the hospital nearest his home, Lawrence General Hospital. Gardner had been treated there many times for asthma. But Lawrence General's ER had gone on "divert status" two hours earlier. The next-nearest ER was at Holy Family Hospital in Methuen, Massachusetts, a mile farther away.

As the ambulance navigated through heavy rush-hour traffic at only twenty-two miles per hour, Gardner experienced increasing distress. Medics were so preoccupied tending to him that Holy Family had not been notified of his pending arrival by the time the ambulance pulled in at 5:30 P.M., according to a state investigative report. One EMS worker rushed in to alert the staff as Gardner was wheeled into the ER. Within minutes his heart stopped beating. Despite all efforts to revive him, at 6:08 P.M. he was pronounced dead.

His sister, who had gone to Lawrence General to check on her brother, did not understand why he had been driven the extra distance to Holy Family. "I think the ten minutes would have made the difference," she told the Lawrence, Massachusetts, *Eagle-Tribune*. "If he went to Lawrence General, he could have been saved." A Massachusetts Department of Public Health investigation concluded that the diversion "had no material bearing on the patient's outcome." But as to why Gardner died, the department said it was "unable to determine a direct cause."

Ambulances have been diverted for years, but the practice periodically reaches crisis proportions, putting a huge strain on patients, families, emergency personnel, and vehicles. On one occasion, fourteen of the sixteen emergency rooms in St. Louis and St. Louis County diverted ambulances at the same time—including one hospital that did it for forty straight hours. A frustrated St. Louis paramedic told of one day in 2002 when his ambulance spent forty-five tense minutes on the highway trying to find a hospital to accept a woman who was suffering chest pains. "We were going up and down the interstate, shopping for hospitals," he told the *St. Louis Post-Dispatch*.

In Denver, as many as five hospitals in the same area have temporarily closed their ERs. "Now the ambulance people are driving around going 'Where do we go? What do we do with this patient?'" said a physician at St. Anthony Hospitals. Rhode Island adopted a statewide policy on diversions in 2003 after a crisis in which some ambulances drove as far as forty miles to find a hospital that would accept a patient. The Florida Agency for Health Care Administration says that, unlike in the past, "ambulance diversions now occur year-round," leading to "unacceptably long transport time intervals."

Diversions have become such a constant in the Boston area that the question isn't whether they will occur, but how severe they will be and how long they will last. The region has world-class medical institutions, including Massachusetts General and the Harvard School of Medicine, but ordinary citizens who call for an ambulance can only guess where they might end up or how soon they might get there. An investigation by the U.S. House Government Reform Committee found that as many as six Boston hospitals have diverted ambulances at the same time, stretching the resources of those still accepting patients. "Public health authorities are investigating at least two deaths associated with the diversions," according to the report.

Few cities have been immune, and what's happened in the Cincinnati area, the nation's twenty-third-largest metropolitan region, is typical. Before 1998, diversions were so rare that Cincinnati didn't even track them. The situation deteriorated so quickly that by 2002 health officials had begun working together to seek solutions. Since then, despite measures to improve the system, diversions have continued to skyrocket. In 2002, the total number of hours that hospitals were on divert status jumped to an all-time high—1,970 hours—the equivalent of eighty-two days. The next year, 2003, the figure more than tripled, to 6,377 hours. December 2003 was a particularly rocky month for patients who needed to get into a Cincinnati ER. Reporting hospitals were on divert status for 1,935 hours, compared to 515 in that month the year before.

"It puts a strain on the entire system," says Colleen O'Toole, vice president of the Greater Cincinnati Health Council. Fire-service vehicles used for EMS are in service for longer periods of time and must cover greater distances, which ties up more equipment. Patients may go to unfamiliar hospitals where their doctors do not have staff privileges, and their families may have to deal with new physicians. An insurer may balk at paying if the hospital to which a patient was diverted is outside its network.

O'Toole said that Cincinnati's health council helped work out a partial solution in which insurers agreed to pay out-of-network rates for diverted patients—at least for short stays. "If it was an extended stay," she said, "insurers wanted that person transferred back to the in-network hospital. That's the good news. The bad news for the patient is there is no automated way for the computer to catch that ahead of time. The claim is submitted and rejected, then it's appealed. It's a pain for the hospitals and the patients."

The House Government Reform Committee concluded in 2001 that diversions have become widespread and are likely to continue. The investigative report said that diversions "have impeded access to emergency services in metropolitan areas in at least 22 states since January 1, 2001 . . . with the result that patients had to delay needed care." In nine metro areas, medical personnel believed the diversions "either caused or risked severe injury or death to persons needing emergency care."

The crisis in the ER is a symptom of shortages throughout hospitals caused by insurers' cost-cutting that has reduced beds and staff. From 1980 to 2001, American hospitals lost 29 percent of their beds. The total plummeted from 1.4 million in 1980 to 987,000 in 2001, during a time when the population went up by 24 percent.

In years gone by, when a doctor decided to admit a patient from the ER into the hospital, aides transferred the person to a bed in the appropriate ward. All too often nowadays, the ward can't immediately accept a new patient because it doesn't have an empty bed. It's full. So the patient stays put in the ER, perhaps for hours, while waiting for a bed. That keeps the ER full, which triggers ambulance diversions.

According to the American Hospital Association (AHA), more than one hundred thousand medical/surgical beds and one in six ICU beds were eliminated in the 1990s alone. Massachusetts lost 24 percent of its hospital beds between 1988 and 1998. In big cities, the statistics are even more grim. Nine acute-care hospitals in the Cincinnati area have closed since the mid-1980s, and the area has lost 44 percent of its inpatient bed capacity since then. Recounting a story one could hear in any city, O'Toole explained: "There was a lot of pressure from the business community and the insurance companies to get rid of excess capacity in hospitals. It was perceived to be expensive and underutilized. Businesses thought they were paying too much in premiums for this capacity." The capacity is so tight on a daily basis that Cincinnati health officials worry constantly over how the system might handle any multicasualty disaster or sudden outbreak of disease.

At the same time that staff and beds in patient wards have become scarcer, emergency rooms have been closing. AHA data shows that 1,128 emergency departments closed from 1988 to 1998, a time when emergency room visits increased by 15 percent. Even many emergency rooms that are ostensibly still in operation function on scaled-back schedules due to a lack of resources.

The popular perception is that much of the overcrowding in emergency rooms comes from large numbers of the poor and uninsured who turn to ERs for the only medical treatment they can get. While this is a major factor in many communities, ERs also are inundated by an entirely different category of patients—people *with* health insurance. A report by the Washington, D.C.–based Center for Studying Health System Change noted in 2003 that emergency department visits rose by 16 percent from 1996–97 to 2000–2001, a surge due largely to increased use by insured people. "Emergency department visits by privately insured persons increased 24 percent between 1996–97 and 2000–2001, far outpacing the 4.7 percent increase in the number of privately insured people during this period," the Center noted.

Insured patients are flocking to emergency departments as a last resort—because they can't get appointments to see their own doctors, or because they face long waits to be seen. The Center confirmed that "more physicians report having inadequate time to spend with their patients and are increasingly closing their practices to some new patients, despite spending more time in direct patient care activities. With extended hours and no appointment necessary, emergency departments increasingly may be viewed by many patients as more convenient sources of primary care than their regular physicians."

ER overload is further compounded by the demands of managed care. Because of the reduced reimbursements they often receive from health insurers, more and more doctors are sending patients to emergency rooms for routine medical needs that they once provided in their offices. Which is why ambulance diversions, while they may wax or wane from season to season and city to city, will be with us for a long time to come.

AMERICA'S UNKNOWN KILLER

Because Washington fails to assure that all citizens have basic health care coverage and are protected from catastrophic medical bills, other breakdowns within the system are allowed to fester, priorities are misordered, and taxpayer dollars are not allocated where they will achieve the greatest return.

Over the decades, presidents and lawmakers from both parties have spent more than one hundred billion dollars on a never-ending war on cancer. For politicians, celebrities, and entertainment personalities who lend their names to the cause, it makes for great photo opportunities. After all, everyone supports apple pie, motherhood, and a cure for cancer. Lawmakers recognized the potential back in 1937 when, in a rare display of Capitol Hill unity, they voted unanimously to create the National Cancer Institute. Some three decades later, in 1971, President Richard M. Nixon called for a War on Cancer, and Congress again responded by opening the doors to the U.S. Treasury.

At first glance, it might seem that all those billions have bought substantial progress. Special-interest groups, from the American Cancer Society to leading cancer-research institutions, routinely issue press releases touting the achievement of the week. The news media trumpet the latest advances and profile the victims who have managed to survive. But there is much less to the progress than meets the eye. To be sure, people with some types of cancer who once would have died now lead productive lives thanks to modern treatment. Yet the inescapable fact is that the death rate is unchanged: In 1950, the death rate from all cancers was 194 out of every 100,000 people. A half-century later, in 2001, it was 196 out of every 100,000 people. When assessed by the only yardstick that counts—the overall death rate from all cancers—progress has been nonexistent.

More than a half-century ago, cancer was the second-leading cause of death in the United States. It remains so today. In 2001, according to CDC data, the deaths of 553,800 persons were attributable to cancer. Heart disease, long the No. 1 killer, claimed 700,100 lives. The third and fourth causes were strokes at 163,500 and chronic low respiratory disease at 123,000.

Yet one of the deadliest killers is not even on the list. It attracts little or no attention from Congress. No celebrities rush to Capitol Hill to testify for more funding to wipe it out. No television entertainers proselytize for a cure or urge more testing. The anonymous killer? Mistakes—the kind that are another symptom of a failed system.

Benjamin Jones Jr., a fifty-nine-year-old retired toolmaker, entered the Osteopathic Medical Center of Texas in Fort Worth in July 1991 for lung cancer surgery. The operation was a success. As doctors told Jones, the right lung they removed was cancer-free. What they neglected to mention was that they had taken the wrong one. The cancer had been in his left lung. Although the hospital learned of the mistake about a week after the operation, an official said he relied on the doctors to tell Jones because he did not want to interfere with the doctor-patient relationship, some relationships being just too sacred to violate. Not until a year later, while Jones was poring over his medical records, did he discover that the cancer had been in his left lung all along. By then it was too late. He died of lung cancer in February 1994.

Briana Baehman was thirty-four months old when she went into the Fairview-University Medical Center in Minneapolis, Minnesota, for a liver transplant in December 2002. Risks in such procedures, especially for children, are well known. But Fairview-University, affiliated with the University of Minnesota Medical School, had been doing such transplants longer than anyone, having performed the first in 1964. Moreover, the program was characterized as having "world renowned success with infants and children," and the hospital was listed as one of the nation's best by *U.S. News & World Report*. The prognosis looked especially good for the little girl from Wichita, Kansas; her grandfather had contributed the liver. The day after surgery, she was alert and playful. By the second day, something clearly had gone wrong. As the family would learn later, the surgery was a success. The care that followed was not. A nurse had mistakenly set up a computer-controlled drip so that intravenous doses of heparin—an anticoagulant to prevent clots from forming—were administered to the tiny girl "at ten times the rate ordered," according to a state health department investigation. Two other nurses checked the drug and the equipment that delivered it. Still, the mistake went unnoticed for twelve hours. By then it was too late. Follow-up surgery failed. In less than two weeks, Briana was dead.

Depending on how they are counted, mistakes are either the third or ninth cause of death. Part of the uncertainty is attributable to varying definitions of what constitutes a "mistake." Many health care professionals, for example, do not consider as a mistake those patients who die from infections acquired while in a hospital. They reason that hospitals are breeding grounds for germs and hence a certain number of deaths are inevitable. But it's unlikely that patients share that view. People enter a hospital expecting to get well, not contract an infection and die. Nor do hospitals advise patients beforehand of that possible outcome. There is no friendly warning that although you are hospitalized to have your appendix removed, it's possible you may pick up some germs that will kill you.

Before going any further, a little linguistic background is in order. The medical world, like the military, thrives on euphemisms, those inoffensive words or phrases used, according to one dictionary, "to avoid a harsh, unpleasant, or distasteful reality." When the Army kills innocent civilians, the dead are called "collateral damage." When the Army kills some of its own by mistake, the dead are referred to as victims of "friendly fire."

Medical professionals also avoid the distasteful with obscure jargon. When someone dies or is sickened in a health care setting, he or she is a victim of an "adverse event," defined as "unintended injuries caused by medical management rather than the underlying condition of the patient." Sometimes the phrase is more specific. If a patient dies from an infection because a nurse or a doctor inserts a dirty catheter, or an infusion pump delivers a lethal dose of a narcotic, the result is an "adverse medical device event" (AMDE). If a physician prescribes an inappropriate drug and the patient dies, it's an "adverse drug event" (ADE), although some prefer "adverse drug reaction" (ADR). And if a patient dies following surgery in which the wrong side of the brain is operated on for cancer, it's a plain-vanilla "adverse event" (AE). Sometimes the mistakes are classed as a "medical misadventure," such as when a patient dies from a heart attack "due to dissection of left coronary artery during catheterization" or "peritonitis due to perforation of the ascending colon during colonoscopy."

The FDA has extensive rules covering the reporting of "adverse events." The agency also suggests how much information can be submitted without violating the federal government's privacy rules, which are designed to protect the system rather than public health. From the patient's point of view, it's all irrelevant semantics. He or she is either suffering from a condition that did not exist before they came in contact with the health care industry, or they're dead. We will use "mistake" and "error" as broad, inclusive terms to mean that someone did something they were not supposed to do. It's not a matter of casting blame. Many more mistakes can be attributed to systems errors than to human frailties. Fix the system, and those mistakes and deaths that follow are prevented.

Health care has become impossibly fragmented. Patients, especially those who are older, often see multiple doctors, each of whom may write prescriptions unaware of what his colleagues are doing. To make timely and correct decisions today, doctors must absorb information from many sources—information that changes by the day. As one medical professional explains, "the amount of knowledge necessary to practice high-quality health care is just too large and changing too rapidly to be carried around in any person's brain."

Consequently, mistakes occur everywhere—in the nation's most prestigious university teaching hospitals, in community hospitals, in for-profit and not-for-profit hospitals. The precise number is unknown. Death certificates never list "mistake" as the cause of death. A widely quoted study by the Institute of Medicine placed the number between 44,000 and 98,000. Another study, which counted prescription drug deaths and was more inclusive, put the figure at 225,000, possibly as high as 257,000. As for the drug-death mistakes alone, more than five times as many people die from drugs prescribed by physicians than from street drugs like cocaine, heroin, and Ecstasy.

The real number of deaths is almost certainly much higher than these estimates. One reason is the natural instinct to conceal fatal errors, when possible, to escape the potential for malpractice awards. Second, and more important: No independent authority examines the records of hospitals, doctors, and drug companies to detect such deaths. No autonomous agency coordinates ongoing surveillance, conducts interviews, reviews charts, and orders autopsies. When lawsuits are filed and settled, the documents that recount events leading up to death are sealed. This practice guarantees the mistakes will be repeated elsewhere, causing still more deaths. A study at one hospital sums up the attitude of the medical profession toward finding out why things happen. When requesting an autopsy, physicians must give a reason from a menu of options. One of the choices: "Evaluation of therapeutic or diagnostic procedures or devices." Of 387 forms completed over six years, that item was checked on 1 percent—or four forms, to be exact.

In case there is any doubt about the need for independent oversight, consider the story of Charles Cullen, a health care worker who deliberately committed mistakes. For sixteen years, Cullen, a registered nurse who last lived in Bethlehem, Pennsylvania, wandered from one hospital to another across eastern Pennsylvania and New Jersey, killing as many as forty patients under his care. No one noticed until the very end. This even though he all but had "killer" tattooed across his forehead. Although several nurses questioned his behavior to superiors, no one in authority thought it important enough to warn other hospitals that hired him. Indeed, the health care system seemed to go out of its way to make it possible for Cullen, a critical-care nurse, to continue his killing spree.

Cullen had grown up in West Orange, New Jersey, and served a stint in the U.S. Navy. There had been bouts of depression, attempted suicides, several stays in mental hospitals, and an arrest for breaking into the home of an acquaintance while she and her six-year-old son were sleeping. In all, he was fired, forced to resign, or investigated at seven of the nine hospitals where he worked. Yet he never received a bad recommendation. This, remarkably, was due in no small part to the reluctance of health care institutions to risk litigation by giving an unfavorable assessment of an employee and thus acknowledging a problem in their midst. Fear of litigation trumps patient care.

At Saint Barnabas Medical Center in Livingston, New Jersey, his first job, he was fired for unknown reasons. At Warren Hospital in Phillipsburg, New Jersey, he resigned after the suspicious death of a patient. At Liberty Nursing and Rehabilitation Center in Allentown, he was fired for failing to follow medication procedures. At St. Luke's Hospital in Fountain Hill, Pennsylvania, ranked as one of America's best hospitals by *U.S. News & World Report*, he resigned voluntarily after being accused of concealing unopened bottles of heart and blood-pressure medicine. With a trail of corpses in his wake, Cullen finally ended up at the Somerset Medical Center in Somerville, New Jersey. There, hospital officials eventually detected suspicious medication levels in his patients and began investigating. The inquiry plodded along as hospital officials looked for every explanation possible—including herbal tea—other than the obvious one. Finally, they called in local law-enforcement authorities. Four patients had raised insulin levels and two had lethal levels of digoxin, a heart medication. After the forty-four-year-old Cullen was charged with murder in the death of a Catholic priest and attempted murder of another patient, he confessed to killing between thirty and forty patients at hospitals and a nursing home where he had worked.

Even after his confession, there was little interest by either the hospitals or the regulatory agencies overseeing the institutions to determine what went wrong. In news media interviews, several hospitals made it clear they had little desire to probe patient deaths under Cullen's watch. The Lehigh Valley Hospital in Allentown, Pennsylvania, one of Cullen's employers, issued a press release saying it had conducted reference checks with a previous employer about Cullen and that "no problems were indicated." Of course, the hospitals had a built-in reason for not wanting to look too deeply: Every death attributed to Cullen represented potentially devastating damage claims against the hospitals. By the spring of 2004, more than a dozen had been filed.

State licensing authorities did not move to permanently revoke Cullen's nursing license until after he had confessed to murder. The Pennsylvania Department of Health, after conducting an examination that consisted of some interviews and records checks, concluded that hospitals within the state had complied with regulations and had done nothing wrong. But Pennsylvania has one of the country's worst records for weeding out incompetent doctors—a failure that raises quality-of-care issues and has contributed to the growth of medical malpractice lawsuits in the state.

To escape the death penalty, Cullen agreed in April 2004 to plead guilty to thirteen murders in Somerset County, New Jersey, and to work with law-enforcement authorities in other New Jersey and Pennsylvania counties to identify all the people he killed. Three more were added to the list by June. How close the two states come to confirming the names of the forty murder victims Cullen claimed originally will turn on how willing local governments are to spend the money on the costly investigations. James B. Martin, the district attorney in Lehigh County, Pennsylvania, where it's believed Cullen killed twelve people, told the *New York Times,* "Our hope is to provide closure for as many families as possible, but in reality, it is highly unlikely that we'll get them all."

Given the background of this horrendous case, it's obvious that hospital deaths brought about by medical mistakes are grossly understated. After all, if hospitals refuse to see murders on their wards, why assume they are recording deaths by mistake? Hospitals and doctors usually attribute the deaths of patients to the conditions for which they were admitted. The assumption often leads to erroneous conclusions, especially in the case of older patients, as amply demonstrated by Cullen. But even the deaths of younger patients are misinterpreted and mistakes missed. Consider the story of Edward Kyllonen.

Kyllonen was thirty-seven years old when he checked into Fairview Ridges Hospital in Burnsville, Minnesota, in November 2001 to have his left hip replaced after a snowmobile accident. The hospital advertises itself as providing "quality care and customer service at its best," a place where "you and your family will receive expert, personal attention from diagnosis through treatment." In Kyllonen's case, he never checked out.

By all accounts, the surgery, which took place on Friday, November 2, 2001, went well. Following the one-hour-and-thirty-six-minute operation, he was moved into the recovery room at 9:32 A.M. According to medical records, "there were no apparent complications." His wife, who was several months pregnant with the couple's first child, and other family members visited. They left later in the day. Although he complained of pain, hospital records show that he was "alert" and "stable."

Shortly after 6 A.M. on Saturday morning, twenty-four hours after the surgery, a laboratory staff member went into Kyllonen's room to draw blood samples. He wasn't breathing. CPR was started. A Code Blue page for more staff was announced. A call was placed to Kyllonen's wife, who was urged to return to the hospital. Her husband had taken a turn for the worse. CPR continued until 7:20 A.M., when a pulse was felt. He was transferred to the Coronary Care Unit. There, a second Code Blue alert was sounded. Doctors and nurses sought to stabilize him. CPR was renewed. A final effort was made at 11:00 A.M., but he "lost blood pressure and pulse." At 11:14 A.M., he was "declared dead due to shock—no pressure or pulse." The physician observed at the time:

"The patient experienced cardiopulmonary arrest somewhere between 5:30 A.M. and 6:30 A.M. this morning which appeared to be most likely on the basis of a pulmonary embolism . . . Despite prolonged efforts at resuscitation, the patient was unable to be stabilized, with a downhill spiral from multi-organ damage."

But Kyllonen's family did not like what it saw, and his wife asked for what most families in similar situations shun: an autopsy. Two months later, the medical examiner issued a report with this curious—and rather obvious—explanation for the cause of death: "Sudden unexpected death following left hip surgery."

Now the Minnesota State Health Department investigators were skeptical. From hospital records they knew that Kyllonen had received morphine for his pain. Yet the medical examiner's toxicological report made no mention of it. They asked that the test be rerun for blood opiate. This time the report came back with a startling finding. Kyllonen's body contained a potentially lethal dose of morphine. As the state investigator put it, "the blood total morphine concentration . . . would likely cause toxicity and probably contributed to his death." No one, it turned out, was keeping track of all the morphine and other painkillers pumped into Kyllonen after his operation.

Not all victims of medical mistakes die. Many survive, but they leave hospitals in far worse shape than when they arrived. Some are paralyzed; some are brain-damaged; some contract virulent infections. Some lose a body part; some lose the wrong part—which is what happened to Willie F. King in 1995 when he was admitted to University Community Hospital in Tampa, Florida, a 430-bed institution that had opened in 1968. The fifty-one-year-old King, a diabetic, entered the hospital to have his right foot amputated. Instead, the surgical staff removed the left one. A month later, King returned to the hospital to have the right foot amputated, consigning him to a wheelchair for the rest of his life. He died from a blood clot in October 2001 at age fifty-eight.

Then there was Linda McDougal, a forty-six-year-old accountant from Woodville, Wisconsin, who was diagnosed with breast cancer. On the recommendation of her doctors, in June 2002 she underwent a double mastectomy at United Hospital in St. Paul, Minnesota. Her choice of hospitals seemed well founded. *AARP Modern Maturity* magazine that same month singled out United as one of "the nation's fifty leading metropolitan hospitals." As it turned out, the operation was a success. Unfortunately, McDougal was the wrong patient. "Forty-eight hours after the surgery," she explained, "the surgeon walked into my room and said, 'I have bad news for you. You don't have cancer.' I never had cancer. My breasts were needlessly removed."

The laboratory had mixed up her tissue samples with a woman who did indeed have cancer. As a result of the error, McDougal ended up with nearly three feet of incisions across her chest and recurring infections. McDougal's experience was not at all unusual. Laboratory analyses of blood work and tissues are a huge source of medical mistakes. So, too, are diagnostic tests of all kinds, from mammograms to PSA readings for prostate cancer. Sometimes the test results are misread. Sometimes the tests show no evidence, say, of cancer when cancer is actually present. Sometimes they show cancer where there is none. As is the case with hospital mistakes, there is no independent monitoring of laboratory or diagnostic test results.

Jennifer Rufer of Spanaway, Washington, learned about false-positive test results in the most painful way imaginable. Married to her college sweetheart and hoping for children, Rufer was twenty-two years old when she went to her gynecologist in January 1998 after experiencing abdominal pain and vaginal bleeding. A test showed elevated levels of the hCG hormone normally produced by a developing placenta and thus a predictor of pregnancy. Marketed by Abbott Laboratories, the AxSYM hCG assay is one of the most widely used blood pregnancy tests. More tests with positive outcomes followed. But there was no evidence of a baby. Finally, Rufer's doctor sent her to a specialist at the University of Washington Medical Center (UWMC) in Seattle.

Because the high hormone level also can be a sign of a gestational trophoblastic tumor, a rare form of cancer that grows rapidly, the university doctors began aggressive chemotherapy. By August, tests continued to show abnormally high hormone levels, so a hysterectomy followed. The chemotherapy treatment continued. When "scans revealed two small nodules in her lungs" and the hormone level remained elevated, doctors feared the cancer had spread. That December, they removed a portion of her right lung. As Rufer began preparing for her own funeral, doctors gave her the good news. She never really had cancer. But now she will never have children. The more than forty tests suggesting that she either was pregnant or had cancer were, in fact, all false positives. She was neither pregnant nor had cancer.

Rufer and her husband sued Abbott Laboratories, UWMC, and the cancer specialist who treated her. UWMC and the doctor argued that they had relied on the Abbott test results. Abbott denied all responsibility, even though the literature distributed with its tests made no mention of the potential for false positives. What's more, according to a court opinion, it turned out that "Abbott also had access to reports that false positive results on its assay led to unnecessary cancer treatment before 1998. It received over forty complaints of false positives, including multiple complaints of unnecessary chemotherapy and surgery before Jennifer Rufer's first treatment in April 1998. Industry standards require manufacturers to warn about their experience of problems with a product. Abbott's insert completely omitted mention of reports of false positives resulting in unnecessary treatment." A jury awarded the Rufers $16.2 million in damages.

FAVORS AND FRAUD

One reason that Washington has resisted all efforts to overhaul health care during the last half century is that key players have their hands in what will soon be a multitrillion-dollar health care till, creating conflicts of interest everywhere. Wherever there is too much money, politicians and businessmen meld like Hollywood's hottest couple of the hour. Label it health care cronyism. It's a disease that has overwhelmed academic and professional integrity. It infects for-profit and not-for-profit institutions alike and runs through prestigious university medical centers and government research institutions once thought to be immune, as well as private and publicly owned corporations and businesses—even doctors.

Pharmaceutical companies pay doctors to attend dinners and talk about the curative powers of their latest drugs. The companies underwrite continuing-education seminars that feature their drugs. They invite doctors to sit on so-called advisory committees dealing with their drugs in return for generous fees. At conventions, some panel members walk away with $10,000 to $15,000 stuffed in their pockets. Companies pay doctors for access to patient drug records. Although names are deleted, the data is invaluable in helping pharmaceutical firms plan sales strategies. All this is done with the expectation that doctors who take part will write more prescriptions for their drugs. And write they do. Companies jack up the wholesale price of select drugs—especially more expensive medicines used for treatments such as cancer—and then give doctors a steep discount so they can collect more money from government and other third-party reimbursers. The price they pay is based on a fictitious average wholesale price that may be many times more than the true cost of the medicine.

Drug companies market their products, in part, on the profit potential for physicians who prescribe them. National Institutes of Health doctors conducting clinical trials receive a government salary from taxpayers and collect consulting fees on the side from companies whose drugs they test. Government officials, in turn, enact rules to make it legal for them and their colleagues to keep secret the amount of cash and stock they receive from private companies. Drug companies pay managed-care organizations to require doctors to prescribe their products. Surgeons collect bonuses based on the number of operations they perform under Medicare—whether the patients need the operations or not. Doctors and academics put their names on medical studies that are authored by ghostwriters and paid for by those who stand to profit from the subject. Physicians send patients to testing facilities in which they hold a financial interest.

This culture of cronyism has created an environment in which fraud thrives. So much so that the United States not only has the world's most expensive health care, but also the most fraudulent.

In October 2001, TAP Pharmaceutical Products Inc., a corporation formed by a partnership of Takeda Chemical Industries Ltd. and Abbott Laboratories, agreed to pay $875 million to settle criminal charges and civil liabilities for its fraudulent pricing and marketing schemes. That included a $290-million criminal fine, the largest ever in a health care fraud prosecution; $559.5 million to the U.S. government in civil damages for filing false and fraudulent claims with the Medicare and Medicaid programs; and $25.5 million to state governments for their losses.

Through the 1990s, TAP's two principal drugs were Lupron for prostate cancer and Prevacid for acid reflux disease. Lupron suppressed or eliminated production of testosterone, which promotes the growth of prostate cancer. Patients receive the injectable treatments for the rest of their lives. Because the drug is injected, Medicare paid physicians 80 percent of the average wholesale price of the drug.

That may sound reasonable unless you know that "average wholesale price" is a fictitious dollar amount fixed by companies to secure over-payments from taxpayers and other third parties and to boost profits. The price, which seldom bears any relation to actual production costs, is recorded in what the industry calls the Redbook. With that background, in 1999, Lupron's average wholesale price was $594.65. Medicare paid physicians 80 percent of that amount, or $475.72. But TAP sold the drug to physicians for less than half that amount—$207.

How much could a doctor make by prescribing Lupron instead of an alternative medication? "For a doctor with thirty patients in his practice receiving monthly injections of Lupron," the government contended, "the profit potential from prescribing Lupron was, in 1996, $50,490." In addition, some doctors who received free samples billed both Medicare and their patients for the drug. The value of the free samples was estimated at between $31 million and $78 million. To discourage physicians from talking among themselves about the varied discounts they received, TAP's sales management spelled out in slide presentations how its sales force should deal with the subject:

Explain to physicians that discussing price could potentially put reimbursement in jeopardy.

"Doctor, by discussing your costs of Lupron with other physicians, you run the risk of that information getting back to HCFA [Medicare's Health Care Financing Administration]. If HCFA then realized that AWP [average wholesale price] is not a true reflection of the price, the AWP could be affected, thus lowering the amount you may charge."

A small number of doctors raked in most of the money. In 1997, according to legal documents, "there were 14,316 urologists nation- wide who submitted claims to Medicare for Lupron prescribed to patients. Of that number, 3.4 percent, or 482 urologists, received 25 percent of all monies paid out by Medicare," or $126 million out of $504.1 million. The top 25 percent, or 3,574 urologists, collected 82 percent of the Medicare money, or $411.6 million. For some doctors, their income in any given year from Lupron alone ranged between $400,000 and $1 million.

How much money was at stake for Abbott Laboratories? Medicare payments for Lupron totaled $2.5 billion in taxpayer dollars in the 1990s.

Are Abbott and its Lupron aberrations? Not at all. Settlement agree- ments in fraud cases with other pharmaceutical companies in recent years included $49 million from Pfizer Inc. over Lipitor, the choles- terol-lowering drug; $88 million from GlaxoSmithKline over Paxil, the antidepressant, and Flonase, the nasal allergy spray; $257 million from Bayer over Adalat, for high blood pressure, and Cipro, an antibi- otic; and $355 million from AstraZeneca over Zoladex, the chief com- peting product against Lupron in the treatment of prostate cancer.

Beyond the traditional government investigations of civil fraud and overbilling, authorities are taking a hard look at a new realm of drug- company practices that have proven especially lucrative. This is the rapidly expanding market for so-called off-label prescriptions. While doctors are permitted to prescribe drugs as remedies for which they were never approved by the FDA—hence the term "off-label"—phar- maceutical companies are prohibited from actively marketing drugs for such purposes. Nevertheless, many, if not most, do so behind the scenes, since it's an easy way to sell more pills without having to spend millions on clinical trials to prove effectiveness and win FDA approval.

In January 2004, Pfizer disclosed in a U.S. Securities and Exchange

Commission (SEC) filing that it was taking a $427 million charge "in connection with the previously reported investigations by the U.S. Attorney's office in Boston, as well as various state authorities, into Warner-Lambert's promotion of Neurontin prior to Pfizer's acquisition of Warner-Lambert in 2000." Pfizer said that it "has cooperated fully with these inquiries" and that it believed the $427 million set aside "will be sufficient to resolve all outstanding federal and state governmental investigations related to Neurontin as well as the pending civil qui tam [whistle-blower] suit concerning this matter."

Neurontin started life with a narrow scope under Parke-Davis, a division of Warner-Lambert. The FDA approved it in 1993 as an anticonvulsant for epileptics when their regular drugs needed a boost. It was never intended as a first-line drug, but to be used in conjunction with other medications. With such a limited market, it never had much profit potential. But if it could be sold to treat other ills, Parke-Davis could reap substantial rewards. It did. As did its parent companies, Warner-Lambert and then Pfizer. In 1994, when Neurontin was just a supplemental epilepsy drug, Parke-Davis estimated lifetime sales of $500 million. In 2003, Pfizer took in just about that much money every two months, as worldwide sales reached $2.7 billion. What accounted for the explosive growth? Off-label prescriptions. Neurontin, whose chemical name is gabapentin, is the poster child for off-label prescriptions. It evolved into a self-styled magical cure-all, thanks to aggressive marketing by Parke-Davis through the 1990s. It gradually was sold as a remedy for various kinds of pain; hot flashes with menopause; restless leg syndrome; partial seizures in adults and children older than three; drug- and alcohol-withdrawal seizures; attention deficit disorder; migraines; amyotrophic lateral sclerosis (Lou Gehrig's disease); and assorted psychiatric conditions, including bipolar disorder, panic disorder, post-traumatic stress disorder, and social phobias.

To spread the word about the off-label uses, since it could not legally promote Neurontin either to the public or physicians for purposes other than those the FDA originally approved, Parke-Davis launched a massive covert marketing campaign. It recruited key physicians in "major teaching hospitals to serve as 'Neurontin champions.'" The company paid tens of thousands of dollars to select doctors to extol the wonders of Neurontin. It paid other physicians to listen to the sales pitches. It also let it be known in teaching hospitals that money was available for doctors to conduct research and clinical trials. Physicians were singled out as Neurontin cheerleaders "based on their potential to write prescriptions."

Doctors served as paid "consultants" and "preceptors." They received money to promote Neurontin's off-label uses in teleconferences and to conduct studies. They were paid to attend dinner meetings and to proselytize at medical education seminars. Parke-Davis marketing specialists, "using a combination of misrepresentation and cash incentives, encouraged many physicians to experiment with their own patients by prescribing very high levels of Neurontin for a variety of 'off-label' indications." They paid doctors to keep their patients on the drug. In addition, Parke-Davis paid for a series of "scientific" articles published in medical journals that were more promotion than science. Under FDA rules, Parke-Davis operatives then could drop off the favorable articles at doctors' offices.

What the Parke-Davis sales force neglected to mention to doctors was that clinical trials had raised serious doubts about the drug. One trial concluded that Neurontin "is probably no more effective than placebo in the treatment of painful diabetic neuropathy." Another study of Neurontin's use in treating depression and bipolar disorder produced similar results. The company "falsely promoted Neurontin as effective for treating bipolar disease, even when a scientific study demonstrated that a placebo worked as well or better than the drug." In other words, a sugar pill was as good as Neurontin.

Finally, in May 2004, it became clear why Pfizer had set aside nearly a half-billion dollars in January to settle Neurontin claims. On May 13, the U.S. Attorney's Office in Boston and the U.S. Department of Justice announced that the Warner-Lambert subsidary of Pfizer "has agreed to plead guilty and pay more than $430 million to resolve criminal charges and civil liabilities in connection with its Parke-Davis division's illegal and fraudulent promotion of unapproved uses for one of its drug products [Neurontin]." The criminal fine alone amounted to $240 million, the second largest ever imposed in a health care fraud prosecution.

POLITICS AND PROFITS

To protect its interests and expand its influence, the health care industrial complex has done what all successful special interests do: It's become a big donor and a high-powered lobby in Washington. In the last fifteen years, HMOs, insurers, pharmaceutical companies, hospital corporations, physicians, and other segments of the industry contributed $479 million to political campaigns—more than the energy industry ($315 million), commercial banks ($133 million), and big tobacco ($52 million). More telling is how much the health care industry spends on lobbying. It invests more than any other industry except one, according to the nonpartisan Center for Responsive Politics. From 1997 to 2000, the most recent year for which complete data is available, the industry spent $734 million lobbying Congress and the executive branch. Only the finance, insurance, and real estate lobby exceeded that amount in the same period, with a total of $823 million. In contrast, the defense industry spent $211 million—less than one-third of the health care expenditure.

In Washington, where administrators and executives move easily through the revolving door between public policy and private interest, few have mastered the technique more effectively than those in the health care industry. Look no further than the Medicare Prescription Drug, Improvement, and Modernization Act of 2003, which might more aptly be called the Pharmaceutical Company and Health Care Industry Welfare Act. In the fall of that year, when Congress enacted a Medicare prescription drug benefit for the first time, the White House point man on the half-trillion-dollar-plus taxpayer-funded program was Thomas A. Scully, administrator for the federal Centers for Medicare and Medicaid Services (CMS).

Before he became Medicare's top official, Scully was president of the Federation of American Hospitals, a 1,700-member trade association of for-profit hospitals "dedicated to a market-driven philosophy." Its business plan, it should be noted, depends heavily on federal tax dollars for Medicare patients.

Scully helped craft the final version of the Medicare bill, which blocked imports of low-cost drugs from Canada, a top priority of pharmaceutical companies. Also, bowing to the wishes of other industry lobbyists, the act provided billions of dollars in tax subsidies to HMOs, private insurers, and corporations to provide drug coverage. Thus, the congressional supporters of market-driven medicine were giving billions of tax dollars to private business to pretend the market system was functioning.

At the same time Scully represented taxpayers and the government, he negotiated to go back to work for the industry that would benefit from the bill he was overseeing. Scully's potential employers, according to an internal Health and Human Services Department (HHS) document, were "law firms, consulting firms, and health care investment firms" that had "substantial interests pending before the department."

Ordinarily, that would suggest a conflict of interest, but in the spring of 2003, before the Medicare bill negotiations got under way,

Scully sought an official waiver from government ethics law from his boss, HHS Secretary Tommy G. Thompson. In an internal decision, Thompson ruled that Scully's job search in the private sector was not "likely to affect the integrity of the services which the government may expect from him."

Ten days after the bill was signed, Scully returned to the private sector. He left government to join the Washington office of an Atlanta law firm, Alston & Bird, and the investment banking firm of Welsh, Carson, Anderson & Stowe. Both had a long list of clients and interests in health care, including pharmaceutical companies, HMOs, and trade groups.

As it turned out, the Medicare drug law that Scully helped mold will be much more lucrative for the industry and much more costly to taxpayers than even its harshest critics realized. The Bush administration sold the legislation to skeptical lawmakers on the basis that it would cost taxpayers about $400 billion over ten years. The actual estimate was closer to $550 billion. But when Medicare's chief actuary, Richard Foster, sought to convey the real number to lawmakers while they weighed the bill, he was silenced by Scully, his boss.

Foster later told the House Ways and Means Committee that Scully "made it clear that we were not [to] respond directly to requests from Congress anymore but instead we were to give any such response to him and he would decide what to do with it." When Scully did not send the estimates to the Hill, Foster was upset. He told lawmakers later: "From a professional standpoint, I felt and believe there is an obligation, on behalf of the public, for my office to give you the best advice possible when requested." Foster said he thought about ignoring Scully's directive and sending the data to Congress, a move that he knew would almost certainly get him fired. He also considered resigning, but his staff talked him out of it, and he decided he would be "better off working inside the system."

After Congress passed the bill—the House did so by the narrowest of votes, 220 to 215—the Bush administration revised its cost estimate. The new figure was $534 billion—35 percent higher than the amount floated to win support for the program, and remarkably close to the estimates of Foster and his actuarial colleagues at Medicare. This meant the Medicare bill, the single largest corporate welfare bill in Congress's history, would almost certainly never have passed if lawmakers had known how much it was really going to cost.

Of course, Congress could repeal the act. But lawmakers would need to get it by Senate Majority Leader Bill Frist, the Tennessee Republican who played a pivotal role in pushing the Medicare bill through in the first place. The health care industry has no more ardent supporter in Washington than Frist, a heart surgeon and staunch advocate of free-market medicine. His father, Thomas F. Frist Sr., and his brother, Thomas F. Frist Jr., founded what has become HCA Inc., the nation's largest hospital chain with nearly 200 hospitals and revenue of $21.8 billion in 2003. His brother held a variety of top HCA posts over the years and still is the single largest individual stockholder, with seventeen million shares. And it was the hospital chain that allowed Senator Frist to start his career as a millionaire, with many of the millions coming from a business built on the solid foundation of taxpayer money. Over the years, HCA derived about one-third of its revenue from the federal government's Medicare program and the joint state-federal Medicaid program.

In addition to owning the largest number of hospitals, HCA also can lay claim to one other distinction, albeit a dubious one. The company has defrauded Medicare, Medicaid, and TRICARE—the military's health care program—of more money than any other health care provider in America, no small achievement in a field where the competition is intense. In June 2003, HCA agreed to pay $631 million in civil penalties and damages growing out of false claims to the government health care programs. That came on top of $840 million in criminal fines, civil restitution, and penalties the company paid in 2000. That same year, the company agreed to pay $250 million to settle other Medicare overbilling claims. In all, HCA has paid $1.7 billion as a result of its fraudulent practices.

This, then, is the sorry picture of health care in America. We spend more money than anyone else in the world—and have less to show for it. We have a second-rate system that doesn't adequately cover half or more of the population. We encourage hospitals and doctors to perform unnecessary medical procedures on people who don't need them, while denying the procedures to those who do. We clog our emergency rooms with patients who have insurance because they can't get in to see their doctors. We stand a good chance of dying from a mistake if we are admitted to a hospital, and an equally good chance of dying from a prescription drug taken at home. We charge the poor far more for their medical services than we do the rich. We force senior citizens with modest incomes to board a bus and travel to Canada or Mexico to buy drugs they can't afford here. We require ambulances to drive around a city until they can find a hospital willing to accept a patient for emergency treatment. We have a system in such constant turmoil that almost everyone involved is unhappy—patients, doctors, nurses, aides, technicians. Almost everyone. But for a lucky few, the turmoil is worth a lot of money.

Wall Street Medicine

Wall Street thrives on buying and selling. For America's most aggressive deal makers, health care has become the source of unexpected riches that even the most optimistic investment bankers did not foresee two decades ago. The move of the moneymen into health care triggered an ongoing wave of mergers, acquisitions, consolidations, hostile takeovers, initial public offerings, spinoffs, failures, and bankruptcies. A field once known for stability of ownership has been traumatized by almost constant upheaval. This has made life miserable for doctors, nurses, and, most of all, patients and their families. But it has been wonderful for the Street, creating endless opportunities to profit.

A hospital acquired by a for-profit corporation is suddenly sold a year later when the company decides the facility isn't a good "fit" for its business plan. A respected community hospital that has served a middle-class urban neighborhood for more than a century is closed when its operating profit falls below the corporation's targets. Nursing homes that once looked after the nation's weakest citizens are snapped up by indifferent chains interested not in people but in assuring a yearly increase in revenue. As for all the failed endeavors, they, too, represent more money for the Street, which collects additional fees for regrouping, restructuring, and recapitalizing the businesses it misguidedly assembled in the first place, as well as bringing out of bankruptcy those that collapse.

The business practices that the Street has introduced—cutting corners, trimming costs by eliminating nurses, hiring less-qualified physicians, replacing skilled employees with the unskilled, paying poverty-level wages to many workers, driving down the salaries of professionals, even curtailing the cleaning of hospital rooms, operating rooms, and doctors' offices to meet financial projections—have also been adopted with a vengeance by the so-called nonprofit side of medicine, so much so that the two now are often indistinguishable. Many of the institutions that remain, for-profit as well as not-for-profit, have lower standards and provide mediocre care. Rather than hold down overall spending, as once promised, the endless financial transactions inspired by the market have accelerated it.

In the earliest days, few on Wall Street recognized the enormous opportunities to make money from sick people. One who did was Benjamin Lorello, who would become one of the most spectacularly successful investment bankers in the new field. The son of an Italian family in Providence, Rhode Island, Lorello arrived in New York City in the late 1970s, fresh out of graduate school at MIT, just as the national debate over market forces and competition in health care began to heat up. He started at Shearson Hayden Stone. In 1985, he moved onto a broader stage when he was recruited by Smith Barney, Harris Upham to create a health care group from scratch for the venerable investment house.

Health care became an especially fertile field for deal making because it was so highly fragmented, with thousands of separate parts—hospitals, care providers, drug companies, biotech researchers, health maintenance organizations, orthopedics businesses, medical leasing companies, assisted living centers, pharmacies, insurers, medical-apparatus makers, nursing homes, specialty medical practices, testing facilities, mental health clinics, and medical information companies, among others. Best of all, the amount of money flowing through the various entities was growing exponentially, on its way to becoming a multitrillion-dollar marketplace, with a solid, guaranteed chunk of the cash coming from the federal government's Medicare and Medicaid programs, or, more precisely, taxpayers. What's more, there was little likelihood of a downturn. After all, disease and sickness—and equally important, the fear of both—were as certain as death and taxes. The remaking of this vast sector offered what the *Investment Dealers' Digest* called a "once-in-a-lifetime opportunity for creative investment bankers . . . a field that rewards creativity and bold thinking." Lorello could not have picked a better arena in which to prosper.

Over the next few years, he built a health care department for Smith Barney that became the most resourceful and successful on Wall Street. He focused on companies that he perceived could have a niche in the market, as well as seemingly attractive businesses that had been passed over by other investment bankers (though later it would be clearer why that was so). Putting together billions of dollars in private placements, public bond offerings, and initial public offerings, Lorello's efforts earned handsome fees for Smith Barney and brought luster to his department.

Assertive and tough-talking, with his loud ties and a rumored fondness for strip clubs, Lorello didn't fit the mold of a polished Wall Street financier. He could be gruff, insulting, and intimidating, but if he supported you, you could have no more forceful advocate. "When you've got Ben on your side, it's like guerrilla warfare," claimed the financial officer of a Lorello-backed company. Those on the other side could expect withering insults. According to *Fortune*, he was once overheard telling a foe: "If you were a stock, I'd short you."

His results for Smith Barney were dazzling. By the mid-1990s, the company was Wall Street's preeminent health care powerhouse. In one year alone, 1994, Smith Barney averaged a health care transaction a week. Lorello's one-man department had grown to nineteen investment bankers and ten analysts, the busiest and biggest on the Street.

To be sure, all the deals did not work out as promised, although they sure looked good in the beginning. So it was with Integrated Health Services (IHS), a nursing home operator and subacute-care provider founded in the mid-1980s by a beguiling free market entrepreneur, Dr. Robert N. Elkins. Like so many investors mesmerized by the mountain of cash available for tapping in the health care industry, Dr. Elkins, a Harvard-educated psychiatrist by trade, spotted an opening in the system. Many hospital patients needed ongoing care, but it was the kind of care and rehabilitation that could be provided in a much cheaper setting. That's when Integrated, based in Hunt Valley, Maryland, just north of Baltimore, turned a nursing-home wing into a subacute facility. More followed. By the time Smith Barney took the company public in April 1991, it had grown to some forty geriatric-care facilities with 5,600 beds in fifteen states. They included fourteen medical specialty units (MSUs) that looked after patients discharged from hospitals who still needed special care. For these services, Integrated charged $500 a day, with much of the money coming from taxpayers in the form of Medicare payments. The company also branched out into other specialized treatment—physical, speech, respiratory, occupational, and psychiatric therapy.

Three months after Integrated began trading on the NASDAQ stock market—its stock went up 11 percent the first week—Elkins was named 1991 Maryland Entrepreneur of the Year, an award sponsored by Merrill Lynch, Ernst & Young, and *Inc.* magazine. At a banquet in Baltimore, William E. Cole Jr., director of Entrepreneurial Services for Ernst & Young, said Dr. Elkins was chosen "from among very compet-

itive candidates," and that his "outstanding accomplishments, entrepreneurial spirit, and integrity have helped make IHS one of the most
respected health care service companies in the USA today."

Armed in part with cash raised on Wall Street by Lorello's team at
Smith Barney, Elkins continued his buying spree, snapping up nursing
homes across the country. By 1995, Integrated had nearly 200 facilities
with 25,000 beds in thirty states. The company's stock had moved into
the $40 range. By then, other Wall Street firms had jumped on
Lorello's Integrated bandwagon. Not even a *Wall Street Journal* story
suggesting accounting irregularities and medical misconduct at Integrated could dim enthusiasm. In a June 1995 report urging investors
to put their money in Integrated because it's "likely to outperform the
market," Salomon Brothers defended the company against the *Journal*
story, asserting that audits "by Federal Medicare auditors have revealed
no instances of improper practices." Furthermore, the Salomon Brothers analyst said, "the company has published a four-page response to
this article that clearly explains that no such practices have taken place
and that the company's accusers have questionable motives."

For its part, Smith Barney continued to underwrite the company,
arranging $950 million in high-yield debt in 1997 alone. The timing
was not good for Integrated, but that was of little concern to Wall
Street. That same year, as part of the Balanced Budget Act, Congress
slashed the Medicare giveaway payment system from which Elkins had
profited so handsomely. No more open-ended charges. Not only were
payments reduced, but also per-case and per-day limits were imposed.
Conditions at Integrated deteriorated as the company's profit of $41
million in the second quarter of 1998 was followed by a loss of $158
million in the third quarter. Its stock plunged from $40 a share in
1998 to pennies a share in 1999, when losses mounted to $2.2 billion.
Faced with nearly $3 billion in debt and falling government reim-
bursements, Integrated filed for bankruptcy in February 2000. As for

Dr. Elkins, he walked out the door with a $55 million severance package, largely in the form of debt forgiveness and income tax payments on his behalf.

Other Lorello-backed companies met a similar fate. Years later, one anonymous investment banker who had long competed against Lorello told the *New York Post*: "Ben does deals no one else will touch." But by the time the transactions he had put together came apart, Lorello had moved on to other deals.

In 1999, Lorello himself moved on—to even greener pastures. UBS Warburg, the Swiss banking giant, seeking a larger piece of the American financial market, recruited him to head its global health care services division for a reported $70 million compensation package over three years. Lorello's principal associates—and, more important, his biggest accounts—followed.

The most important client who accompanied Lorello to UBS Warburg was HealthSouth Corporation, America's largest operator of outpatient surgery centers and rehabilitation facilities. Founded in Birmingham, Alabama, in 1984, HealthSouth had grown into a Fortune 500 company, with $4 billion in revenue and 52,000 employees by the end of 1998. It boasted 1,900 inpatient and outpatient rehabilitation facilities, outpatient surgery centers, and occupational health and diagnostic centers in all fifty states and abroad. More than anyone else on Wall Street, Ben Lorello helped put the company on the map. He took it public in 1986 while at Smith Barney, then served as the underwriter on billions of dollars in debt and stock offerings that enabled it to gobble up competitors and branch out into other fields. Overall, Lorello would do more than $10 billion in deals with HealthSouth.

He developed a close relationship with HealthSouth's charismatic founder, Richard M. Scrushy, a controversial good old boy from Selma, Alabama. Scrushy liked to tell the story of when he was seventeen, working at a gas station to support himself and his pregnant teenage wife, and decided to make something of himself. He went back to school, obtained a degree as a respiratory therapist, and hatched the idea of becoming a health care baron. Charming and persuasive, Scrushy brushed aside doubters. One executive who later went to work for him described the impact of their first meeting: "I went home and told my wife that I just interviewed with the biggest con artist I ever met, or the most brilliant young man I ever met."

Ultimately, everyone would know the answer. "I want to be the highest-paid CEO in the world," Scrushy boasted. HealthSouth's eleven jets, the largest private fleet at Birmingham International Airport, allowed him to indulge his whims, such as ferrying himself and his country-and-western band, Dallas County Line, to gigs throughout the South, where Scrushy, dressed in black from head to toe, would belt out, "Honk If You Love to Honky Tonk." To celebrate his third marriage, Scrushy chartered a Boeing 727 to fly 150 invited guests, including Martha Stewart, to Jamaica in 1997.

If his flamboyant forays into country music and his courtship of the glitterati amused outsiders, inside HealthSouth, Scrushy was feared for his temper and dictatorial style. "King Richard" could be awfully high-handed, directing inspectors to subject department heads to a dreaded "white glove" spot check by sweeping surfaces for specks of dust. Those whose facilities didn't pass the test were penalized.

During the entire period when HealthSouth mushroomed from a regional rehabilitation business in the South to a nationwide corporation, Lorello's shop was closely involved in the company's growth. He or his deputy, William C. McGahan, often attended HealthSouth board meetings—nine from 1997 to 2002 alone. Stock analysts who were at Smith Barney and later UBS Warburg at the same time as Lorello regularly heaped praise on HealthSouth: "This company embodies nearly all the positive trends in this industry: consolidation, cost efficiency, good use of information systems," Geoffrey Harris, Smith Barney's head health care analyst, told *Fortune* in 1996.

Other Wall Street firms were equally bullish. Credit Suisse First Boston proclaimed that HealthSouth "should be considered a core holding in any health care and growth investment portfolio." A Credit Suisse analyst reported that "after spending some time recently with the chief executive of HealthSouth we continue to believe the company represents one of the most attractive investment opportunities in any of the health care service sectors." The data seemed to support Wall Street's endorsement. When *Fortune* published its list of 100 fastest-growing companies in 1996, there was HealthSouth, planted firmly at No. 40.

After Lorello moved to UBS Warburg, HealthSouth became a fixture at the investment firm's annual Global Health Care Services Conference in New York. A regular feature of health care banking on Wall Street, these conferences are a crucial part of market-based medicine, a way for investment bankers to introduce investors to large firms and start-ups. UBS showcased HealthSouth at annual conferences after 1999 and made it the subject of a keynote address at its 2002 meeting. Positive in-house assessments by UBS Warburg analysts helped cast a favorable light on the company's stock, which made it possible for UBS to do even more deals.

Things were so tight between Lorello and Scrushy that when UBS Warburg needed to assign a new analyst to the account, Scrushy was given the right to pick whom he wanted. He tapped Howard Capek, then with Credit Suisse First Boston, who had issued glowing reports on HealthSouth. After joining UBS, Capek continued to issue "strong buy" recommendations for the stock. Privately, though, he had serious doubts about the company. In confidential e-mails to a client in 1999, Capek said of HealthSouth: "I'd love to publish on this pig, then I wouldn't be spending so much time in Birmingham in July/August."

He offered to send "a few charts and graphs which should glaringly highlight the company's inability to collect and convert sales into cash." He later added: "What a mess. I wouldn't own a share."

Of course, that wasn't what Wall Street was telling investors. A Deutsche Banc Alex. Brown analyst put out a "buy" report in April 2000, saying that "the recent string of positive news flow related to nearly every aspect of HealthSouth's business, including pricing, purchasing, cost reduction, and inventory management leads us to believe that the 'tide has turned' in Birmingham, Alabama," and the stock is headed up. It was, which prompted the company to observe in its next annual report: "In 2000, our stock rose to promising heights, closing up 203 percent for the year and earning HealthSouth recognition as a top-five performer in the S&P 500. We also fulfilled Wall Street expectations for another year, maintaining our position as the Fortune 500 company with the second-longest streak for meeting or exceeding analysts' expectations."

Despite Wall Street's strong support, the foundation began to crumble during 2002. Although the company had long known that a change in federal law would reduce Medicare reimbursements, it waited until August 2002 to disclose that the new formula would cut earnings by $175 million, or about 15 percent for the year. Shareholders sued, claiming they had been misled. The SEC opened an investigation to determine if securities laws had been breached and whether Scrushy, who had sold half his stake in the company for $25 million only weeks before the disclosure, had benefited from inside information. Even after these bombshells, UBS Warburg hung tough with its "strong buy" recommendation, if only for a few more days.

Over the next several months, a series of revelations exposed HealthSouth as a monumental accounting fraud. For years, the company had been cooking the books through a scheme that inflated earnings to meet Wall Street's projections, enabling it to borrow more money to cover up ongoing shortfalls. The company needed constant injections of fresh capital to camouflage its mediocre performance and to help pay for acquisitions. It was a Ponzi scheme of sorts, using new money to plug holes from past problems, dependent on bogus numbers to create the illusion of a robust company worthy of investors' confidence.

HealthSouth's felonious accounting gave new meaning to the concept of playing with the numbers, according to SEC and shareholder lawsuits. Before announcing quarterly returns, the company's top financial officers would provide Scrushy with the company's operating results. "When Scrushy and his chief lieutenants saw that actual results were well below forecasted results and those necessary for the scheme to continue," a shareholder complaint contended, "Scrushy and HealthSouth's then-CFO would direct accounting subordinates to 'fix' the shortfall through the entry of false accounting entries to create made-up revenue and income on HealthSouth's records." The select few who got together to doctor the books were known in the corporate culture as "family" members. Their gatherings to massage the numbers were called "family meetings." Plugging gaps in the company's books was called "shoveling dirt into the hole." The hole eventually became too deep.

In March 2003, the SEC charged Scrushy and HealthSouth with massive accounting fraud—for having overstated earnings by $1.4 billion since 1999. Even by Enron and WorldCom standards, the Health-South fraud was shocking. The government charged that company accountants routinely created "false documents to support its fictitious accounting entries." When an auditor questioned an entry on the company's books, the SEC alleged, the accountants would take an invoice from an unrelated transaction and alter it to make it appear to be the entry in question, then pass it on to the outside auditors to "indicate that the facility in question had actually purchased the asset."

In November 2003, Scrushy was indicted on eighty-five counts of fraud, conspiracy, money laundering, and making false statements in what the U.S. Department of Justice charged was a seven-year scheme to add $2.7 billion in mythical income to HealthSouth's books and defraud investors, the public, and the U.S. government. During the time Scrushy earned $267 million in salary, bonuses, and stock options, the government claimed that he also illegally acquired $279 million in property—including multiple residences, a yacht, and an assortment of boats, jewelry, luxury cars, aircraft, and paintings by Picasso, Chagall, and Renoir. His compensation package was tied to the company's financial performance, which, as it turned out, consisted of counterfeit numbers. In time, more than a dozen current or former top financial officials of HealthSouth would be charged and plead guilty to manipulating the company's earnings to prop up the stock price.

What did Wall Street know about all this? When called before a congressional committee investigating the scandal in November 2003, UBS's Lorello professed ignorance. "I was not aware of nor did not suspect that anyone at HealthSouth was engaged in any improprieties," he told a House subcommittee on investigations, adding that UBS relied on HealthSouth's "audited financial statements." He blamed the company's management, which he said engaged in an "elaborate conspiracy to cover up, conceal and keep secret the fraud from its auditors, its underwriters, and lenders such as UBS." He had worked with Scrushy for more than fifteen years, attended numerous board meetings, knew top management, but was completely unaware of the doctored books.

Many of HealthSouth's outraged investors were not so sure. One HealthSouth executive who later pled guilty to fraud and was sentenced to prison told of hearing a voicemail message from a "Ben" at UBS Warburg, impressing upon company executives in no uncertain terms the importance of hitting their numbers. Emery W. Harris, HealthSouth's vice president for accounting and assistant controller, said the voicemail was played by Michael D. Martin, HealthSouth's chief financial officer, to emphasize why he was asking Harris and his associates to make sure the numbers met the Street's expectations. In playing the message for them, Harris recalled Martin saying: "This is what I'm up against and this is why I asked you to do the things I asked you to do." In the voicemail, Harris said "Ben" told Martin that "it was important for him to lay down for the family and do what was right. And there was a lot of people counting on you to make things happen this quarter. We're expecting big things, you know. If you don't lay down for the family, you'll get whacked."

Many of Ben Lorello's widely celebrated health care ventures flamed out. So, too, did many more ill-advised deals put together by other investment bankers. But Wall Street never looks back. It simply moves on to the next target in a never-ending search to feed its perpetual-motion machine of fees, IPOs, debt offerings, and restructurings.

So it was that Wall Street saw fresh opportunities in the temporary staffing of nurses. Because some nurses prefer a flexible schedule and the chance to work in different hospitals and health care settings, small independent staffing agencies have long served that need. They arrange assignments as short as a single shift, or for days or weeks, to meet the requirements of hospitals and other health care facilities. But as Wall Street moved into hospitals, creating turmoil and dissatisfaction, nurses began moving out. Suddenly, thanks to Wall Street, there was a new demand for services that provided temporary workers.

Through the 1990s, the Street brought to market several large staffing companies, among them Cross Country Healthcare Inc., Medical Staffing Network Holdings Inc., AMN Healthcare Services Inc., and On Assignment Inc. Morgan Stanley even picked up 13.6 percent of the stock in Cross Country Healthcare, a Boca Raton, Florida, firm that describes itself as "one of the largest providers of healthcare staffing services in the United States" with revenue of $687 million in 2003. Warburg Pincus & Company, a private equity investor, took a 47.9 percent stake in Medical Staffing Network Holdings Inc., also of Boca Raton, which had 2003 revenue of $513 million.

AMN Healthcare Services was typical of the new arrivals, which sought to take advantage of the heavier workloads, mandatory overtime, and more demanding work environments—often resulting from business practices designed to make hospitals more "efficient"—that were driving nurses out of the profession. During nursing shortages, says AMN, "permanent staff nurses are often required to assume greater responsibility and patient loads, work mandatory overtime and deal with increased pressures within the hospital. Many experienced nurses consequently choose to leave their permanent employer, and look for a more flexible and rewarding position."

After championing the ill-conceived business practices that helped cause a shortage of nurses, Wall Street thus bankrolled companies to solve the problems that it created. AMN was founded in 1997, went public in 2001, and floated another stock offering a year later. The company's stock performed marvelously, climbing from a low of $21 in the fourth quarter of 2001 to a high of $37.40 in the second quarter of 2002.

AMN sees a bright future given the "favorable industry trends" caused by the flight of nurses out of their long-time jobs. Or, as the company puts it: "Temporary staffing has emerged as an increasingly utilized method to efficiently deliver health care services. . . . We believe that this expanded demand and supply pattern will continue over the long term." The potential seems limitless. In 2002, temporary health care staffing generally represented a $10.6 billion industry, one that was growing at an annual rate of 16 percent. As for AMN, its revenue spiraled from $88 million in 1998 to $776 million in 2002—an increase of 782 percent. Those were just the kind of numbers that Ben Lorello liked. His group at UBS Warburg had been a lead underwriter on AMN's first two public offerings.

HOW PROFIT BECAME POLICY

It was no accident that American health care became a profit center for Wall Street. The transformation of many not-for-profit providers into for-profit corporations was engineered by Washington in the early 1980s. The Reagan revolution had swept into power conservatives who were determined to alter health care drastically by reducing government funding and by introducing competition to give consumers and companies more choices in selecting providers. The goal, as *Congressional Quarterly* put it, was "to unleash 'free market forces' to attack the persistent problems of the cost and accessibility of health care."

One of the administration's first moves was to cut off federal funding for the burgeoning nonprofit HMO movement. Eight years earlier, in an unlikely alliance, President Nixon had embraced HMOs as a way to restrain health care costs and open the door to coverage for more Americans. Using the successful Kaiser Permanente system in California as a model, Congress passed the HMO Act of 1973, which provided seed money to start similar care-providing networks in other states. The idea was to deemphasize fee-for-service medicine, which was seen as the major force driving up costs, and replace it largely with a system of flat fees. There was reason for optimism. The Kaiser HMO was created just before the outbreak of World War II by the industrialist Henry J. Kaiser, whose stunning achievements included building Hoover Dam and a fleet of cargo ships during the war. The goal of his health system was not to make money but to keep workers healthy so they could remain on the job, building ships that helped America win the war. It worked splendidly. Of course, critics labeled it a dreaded socialist experiment and doctors who worked for it in the beginning were shunned by much of the medical world.

By establishing fees up front, HMOs were expected to create financial incentives for both patients and doctors to avoid elaborate and sometimes unnecessary procedures. To Americans today, the mere mention of HMOs conjures up all that has gone wrong with health care. But years ago, when HMOs were perceived as not-for-profit operations, the view was much more positive. HMOs were seen as a way to include more Americans, promote quality care, and hold down costs. With the new federal support from the Nixon law, the number of HMOs multiplied from thirty in 1970 to nearly 300 in 1980. Enrollment tripled from three million to more than ten million.

By Washington standards, the government-backed HMO experiment was never very costly—just $350 million in loans and grants over the seven-year period from 1973 to 1980. But even that was too much for the Reaganites, who intended to wean the system from government funding and transform health care into a business like any other. After September 1981, when federal funding ceased, each HMO had to sink or swim, at the mercy of the marketplace.

To encourage Wall Street to step in, the Reagan administration embarked on an ambitious plan to sell investors and venture capitalists on investing in health care. The U.S. Department of Health and Human Services (HHS) commissioned a study by the accounting firm Touche Ross & Co. extolling the benefits of a market-driven system. "The Investors' Guide to Health Maintenance Organizations" provided an introduction to the far-flung health care industry and assurances that "effectively managed H.M.O.'s are good investments."

HHS sponsored workshops in New York, Washington, and Chicago to show investors the profit-making potential of health care. Frank H. Seubold, director of HHS's office of HMOs, said that federal funding had proven the feasibility of HMOs. "Now it's time to shift gears," he said. There were uncertainties, he acknowledged, but the evidence indicated that HMOs "are good businesses and can provide a good focus for investment." The author of the Touche Ross study, James M. Turnock, put it in terms investors could grasp: HMOs, he said, were "just like any business. If you can pick a winner, you can make a lot of money."

Government policy makers envisioned vigorous competition, giving consumers choices among multiple HMO providers. They then could weigh their options and decide what they needed, much like buying a car. The concept, as *BusinessWeek* put it, was to make workers, companies, and Medicare recipients more cost-conscious: "Such a change is expected to induce insurers, doctors, and hospitals to organize into rival health care delivery groups that compete on price and quality of service." Just exactly how consumers would judge the merits of various health care plans, in contrast to comparing models of a standard consumer item, was unclear. Even more puzzling was how they would make this decision in an ambulance on the way to a hospital emergency room after an accident. Nevertheless, ardent supporters such as Representative David Stockman, a Michigan Republican who would later be Reagan's first budget director, were convinced that competition was the key. "The secret is to *liberate* health consumers from the policy-induced stupor that has reduced them to passive, indirect *payors* when by nature they are accomplished, resourceful *shoppers*," he wrote in 1979. "The activation of 150 million adult health care shoppers would dramatically transform the medical marketplace. . . ." He was right, of course, but not in the way he imagined.

The person generally credited with spawning the idea that competition would be the salvation of American health care is Alain C. Enthoven, a professor of public policy at Stanford University. A technocrat with a coldly analytical belief in the power of computers to solve public problems, Enthoven was Robert McNamara's chief whiz kid at the Pentagon during the Vietnam War.

As head of systems analysis for McNamara, Enthoven's office devised the infamous "body count," the controversial program that purported to measure the progress of the war by tabulating the number of enemy dead. Working with reports from U.S. commanders in the field, Enthoven's numbers crunchers factored Vietcong kills into a complex computer analysis that was then used by U.S. civilian and military leaders to show how the United States was winning the war.

To believe that quantitative methods could be applied in such a complex human endeavor as war was, in the words of one military historian, "the height of arrogance." Moreover, it was open to manipulation, error, and abuse. Because favorable body counts caught the attention of the top brass, some units inflated their numbers. Some officers won promotions based in part on mythical kills. The system "proved so morally corrosive that it led to a crisis of soul-searching in the post-war officer corps," according to historian William S. Murray. Ultimately, the entire concept was discredited, "a notorious symbol of the errors of the war," as McNamara biographer Deborah Shapley wrote.

After Vietnam, Enthoven went on to his next career, this one in health care, as a professor at the Graduate School of Business at Stanford. In 1977, the Carter administration asked him to develop a plan to extend health care benefits and curb costs. His *Consumer Choice Health Plan* concluded that the key was to encourage competition in the private sector. Arguing that government regulation would "raise costs," Enthoven advocated that Washington "change financial incentives by creating a system of competing health plans in which physicians and consumers can benefit from using resources wisely." Enthoven contended that this "would give people an incentive to seek out systems that provide care economically by letting them keep all the savings." Enthoven foresaw government creating numerous HMOs that could then compete for consumers' business.

Although the Carter administration rejected Enthoven's proposal, his ideas were embraced by conservatives who saw in them a way to apply their own free-market, antigovernment theories to health care reform. After Reagan won the 1980 election, the stage was set to implement these ideas in the marketplace.

The nudge from Washington was all Wall Street needed to ignite an explosion of activity to convert nonprofit HMOs into investor-owned corporations. "Word of phenomenal growth and hefty profits has forecasters abuzz," gushed an article in *National Journal*. "HMOs are one of the hottest, if not the hottest, stocks on Wall Street," said Eric Schlesinger, a consultant with Boston Consulting Group Inc. of New York City. "They are loved on Wall Street. They have made dollar signs dance in the eyes of HMO administrators who think they can become millionaires overnight."

In 1983 alone, five formerly not-for-profit HMOs with hundreds of thousands of enrollees converted to publicly owned corporations. The single most dramatic sign that times had changed was the IPO for U.S. Health Care Systems Inc. in suburban Philadelphia. Once known as HMO of Pennsylvania and the recipient of federal seed money, the HMO had converted to for-profit status in 1981 and two years later became the first to go public. The stock was priced at $15 in advance of the sale, but there was so much interest, it sold at $20 on the day it debuted. Even so, the issue was oversubscribed, and within a week U.S. Health Care stock was trading at $33¼. Within three months, the company declared its first dividend. "It was one of the hottest stocks in the country," said the company's lawyer. "Everybody wanted it."

Renamed U.S. Healthcare, the company would soon earn a dismal reputation among doctors, who would chafe under its reimbursement and referral practices. However, founder Leonard Abramson, who started the company in 1981, prospered nicely. A former pharmaceutical salesman, he turned up on the Forbes 400 list of richest Americans within two years of taking the company public. Eventually, U.S. Health-care would be bought by Aetna, providing yet another fortune to Abramson. The lesson of this stunning financial success—that you could make a lot of money in a very short time from health care—was not lost on other entrepreneurs and investors, and in subsequent years dozens of nonprofit HMOs would convert their status just like U.S. Healthcare.

The move to for-profit health care companies was a profound trans-formation that would affect millions of Americans. It was rationalized, explained, and justified for one reason—as the only way to control costs. "The object will be to slow the explosive rise in the nation's med-ical bill," *BusinessWeek* reported, "and to set in motion free market forces that will reduce the waste, inefficiencies, and misuse of health ser-vices that have eluded the corrective thrust of government regulations."

For-profit HMOs were the "Johnny-on-the-spot answer to the health care cost problem," said a Piper, Jaffray & Hopwood analyst in 1984. Calling them "clearly an idea whose time has come," the analyst proclaimed that they offered something for everyone: "The employer saves money and administrative hassle, is able to predict medical expenses and contain those expenses within reasonable limits. The patient receives lower cost health care by virtue of deductibles/co-pay-ments . . . and is freed of the need to fill out reimbursement forms. The doctor gains a predictable revenue source and reduced administra-tive burden." To continue the current pattern of ever-greater health care costs was "clearly unsustainable—and unaffordable."

Smith Barney, Harris Upham & Co. said the current system "offers no controls or incentives to monitor costs in an effective way . . . (HMOs) have injected an element of competition into a previously non-competitive industry . . . (They) present economic incentives to monitor and limit unnecessary hospital utilization and medical services."

In Wall Street's view, "the chief beneficiary of all this will clearly be society," claimed Sanford C. Bernstein & Co., a New York investment company. "For the first time, the U.S. health care system will be under control."

At the time, in 1984, health care costs represented 10.5 percent of gross domestic product. Twenty years into the experiment to "slow the explosive rise in the nation's medical bill," health care costs at the end of 2003 exceeded 15 percent of GDP. They are still rising. The last time that so many on Wall Street and in government were so wrong was 1929—but this time many would make a great deal of money.

SELLING THE HOSPITALS

From the 1980s on, hospitals were an inviting target for Wall Street. Here was a field that seemed ripe for consolidation and economies of scale: All hospitals purchase many of the same goods, services, and equipment, use similar technology, negotiate with many of the same insurers, and must abide by the same Medicare and Medicaid regulations. Wall Street reasoned that a portion of America's hospitals could be assembled into national chains, much like department stores and auto-parts distributors, and investors would make a fortune.

For most of their existence, hospitals were largely owned by nonprofit institutions, affiliated with churches, universities, and other tax-exempt organizations. They served neighborhoods and religious communities, as their names often indicated—Baptist, Lutheran, Methodist, Presbyterian, St. Vincent's. Members of their boards were the local elite who brought to the table all the advantages and disadvantages of their specialized expertise. Their mission was to serve patients and meet community needs. "You didn't have to worry if you failed to bring in 10, 15, or 20 percent in profits every year," said Dr. Quentin Young, a Chicago internist who helped found Physicians for a National Health Program, a not-for-profit organization that advocates a single-payer health plan for America. "That wasn't your purpose. You didn't want to lose money, but your purpose wasn't to make money."

Wall Street had begun eyeing hospitals even before the big move into free-market medicine in the 1980s. Several companies already were assembling networks—Humana Inc., American Medical International, and Hospital Affiliates International Inc. But the company that pointed the way was Hospital Corporation of America (HCA), founded in 1968 on the promise to "create economies of scale and enhance the quality of care in communities across the country." HCA's driving force in the early years, Jack Massey, had plenty of experience coordinating the operations of multiple entities. A colorful, cigar-smoking former pharmacist, Massey had made a fortune franchising Kentucky Fried Chicken outlets and believed the lessons learned in the fast-food industry could be applied to investor-owned hospitals. As HCA swallowed up hospitals, *Forbes* enthused that under Massey "HCA dispenses health care as profitably as KFC did drumsticks."

After steady growth through the 1970s, HCA took off when the for-profit boom exploded in the 1980s. During this period, HCA and other chains competed to acquire nonprofit hospitals and clinics everywhere, large and small. Soon many nonprofits central to the health of their communities were converted to investor-owned properties.

Health care conglomerates made thousands of transactions, buying independent hospitals and then selling them, often in rapid succession. Of all the companies that followed this pattern, one of the most zealous was the nation's second-largest for-profit hospital chain, Tenet Healthcare Corporation.

Tenet's story begins in 1993, fittingly enough, when the company was born out of the wreckage of an earlier for-profit hospital chain, National Medical Enterprises (NME), which was run by fervent believers in the free market of health care. As an NME executive once put it: "We must abandon our mystical notions about the art of healing and replace them with a philosophy of offering a good product at a good price." As it turned out, the company's psychiatric unit set the standard for health care fraud. Its doctors and administrators over-billed patients, insurers, and Medicare. They charged for services and treatment never provided. They signed false insurance claims and encouraged others to do so. They paid up to $40 million in kickbacks to doctors to refer Medicare, Medicaid, and privately insured patients to their psychiatric hospitals. They falsified the charts of patients to confine them in the hospitals longer than needed—sometimes against their will—in order to keep the money flowing from insurers.

The company ultimately pleaded guilty to fraud charges and paid the U.S. government $379 million in criminal fines, civil damages, and penalties—the largest sum ever assessed until then. It also agreed to sell sixty of its psychiatric hospitals and substance-abuse facilities. By the time the civil lawsuits by patients were settled, the company had shelled out nearly three-quarters of a billion dollars as a result of its fraudulent conduct.

To clean house, the NME board tossed out the old management and brought in a new leader to run the Santa Monica–based corpora-tion. In any other era, their choice would have provoked skepticism about his qualifications to manage a chain of hospitals. But by the early 1990s, with the belief deeply embedded that corporations and the free market were the answer to health care's woes, not a question was raised.

The new CEO was Jeffrey C. Barbakow, a forty-nine-year-old investment banker who knew little about hospitals but a lot about Wall Street. A managing director of Donaldson, Lufkin & Jenrette, Barbakow had spent much of his career doing deals, mostly in the entertainment industry. A business school graduate of the University of Southern California, he began as an investment banker on Wall Street in 1969 with Merrill Lynch. Three years later, he opened a Mer-rill investment banking office in Los Angeles, where his clients included Columbia Pictures, 20th Century Fox, and National Medical Enterprises.

In 1988, Kirk Kerkorian, the Beverly Hills billionaire who owned Metro-Goldwyn-Mayer/United Artists Communications Co. (MGM/UA), hired Barbakow as MGM's president and CEO. Barbakow pledged to revitalize the legendary studio of *Gone With the Wind*, *The Wizard of Oz*, and other classics, but almost no one believed him. Kerkorian had been selling off pieces of MGM for years, and bringing in an investment banker, *Daily Variety* noted, was the equivalent of trying to "fatten the cow for market."

Two years later, MGM/UA was indeed sold to an Italian financier, Giancarlo Parretti. Credit Lyonnais, which financed the $900 million sale, later sued Kerkorian, Barbakow, and others, charging that they had misled the bank about the true state of MGM's finances. The company was a shadow of its former self by the time Parretti bought it. For Barbakow the litigation was a minor annoyance. According to reports, he had pocketed $30 million or more from readying MGM for sale, and had retreated in semiretirement to his home in Santa Barbara, ninety miles northwest of Los Angeles. He was living there, in the area that has been called the American Riviera, when the call came to run NME.

Barbakow set about to remake the troubled, scandal-plagued company and promised great things. "I believe in NME's future," he said after taking over. "The foundation clearly exists for future success." One of his early acts was to put some distance between the old company and the new by changing its name. After a company-sponsored naming contest, National Medical Enterprises was renamed Tenet Healthcare. Since a "tenet" is a principle or belief held as a truth, the name had special resonance for a company that had been mired in scandal and engaged in unethical conduct. "It's very warm," said Barbakow. "It'll grow on you more and more."

To make Tenet grow and impress Wall Street, Barbakow fell back on a formula that had been one of his own "tenets" as an investment banker—doing deals. His tenure would be marked by one long acquisition binge. In 1994, a Texas-based for-profit hospital chain, American Medical Holdings, was purchased for $3.3 billion, more than doubling the number of the company's hospitals to seventy-one. Two years later, Barbakow engineered the $3.1 billion acquisition of Nashville-based OrNda HealthCorp with fifty acute-care hospitals in fifteen states, including nine where Tenet had no presence.

The growth was yet to translate into a great investment for shareholders, but Wall Street was enamored of Tenet and especially Barbakow. "He basically salvaged the company," said Leo Dierckman, an analyst with Conseco Capital Management. "He's just a good businessperson who happens to be in health care." When a dissident shareholder raised questions about the corporation's operations, he was dismissed as a nuisance by the Street. "Cash flow is improving at a rate never seen, debt is down, and profit margins are up," said Sheryl Skolnick of Robertson, Stephens & Company. "Is this guy complaining that management isn't doing a good job?"

Wall Street was especially charmed by Barbakow's efforts that gave the impression that he was saving money for the corporation and creating value for shareholders. There was often much less to this than met the eye. Early in 1995, Barbakow closed the company's corporate headquarters in Santa Monica and shifted many of its 700 positions to an operations center in Dallas. Longtime employees were given an option of transferring to Texas or losing their jobs without severance. Weary of the occasional commute to Santa Monica, Barbakow transferred his office to Santa Barbara. From a business standpoint, separating the corporate executives from the principal operating division made little practical sense. It was costly, too. Santa Barbara was an idyllic setting for vacationers and retirees, but not a very good location from which to run a national business. Office rents were high, and the town had only spotty airline service. Barbakow solved that by leasing two jetliners that could carry him and other executives to the company's far-flung properties without the inconvenience of flying out of Los Angeles International Airport. The new headquarters was only a few minutes from Barbakow's hillside estate.

By 2000, Barbakow's incessant deal-making had built Tenet into a rival of HCA, the largest for-profit hospital chain. Tenet had revenue of $11.4 billion and more than 100,000 employees in 111 hospitals in seventeen states. The company's financials had remained lackluster until 2000, when Tenet finally was able to string together a series of consecutive quarterly gains. It wasn't much when lumped in with the company's performance for the decade, but was more than enough to let Barbakow toot his horn. "We've weathered a very difficult period and are now positioned for strong growth," he said. Wall Street weighed in approvingly: "They're setting the bar high for the rest of the industry," said Merrill Lynch analyst Albert Rice. "The company is on a roll right now," said John Hindelong, an analyst with Barbakow's old firm of Donaldson, Lufkin & Jenrette. "I expect them to continue to do well."

CORPORATE CULTURE

Tenet was finally fulfilling Wall Street's confident forecasts, largely because of a corporate culture instilled by Barbakow that emphasized hitting the numbers at all costs. Hospital administrators were under intense pressure to maximize profits and minimize expenses, and Barbakow put in place an incentive pay plan that rewarded them with cash bonuses if they exceeded their targets.

Chief executives of Tenet hospitals had an average salary of $200,000 in the 2001 fiscal year. But collectively, the company confirmed, they doubled their pay with cash bonuses, mostly for boosting a hospital's earnings. In conference calls with analysts, Tenet executives stressed the value they placed on cash flow. "We make cash flow an important part of our incentive compensation system," said Tenet's chief financial officer, David Dennis. A hospital's cash flow was closely monitored by headquarters, and administrators who fell short of the goal could be grilled. Making your numbers, a Tenet executive later told the *Los Angeles Times*, was "how you were judged, paid and evaluated."

This tight control over costs and revenue was perfectly in line with business-school models about the most efficient way to run a company: If revenue falls short, then cut back on staff, supplies, or inventory until the business rights itself. But in hospitals, where a sudden spurt in costs or a drop-off in revenue might be due to factors beyond the institution's control—such as a heavier-than-usual flu season—cutting costs isn't something an administrator can do without sacrificing patient care.

Lorraine Lydon of Loxahatchee, Florida, a small town on the edge of the Everglades outside Palm Beach, considered herself a reasonably active middle-aged woman when she entered Palm Beach Gardens Medical Center for heart surgery in 2000. She had selected one of South Florida's oldest and busiest cardiac centers, a hospital that had been a fixture in the metropolitan area for decades. The formerly independent hospital had become part of Tenet five years earlier when the corporation acquired American Medical International. After Tenet took over, Palm Beach Gardens, according to litigation, made "drastic reductions in capital outlay for nursing staff, physical plant maintenance, housekeeping, medical and surgical supplies [and] medical equipment."

Lydon underwent surgery on September 28, 2000, and subsequently was discharged. Before long she was back. She had picked up an infection in the hospital, an increasingly common occurrence in hospitals everywhere. During the weeks to come, she received a series of intravenous treatments with powerful antibiotics. When that failed, surgeons operated again to remove the dead tissue and bone that had been destroyed by the infection—her sternum, clavicle, and parts of ribs. Eventually, she had seventeen operations for complications arising from her postoperative infection. "I was an active fifty-year-old woman before all of this," Lydon later said, "but now I feel like I'm in a ninety-year-old body."

Calvin Warriner, a West Palm Beach lawyer who represents Lydon in her action against the Tenet hospital, says he has documented more than 100 similar cases of cardiac patients who contracted virulent staph infections because of unsanitary conditions at Palm Beach Gardens. Warriner has said most of the cases were caused by penicillin-resistant forms of bacteria. Warriner told the *Jupiter Courier*, "[These people] thought heart surgery would make them better and look at them now."

Though crippled for life, Lydon fared better than some who went under the knife at Palm Beach Gardens. She lived. Warriner says he has documented sixteen cases of patients who died from staph infections.

After the infections became known, the U.S. Centers for Medicare and Medicaid Services threatened to revoke the hospital's Medicare certification unless the problem was brought under control. "This action was taken because of infection-control issues," said Hugh Miller, a CMS official in Atlanta. Months later, after new procedures were implemented by Palm Beach, federal and state officials withdrew their plans to bar treatment there for Medicare patients.

Hospital officials have denied that unsanitary conditions caused illness and death at Palm Beach, but horror stories have turned up at other Tenet-owned hospitals. Surgeons at Tenet's Garden Grove Hospital in Orange County, California, were stunned to learn one day in 2000 that they had been operating on patients with surgical tools that hadn't been properly cleaned. For three months, some instruments that were supposedly sterilized had been testing positive for bacteria. During that time, some 3,000 persons had surgery at the hospital. Although it was obvious to the hospital staff that something was wrong with the equipment, the hospital continued to use the same faulty sterilizers without telling surgeons they were operating with potentially contaminated instruments.

The hospital's chief of surgery, Dr. Charles Rosen, was so upset when he learned about the problem that he resigned. "There are always things that break down in hospitals, and people fix them, but to consciously and deliberately withhold information about an ongoing problem from doctors is outrageous," Rosen told the *Orange County Register*. "It's immoral. It's endangering people's lives."

Cutting back on supplies, staff, and services in hospitals was just one way that Tenet bolstered its bottom line. Another practice seems to have been a conscious policy to concentrate on attracting the sickest Medicare patients, the "outlier" patients whose medical conditions are so severe or treatment so costly that they trigger an additional payment from the federal government.

The source of this initiative within Tenet remains unclear, but there is little doubt the corporation became heavily dependent on Medicare payments of this sort. In the 2000 fiscal year, Tenet took in $351 million in outlier payments, 3.1 percent of its $11.4 billion in total revenue. By fiscal 2002, those payments had more than doubled, to $763 million, or 5.5 percent of its revenue of $13.9 billion. Of Tenet's Medicare revenue, 23.5 percent came from the outlier patients. By contrast, HCA, the largest hospital company, received only about 5 percent of its Medicare revenue from that source. However the change came about, it was the engine that converted a lackluster Tenet in the 2000–02 period into a stock market star.

Wall Street continued to love everything about Tenet, always finding something to praise. In March 2002, analysts for Deutsche Banc Alex. Brown cited Tenet's "effective cost controls" as a major factor in driving earnings.

Frugality did not apply everywhere. In Santa Barbara, at Tenet's office building a few blocks from the Pacific, life had never been better for those at the top. The run-up in the company's stock price seemed to vindicate Barbakow's management philosophy. Tenet thought nothing of spending hospital revenue on corporate jets or staging spectacles to mark company milestones. For a conference extolling the success of the company's "Target 100" customer-satisfaction program, Tenet leased Caesars Palace in Las Vegas and flew in 1,000 employees from around the country for a three-day extravaganza. According to the *Los Angeles Times*, speakers dressed up as Dr. Seuss characters, and "Tenet Chief Executive Jeffrey C. Barbakow, wearing a big red-and-white striped hat, addressed the group as mayor of Tenetville, and souvenir dolls of him in the role were passed out. Senior executives rode around in decorated golf carts, and some emerged on stage as if riding Harley-Davidsons." A former Tenet executive who declined to be identified told TheStreet.com that the company once rented the entire South Fork Ranch—where the television series *Dallas* was taped—to hold a seminar aimed, ironically, at sharpening administrators' budgeting skills. "Tenet paid palm readers, fortune tellers and psychics to be on hand for employees to consult with," he said.

Tenet's most flagrant excesses were corporate salaries. In 2002, Barbakow was the highest-paid corporate executive of any public company in America, pulling in $117 million in stock options and salary. In one sale, on January 16, 2002, he earned $111 million from cashing in options, the largest single insider transaction in corporate America that year. Barbakow also enjoyed personal use of Tenet's corporate jet, a perk that cost the company more than $100,000 for the years 2001 and 2002.

Meanwhile, a small but increasingly vociferous group of shareholder activists led by a Miami physician, Dr. M. Lee Pearce, tried to turn the spotlight on Tenet's culture of wretched excess, as well as its overall poor performance, fundamental weaknesses, and slavish devotion to the stock market. "How much longer will you embrace Wall Street Medicine and its spurious earnings to the detriment of quality care?" he would ask Barbakow in an open letter in 2002. Dr. Pearce sounded the alarm repeatedly about Tenet but had little initial success. He lost a proxy fight in 2000 to unseat Barbakow directors, and Wall Street analysts portrayed him as a troublemaker. Instead of heeding Pearce's warnings, most of which turned out to be right on the money, the financial press continued to shower Tenet with glowing tributes. A *Business Week* story of October 16, 2002, stands out as embarrassingly off base:

> A few years back, Tenet Healthcare was dealing with onerous Medicare payment cuts mandated by Congress . . . [and] a shareholder activist . . . was seeking to oust [Barbakow]. . . . What a difference a couple of years can make. Tenet's 114-hospital chain is posting record profits. . . . In what has been a dismal market, Tenet's stock has been a haven, doubling in two years.

Less than two weeks later, on October 28, Wall Street sent up a warning flag about Tenet's earnings. In an abrupt shift, an analyst for UBS Warburg pointed to Tenet's overdependence on the Medicare outlier payments for very sick patients. UBS Warburg noted that a far higher share of Tenet's revenue came from such payments than did its competitors' and questioned whether the company could sustain such growth. He suggested that shareholders reduce their Tenet holdings. At the same time, an investigator working for an insurance company had reached a similar conclusion and was in the process of alerting Medicare about what he considered Tenet's disproportionate Medicare payments.

Two days after the UBS Warburg report, Tenet was rocked by an even more alarming development. More than forty FBI agents raided

Tenet's Redding Medical Center and the offices of two doctors in northern California in search of evidence to support allegations that the doctors had carried out large numbers of unwarranted cardiac procedures, some on patients with normal hearts. An FBI affidavit stated that Dr. Chae Hyun Moon, the hospital's chief cardiologist, and Dr. Fidel Realyvasquez Jr., a cardiac surgeon, had performed an unusually high number of heart catheterizations and other coronary procedures, of which as many as half might have been "unnecessary by commonly held medical standards."

The FBI investigation of Tenet's Redding cardiac factory revealed a chilling tale of how the lure of profits affected the lives of unsuspecting patients. The 238-bed hospital performed about one thousand cardiac procedures a year—heart catheterizations, angioplasty, and open-heart surgeries—a disproportionate number for a regional medical center. The cardiac unit was hugely profitable for the hospital as well as the doctors. In the 2002 fiscal year, Moon and Realyvasquez were paid $2,403,159 by Medicare alone.

Typical of the cases the FBI uncovered was that of an elderly woman who feared that she had a heart problem and had asked her physician for a referral to see a cardiologist. Although her doctor didn't believe there was anything wrong, he referred the woman to Moon, who soon called to report that he "had discovered a serious heart valve problem with this patient and that he had admitted her for immediate heart valve replacement surgery." A year after the surgery, the woman was airlifted back to the hospital in severe pain. "Moon then discovered," according to the FBI, "that a problem had developed with the patient's new heart valve and that it needed to be replaced." Again, surgeons replaced the heart valve. This time the patient died shortly afterward in the hospital.

In another case, a seventy-two-year-old woman who was complaining of chest pains was diagnosed by her cardiologist as being in "rela-

tively good health and not suffering from any coronary artery disease."
But when she consulted Moon for a second opinion, she was told that
"she suffered from a severe heart valve problem and that she needed a
valve replacement and at least one coronary artery bypass graft." The
woman underwent a heart catheterization the same day as the diagnosis, according to the FBI. Moon further told the woman that she
needed immediate bypass surgery, which she subsequently received at
the Redding hospital.

Investigators saw this pattern in other cases, where relatively healthy
patients were told they suffered from a "grave condition of the heart
which required immediate surgery." The FBI reported that 167 of the
patients operated on by Moon and Realyvasquez later died, though it
did not attribute their deaths to the two doctors. Both physicians
denied any wrongdoing.

What did Tenet's Redding hospital know about the lucrative cardiac
assembly line? Long before the FBI raid, some doctors and friends of
patients had warned hospital executives that they feared too many
heart procedures were being performed and that some of them may
not have been "medically necessary." But Tenet administrators, always
under pressure from the home office to hit their numbers, brushed
aside the concerns, saying that Dr. Moon was "very experienced and
[had] performed more than 35,000 catheterization procedures."

The warning from Wall Street and the revelations about large numbers of unnecessary cardiac procedures sent Tenet's stock into free fall.
Within ten days, it lost more than half its value, plummeting from
around $50 a share in late October to $19.20 on November 8. Tenet
was soon engulfed in a wave of investigations and legal actions. The
U.S. Department of Health and Human Services commenced a
nationwide audit of Tenet's Medicare payments. The Department of
Justice probed whether any criminal laws had been broken. The Internal Revenue Service levied a claim for back taxes. The Securities and

Exchange Commission investigated charges of insider trading. Dozens of shareholder lawsuits were filed, claiming the company had deceived shareholders about its true financial condition. Numerous states where Tenet had hospitals launched probes as well; hundreds of lawsuits were filed in California and in other states, naming Tenet as a defendant in cases where physicians at Redding Medical Center and other hospitals knowingly performed unnecessary procedures on unsuspecting patients.

Initially, Barbakow tried to blame others in the corporation for Tenet's problems. His two top aides, Thomas Mackey, chief operating officer, and David Dennis, chief financial officer, left the company within days of the Redding raid. In the beginning, Barbakow acknowledged that "Tenet does receive higher-than-average Medicare outlier payments." He maintained there were "numerous reasons for that, including our charge structure, the acuity of our hospitals, the preponderance of large urban hospitals and many other factors." He later amended that version, saying that after studying the company's Medicare outlier policy, he had concluded that Tenet's aggressive pricing strategy was "inconsistent with the position and posture I want Tenet to have within our industry." Barbakow assembled a new management team in an effort to move on, but the damage was too great, and he, too, stepped down, in May 2003.

When he exited, Barbakow was one of the few who made money from Tenet, along with his Wall Street pals who peddled Tenet stock and helped him do deals. In his ten-year tenure he pulled in more than a quarter-billion dollars in salary, bonus, stock options, and assorted perks. His severance package gave him more than $1 million a year for three years, as well as health insurance and a car allowance. After that his pension will pay him a half-million dollars a year.

By the end of 2003, Tenet was more or less back where it had started ten years before when it was National Medical Enterprises—

battling government investigators, facing hundreds of millions of dollars in potential fines, and its Wall Street–sanctioned business model in ruins. The company agreed to pay a $54 million fine to resolve federal charges of unnecessary heart procedures at Redding Medical but still faced hundreds of civil lawsuits from patients there and at other facilities, as well as ongoing federal and state investigations. The company noted in a March 2004 SEC filing that it remained "subject to a significant number of claims and lawsuits," including "coordinated civil and criminal investigations and enforcement efforts" by federal and state agencies.

Tenet's response to the new crisis also was much like NME's a decade earlier: It restructured. The Tenet board replaced Barbakow with another investment banker, Trevor Fetter, who, like Barbakow, had worked at MGM and Merrill Lynch. He had been Tenet's chief financial officer until 2000, when he left to take over the reins of a new company called Broadlane Inc., established to provide "business-to-business e-commerce procurement solutions for the health care industry." The seed money came from none other than Tenet. As of May 31, 2002, Tenet "owned 67.3 percent of Broadlane." In turn, Broadlane provided services to Tenet hospitals and other health care companies. Barbakow and other Tenet executives and employees owned stock in the company.

One of Fetter's first major acts was to start selling hospitals. With his best Wall Street spin, Fetter explained: "We have made the strategic decision to concentrate our efforts on a core group of hospitals in order to produce tangible benefits in quality and service for the communities we serve and to create long-term sustainable growth for our shareholders." Overall, Tenet announced plans to sell a third of its hospitals. If it sounded familiar, that's because one of Barbakow's first steps ten years earlier was to sell many of NME's hospitals—before he went on a buying spree of his own. Now this new turn of events would mean fresh opportunities for investment bankers to earn fees, selling hospitals that had changed hands three or four times in the last decade.

For the hospitals and their patients, it will be one more step down in quality. If a profitable Tenet applied pressure to scrimp on staff, equipment, and supplies, one can only imagine what it will be like inside those hospitals with Tenet deep in the red.

BUYING THE DOCTORS

After transforming many hospitals and HMOs into investor-owned companies, Wall Street turned its attention in the mid 1990s to the third leg of the health care services triangle: physicians. Doctors were ready. The emergence of powerful hospital chains and health plans had eroded their income and usurped their authority to practice medicine. Long the aristocracy of health care, many doctors had been marginalized by Wall Street's push into medicine, and they lacked the negotiating power to do much about it. Frustrated by this turn of events, doctors were receptive to any idea that promised to give them the muscle to fight back.

Wall Street saw physicians as ideal candidates to organize into profit-making corporations. In many cities, individual doctors already had banded together to form group practices, some with just a few physicians and others with dozens of primary-care doctors and special-ists. The thinking on the Street was that if group practices at the local level could be profitable, then group practices across the country united in publicly owned corporations would be even better. Thus was born Wall Street's campaign to create physician practice management companies, or PPMs. The sales pitch to the nation's beleaguered doc-tors was seductively simple: "Treat the patients and leave the business side of medicine to us."

Wall Street began pushing PPMs aggressively and found a favorable response—from doctors as well as investors. "Many independent doctors are beginning to realize they have to do something to compete with the large HMO organizations," said Robert Mescal, an IPO analyst at the Institute for Econometric Research in Fort Lauderdale. PPMs grew quickly by acquiring individual practices and clinics and by pledging to supply doctors with equipment and administrative services in return for a percentage of their revenue. Once again, one of the earliest and most enthusiastic promoters was Smith Barney's Ben Lorello. "From a Wall Street perspective, this is the brave new world of health care services," he said. "[The] Street is backing these companies in a big way."

Publicly traded PPMs proliferated throughout the 1990s. By 1998, it was estimated that more than 10 percent of the nation's 650,000 physicians were affiliated with a PPM. Of those publicly held, Wall Street's favorite was Alabama-based MedPartners, which went public in 1995. Within two years, the company grew to a $6-billion-a-year business, serving two million patients in thirty-seven states through a network of 13,000 physicians. It also operated one of the nation's largest independent pharmacy benefit programs, distributing 43,000 prescriptions daily.

MedPartners appeared to be performing just as Wall Street promised: It was adding doctors; its revenue was multiplying; its stock price was going up. Shares sold for $13 when the company went public in 1995. A month later, they hit $22, and within a year, $36. Its chief executive, Larry House, lived on a grand scale. With the money rolling in from health care, House built a twenty-one-bedroom, twenty-two-bathroom mansion, complete with a movie theater and Italian white marble floors. The estate's guitar-shaped driveway mirrored that of Andrew Jackson's Hermitage in Nashville. Honors flowed along with the money. In June 1997, a pair of corporate jets took House, his family, and friends to Atlanta, where he was hailed at a black-tie awards banquet as regional Entrepreneur of the Year by Ernst & Young, the professional services firm. House was cited for his "innovative approach to health care," with his company poised "for rapid growth" and "projected 1997 revenue of $6.4 billion." If this sounds vaguely familiar, you may recall that Robert N. Elkins won the same award for his entrepreneurial spirit in establishing Integrated Health Services.

With the blessing of Wall Street, MedPartners and its chief competitor, Nashville-based PhyCor, the nation's second-largest PPM, announced plans in 1997 to merge. The alliance would give the new organization revenue of $8.4 billion, 35,000 physicians in the fifty states—or nearly 6 percent of all U.S. doctors—and three million HMO patients, forming what the news media labeled "a blockbuster in the health care industry." One of the most enthusiastic advocates of the marriage was HealthSouth's Richard Scrushy, who was House's mentor and a member of the MedPartners board: "The merger of these two companies is going to clearly create the leader in the industry. This is the model that works."

Not quite. When PhyCor took a close look at MedPartners's books, it called off the marriage, citing "significant operational and strategic differences." In fact, the books showed that MedPartners's performance had been enhanced by creative accounting. On the day the merger was announced, MedPartners released its third-quarter earnings, reporting income of $54.4 million on revenue of $1.61 billion, up 23 percent over a year earlier. By the time the accountants got through deciphering the numbers, MedPartners's mythical profit had vanished into a loss of $840.8 million.

MedPartners continued to unravel through 1998. By the fourth quarter, when losses reached $1.2 billion, the company that had entered the physician practice management business with such fanfare announced that it was getting out to concentrate on its mail-order pharmacy business. Various pieces of the nationwide network were sold off or placed in bankruptcy court.

The company's collapse was no aberration. In 1996, a year after MedPartners began trading, Lorello and his team, who seemingly never met a deal they didn't like, took another PPM public—PhyMatrix Corporation in West Palm Beach, Florida. Its stock shot up 40 percent on the first day of trading. Two months later, Smith Barney analysts reported that "in little more than one year PhyMatrix has developed comprehensive health care networks in three large markets, and generated more than $100 million in pro forma revenues."

Analysts touted the company as a No. 1 buy, though a "high risk" one, and predicted growth in earnings per share of "roughly 35–40 percent during the next three years." Smith Barney reported that PhyMatrix envisioned the consolidation of its various medical operations from oncology to radiation to lithotripsy (the crushing of kidney stones), creating a "health park or a medical mall, which are physical plants that combine physician offices with related medical support services in one building or geographic site." PhyMatrix's operations eventually were indeed consolidated in one location: not in a medical mall, but in U.S. Bankruptcy Court.

In retrospect, PPMs never made much sense to anyone other than Wall Street investment bankers. With health insurers continuing to squeeze doctors, PPMs had little chance to become going concerns. Doctors resented the high fees they had to pay PPM administrators—usually 15 percent of their revenue. Meanwhile, the stock they had received in the companies in exchange for selling their practices soon was worthless.

In the end, the PPMs had no real value. Wall Street papered over this basic flaw by pointing to revenue increases that large groups like MedPartners achieved through acquisitions. "PPMs were built by finance guys," consultant Michael Parshall told *Medical Economics*. "They know how money works, but they don't know how doctors' practices work."

The industry swiftly imploded, swept by waves of bankruptcies, liquidations, downsizings, and sales, wreaking havoc on thousands of doctors and their patients, wasting hundreds of millions of dollars that could have been spent on health care. The speed of the collapse was astonishing. Specialty Care Network of Lakewood, Colorado, a nationwide PPM of orthopedic surgeons, had begun operations in January 1997 after purchasing the assets of 183 musculoskeletal doctors in twenty-four practices. "With its focused strategy, attractive investment opportunities and experienced management team," one analyst wrote at the time, "the company is well positioned to grow earnings at a rate of 30% for the next few years." Three years later, it was out of business. The failure of many PPMs set off a mad scramble and flurry of litigation among physicians to buy back their practices or disentangle themselves from arrangements that threatened them with financial ruin.

Doctors who had been led to believe that PPMs would be beneficial for health care were disillusioned. Family practitioner Steven Myers, who once worked in a clinic owned by a PPM in Pittsfield, Massachusetts, said of his experience: "You kept waiting for the sun to start shining, and it never did." Myers, who later relocated to another state, estimated that in 2000, the last year he practiced in Massachusetts, he earned only $15,000.

Although a few PPMs succeeded, they were the exceptions. *Medical Economics* wrote the epitaph for the industry in 2001: "PPMs will be remembered years from now for their sheer destructiveness."

NURSES WHO BATTLE THE BOTTOM LINE

With Wall Street's entry into health care, it was inevitable that many management practices and business school ideas that had engulfed corporate America in the 1980s would be implemented in hospitals. Sensing a field of almost unlimited potential, consultants began flooding into the hospital industry in the early 1990s with ambitious plans to redesign operations and reorganize work and jobs.

Importing ideas from the auto industry such as "Just-in-Time Inventories" and "Total Quality Management," they also came up with catchy phrases tailored to health: "Excellence in Care," "Patients First," "Patient-Focused Care," and "Population-Based Care." Management consultants such as McKenzie, Booz Allen Hamilton, American Practices Management, Andersen Consulting, the Hunter Group, and a number of lesser lights, would earn hundreds of millions of dollars in fees.

They devised elaborate restructuring models that would radically alter hospitals and patient care. These ideas were promoted on the basis that hospitals needed to be more efficient, to run better. To encourage more productivity and output, hospitals were told they needed to embrace management practices that other industries had adopted. The consultants borrowed heavily from manufacturing. A McKenzie study team visited a Saturn auto-assembly plant and a Levi Strauss apparel plant in Tennessee looking for tips on labor-saving techniques and processes on a manufacturing assembly line that might be adopted by hospitals. Patient care could be industrialized, just like making cars or a pair of pants.

Don DeMoro, executive director of the Institute for Health & Socio-Economic Policy, in Orinda, California, who has been studying the health care industry's transformation for years, says that all the restructuring has been justified for one misguided reason alone: "All this was built around a business school belief in the market. The market says this. The market says that. There is this overriding belief that the market determines everything, as though human beings have no say. Don't interfere with it. Leave it alone. It will do the right thing."

The changes have been momentous, and few who were working the floors of hospitals realized how far-reaching they would be. In the

beginning, the need to modernize and to become more efficient struck
a chord in the inherently chaotic world of hospitals. The best of them
are a dizzying maze of activity—of patients, staff, suppliers, and visitors coming and going, requiring an enormous amount of coordina-
tion. The sheer number of essential tasks and jobs that must be
performed and synchronized is daunting.

Few would dispute that most hospitals could be run more efficiently.
But the main intent of the restructuring was to cut jobs and reduce
payrolls, the single largest cost. Talk to people who work in hospitals
about a typical day, and the picture that emerges is remarkably consistent: how staff is asked to take on more work, how there are fewer
people to perform it, how management is constantly pressuring them
to produce more, how conditions are frequently unsafe or unsanitary.
These changes are hard on everyone, especially the nurses, many of
whom are so burned out and saddened by what is happening to their
profession that they are leaving the field.

From the time she was a child growing up near St. Louis, Sharon
Penrod knew she wanted to be a nurse. She was always "bandaging up
animals and stuff like that," acting out make-believe stories as all little
girls do in the fantasy world of the people they would like to become.
It wasn't until 1983, when she was nearly thirty, married, and the
mother of two children, that she finally earned her R.N. degree and set
out, her "eyes filled with stars," for her first job—as a night nurse at a
community hospital in Sullivan, Missouri.

Sullivan proved to be a wondrous place to start, Penrod remembered. As one of two nurses on the 11 P.M. to 7 A.M. shift, she did a
"little of everything." She was responsible for the ICU (two beds), the
medical-surgical hall, and the ER. When an ambulance brought in an
accident victim, the police would radio ahead, and Penrod would rush
to open the ER to receive the injured patient. The experience went
well beyond her medical training: "I learned how to fix machines, to

work with families, to attend to patients." She learned that nurses "play many roles."

From Sullivan she followed the classic route of many R.N.s—moving to larger, more sophisticated hospitals, gaining wider experience and deeper knowledge of nursing that only hands-on work in operating rooms and surgical wards could provide. In 1988, she went to work at a well-regarded hospital in the St. Louis region, Christian Hospital in Florissant, with roots dating to the turn of the century. In the OR, she assisted with everything from general surgery to childbirth. "It was a good job," she recalled. The doctors were good. The nurses were committed. The hospital was well run. "I enjoyed it," she said.

But in 1993, after Christian merged with Barnes-Jewish Hospital, in one of the mega-mergers that have swept hospitals in communities across America, Penrod said the tenor of work began to change ever so subtly. Even Penrod now admits she didn't comprehend what was happening or understand what was driving the changes in her hospital and subsequent ones where she worked. But they were there.

When she had first gone to the OR, the rooms were cleaned thoroughly. "Every surface, I mean every surface, even the ceiling, underneath the tables, was cleaned before surgery," she said. Then the hospital began to cut back on employees who did that work. When nurses expressed concern, they were told there was "no indication that the cleaning had been a factor in preventing infections." She said managers assured them it was necessary to clean only the immediate area around the operating table, the items they would use in surgery, and the floor.

Then one hospital changed the inventory system in the OR, modifying the nurses' preference cards, which each had developed to assist individual surgeons. "These were the specifics that each doctor wanted, the certain things they preferred," she said. "Maybe they were quirks, but they were individual to each doctor. You were prepared and you knew how to anticipate what each doctor wanted so you could assist in surgery. A doctor might prefer a certain kind of suture. When they standardized the preference cards, all those little quirks were left off."

Perhaps most frustrating, they were always running out of critical supplies, the by-product of the "Just-in-Time Inventory" concept the hospital consultants had lifted from the auto industry and implemented in hospitals, as though spark plugs and heart valves were interchangeable.

Penrod still cringes when she remembers the night in one hospital where she had a patient with a blood clot and requested a Greenfield filter, a small metal device that is inserted in a vein to prevent a clot from moving through the body. "But there wasn't one in the hospital, and that patient lay on the table for two hours, asleep under anesthesia, because we didn't have any," she said. "We had to wait for one to come in from another hospital."

Other times they ran out of sutures. "The surgeons would be furious with the nurses," she recalled. "'Why didn't you notice this?' they would ask. They didn't realize what was happening either, and they blamed the nurses." After surgery, patients were hustled into rooms with little or no time for nurses to review their charts. "When you took time to check charts in detail, managers would often say that's already been done," she said. "That's what really infuriated nurses, the speedup. There was no letup. You had trouble even keeping up with the call lights." Nurses who quit weren't replaced, further adding to the workload of those who were left.

As working conditions deteriorated, Penrod said nurses began to hear more and more from hospital administrators about how health care was evolving and that the hospital would have to change to remain competitive. She could have tolerated a lot of that corporate-speak, but what bothered her the most "was not being able to take care of the patients." Even with all the added pressure, nurses "feel obligated to try to maintain their expectations," she said. "It's that good-girl syndrome. They want to be a good nurse."

As a form of therapy, and a way to remind herself of the harm that comes from mistakes, she began keeping a written record of things that go wrong in hospitals generally—surgical errors, hospital-caused infections, and other failings that bring grief to patients and nurses.

"I didn't want to have to say I didn't give good patient care—that I hurried so fast I didn't check. Or that a patient had an allergy and was given the wrong medicine. A nurse I knew ended up giving medication that a patient was allergic to. It ruined her. I wouldn't want that on my conscience."

Years later, Penrod said she would think back on those times and come to understand what was really happening. All the new ideas of letting the market dictate conditions dated from the restructuring she saw at St. Louis hospitals where she worked. It was all about letting "the market" work in hospitals.

Eventually, she quit nursing. But she did not abandon her colleagues, resolving that the only solution was to organize nurses into a union as a voice against the corporate mentality. Only by demanding better staffing and conditions could nurses serve patients. For guidance, she drew on the work of the California Nurses Association (CNA), the 55,000-member union whose influence stretches well beyond California. An advocate for lower staffing ratios and better patient care, CNA has become a national voice calling attention to the consequences of market-driven medicine in hospitals and its impact on patients and health care workers.

The largest independent union of nurses in the country, CNA has responded much more aggressively to the changes imposed on hospitals—the increased workloads and budget battles with hospital managers—than many old-line organizations. It has waged strikes, job actions, and legislative campaigns on behalf of patients, as well as rallying to the cause of nurses in other states who faced similar challenges. CNA has become a powerful force for patients at a time when they have few advocates. With the profession in turmoil in so many places, CNA has inspired affiliates and like-minded organizations outside such as Sharon Penrod's nurses coalition in St. Louis.

By 2004, Penrod had led two union-organizing campaigns. A rival union won the election to represent the nurses in one, and she barely missed victory on the first try at another. She is undaunted. "This must happen," she says. "And it is going to happen. It is right. It's best for patients."

Thirteen hundred miles to the east, in a small room just off a busy intensive care unit at Boston Medical Center, Karen Higgins eats a sandwich. Energetic and outgoing, Higgins has been an ICU nurse for twenty-nine years, almost all of it at Boston Medical. She is grabbing her "lunch" in between rounds of her severely ill patients. Once upon a time, she might have left the ER to eat. But no more. There would be no one to monitor her patients. So she eats a few feet from them.

She is so busy that she never leaves the floor once she arrives for a twelve-hour shift. "With ICU patients, you have to watch them all the time," she says. "It's their medicine, their heart, other things." And the people who will do that are nurses. "You know what we say about the hospital?" she asks. "Without us, it's just a hotel."

When she first became an ICU nurse, she usually was responsible for two patients—which she considers ideal. Now she often watches over as many as four, which makes every shift a blur. "We joke that we have great bladder control," she says. Now the hospital moves ICU patients much more rapidly out of the unit and onto the floor, where newer, less experienced nurses are forced to take over. "This is an awful lot of pressure on a new nurse," she says, "and many are leaving."

For nurses like Higgins who have been in the profession for years, the hardest part is seeing how difficult it has become to care for patients. "Cost wasn't a big thing in the past," she said. "Now health care is a business. To us patients are patients. They want us to call them customers. They aren't customers. They aren't here by choice. They are in because something is wrong that has to be taken care of."

Conditions like this have helped create what many longtime nurses call an artificial shortage. "There's no shortage of nurses, but there is a shortage of nurses who want to stay in nursing," says Higgins. The work has become so frustrating and unrewarding that it is increasingly difficult to attract and retain the right people. Hospitals continually recruit nurses, but many don't stay in the field. The hospitals that new nurses enter aren't what they had imagined, the kind of places where they thought they could help people and make a contribution. When they get there, they are shocked by the reality.

Trande Phillips, a pediatric-care nurse in northern California, tells the story of the newly graduated nurse who reported for orientation one day in 2000. The woman appeared to be just the kind of person the profession seeks to attract. She had wanted to be a nurse all her life, but her family had discouraged her from pursuing that career when she was younger. She had become a librarian instead. Then, in her midforties, after saving enough money, she enrolled in nursing school, determined to fulfill the dream of her youth. Phillips said the day the new graduate arrived for her first shift at Kaiser's Walnut Creek hospital was a high point in her life. "She was so proud to be a nurse," she said.

Her orientation was fairly typical, Phillips recalled. "She had to follow me around doing all the things we do on every shift—changing patients' dressings, checking on their meds, lifting a patient off a gurney into a bed, and so on." A nurse for more than thirty years, Phillips had seen many changes. She had learned to look after far more patients while spending less time with each one. Like all nurses, she worried about making mistakes, a fear exacerbated not only by the greater number of patients, but also by the growing complexity of technology and medications. All this had come about gradually for Phillips, who at least knew the turf and understood the reality of nursing in the twenty-first century.

So on that first night with the new nurse, as Phillips tells it: "I went racing around as usual. First there was this crisis, then another, and another as I went from one room to the next, with new situations arising as I worked with one patient before moving on to the next. On the second night, it was the same thing—me racing around from patient to patient, doing all the things you have to do to keep up. After the second night, when our shift was over and we were at our lockers changing, she started crying. She said, 'I can't do it. It's just too much.'" Phillips said she tried to reassure her that things would get better and that "she would be fine." Phillips told her to take a couple of days off and then the picture wouldn't seem so bleak.

Two days later, when Phillips returned from her own days off, she noticed that the name of the new nurse was missing from the locker next to hers. When she asked why, one of the other nurses told her that the woman had resigned. Phillips never heard from her again, but she understood that she went back to being a librarian. She was so traumatized by the experience that she did not even come back to the hospital to clean out her locker. When it was opened, they found her stethoscope, the object that symbolized the new career that she had embarked upon with such joy and enthusiasm. In Wall Street medicine, there was no place for such values.

Anatomy of a Systems Failure

The summer of 2000 was the turning point in California health care, a signal of what lay in store for the rest of the country. On Saturday morning, July 1, at the Lakewood Regional Medical Center twenty-five miles south of Los Angeles, a sixty-six-year-old man with a history of chronic obstructive pulmonary disease arrived suffering from acute respiratory distress and shortness of breath. While he was in the ER, his heart stopped beating. Three times, he was defibrillated by electric shock. Finally, he was placed on a ventilator and given dopamine intravenously to raise his blood pressure. Dr. Domingo Barrientos, the physician on call, admitted him to the coronary unit. Because of the patient's existing health problems, coupled with the cardiac arrest, Dr. Barrientos put in hurried calls for two consulting specialists—one for heart, one for lungs.

Dr. Barrientos knew that the pulmonologist under contract to the hospital's physician management firm, KPC Medical Management Inc., had canceled his agreement several weeks earlier. And not without reason—he wasn't being paid. When Dr. Barrientos asked KPC's medical director for a backup specialist, he was given another name. But that doctor refused the request. He said that he had informed KPC earlier that he would no longer treat its patients. The staff cardiologist, Dr. Jerry Floro, did respond, and the two physicians tended to the patient as best they could, but he died without seeing a pulmonologist.

Dr. Barrientos was so shaken by the incident, which he reported to KPC's legal department, that he made up his mind "right then and there that I did not wish to work for KPC any longer than I had to."

While there was "no telling whether a pulmonologist could have prolonged this patient's life," Dr. Barrientos said later, what was clear to him was that under such circumstances, "the standard of care requires that specialty backup be available."

As he made plans to leave KPC and move into another practice, Dr. Barrientos was compelled to deal daily with conditions more apt to be found in an undeveloped country than in the nation routinely hailed as having the best health care system in the world. Not only was he unable to get specialists to treat patients, he often lacked basic medical supplies. KPC hadn't paid its bills. Once a patient showed up for a routine procedure requiring liquid nitrogen, and Dr. Barrientos had to send him home. KPC had run out of it. The supplier had refused to extend further credit. He couldn't order X-rays because the clinic had used up the X-ray solution—again, nonpayment. When he signed the last of the prescription pads with his name and state medical board and DEA numbers, he couldn't get replacements. The printer hadn't been paid. There were no tissues to give to patients to clean themselves following pelvic and rectal exams.

And there were the neverending life-and-death crises. Like the ailing fifty-year-old man with a history of diabetes, hypertension, and obesity who arrived at KPC's Downey Clinic on Firestone Boulevard in southern Los Angeles County. Again, Dr. Barrientos was on duty. He performed an EKG, which showed no abnormalities. Given the patient's multiple risk factors, he "ordered an immediate treadmill stress test . . . to assess the flow of oxygenated blood to the heart." The next available appointment was three weeks away, even after Dr. Barrientos explained the seriousness of the patient's condition. Finally, he "prescribed nitroglycerin to be taken at the onset of chest pain and told the patient to call 911 if the pain did not subside after two doses."

About a week later, the patient returned, complaining of increased chest pain. Dr. Barrientos immediately sent him to the Lakewood ER, where doctors discovered that he had suffered a heart attack and admitted him to the Intensive Care Unit. The next morning, an angiogram showed that three coronary arteries were clogged, and he underwent triple bypass surgery.

It could have been different. "Had this patient been able to obtain his stress test when I requested it," Dr. Barrientos said later, "[he] would have then been admitted to the hospital for an angiogram, and could have been treated before having a heart attack by angioplasty or other less invasive procedure. The delay in obtaining basic service caused my patient to suffer a heart attack needlessly. Had he not come to me that day, he may well have died."

The situation was much the same at KPC clinics throughout the greater Los Angeles area as doctors, nurses, and other staff members wrestled with the consequences of market-driven medicine. On Sunday, September 10, Ronald W. Hudson Sr. was admitted to the San Antonio Community Hospital in Upland, a community of 68,000 in the foothills of the San Gabriel Mountains, about thirty-five miles east of Los Angeles.

The sixty-year-old Hudson, a dialysis patient with high blood pressure, diabetes, and end-stage renal disease, was no stranger to the hospital. During the previous four years, he had been admitted more than a dozen times, primarily "for treatment of problems related to his dialysis," according to the hospital. This time paramedics rushed Hudson to the emergency room with "severe lower abdominal pain" and a temperature of 102.2. The attending ER physician thought it prudent to rule out appendicitis, and Hudson's nephrologist admitted him to the hospital. A surgeon on duty decided that more tests were required.

That's when differences erupted over ultimate responsibility, as physicians debated whether to operate, who should operate, and when. An entity called Inland Global Medical Group, an independent physicians association with hospital privileges, contracted with specialists to see its patients. It also contracted with a group called Sanacare to provide surgical services. Still another entity, Inland Global Services Inc., was responsible for managing all these services—but it subcontracted the management services to yet another company, KPC Global Care Inc.

When the surgeon who first saw Hudson and recommended more tests discovered that Hudson was an Inland Global patient, he said he was "not under contract to treat" Hudson. Other surgeons, he said, were "contracted by Inland Global to treat such patients." The ER staff called a second surgeon for a consultation. He, too, declined, saying he had no contract with Hudson's HMO.

At that time, whenever an Inland Global patient arrived at the emergency room and needed surgical services, the hospital staff was supposed to call in an Inland Global surgeon. When that failed, hospital personnel tried several times to reach yet another surgeon, Dr. Jehan Zeb Mir, but that, too, was unsuccessful. Finally, David Duong, a registered nurse on duty, placed a call on his own. When he got through to Dr. Mir, he advised him there was a request for a surgical consultation. Dr. Mir asked how the patient was doing. Duong replied, "He's fine." Dr. Mir said he would see the patient the next morning. Duong did not describe Hudson's condition. According to Duong, the surgeon asked, "Is the patient okay?" Duong said he replied, "He's okay." Unfortunately, Duong was unaware that Hudson had been diagnosed with possible appendicitis.

Meanwhile, Hudson's condition deteriorated. His appendix ruptured, and peritonitis set in. The infection spread through his body.

Two days after Hudson arrived at the hospital, an Inland Global surgeon performed "emergency" surgery. Eleven days later, Hudson died.

Amid the turmoil that characterized the KPC health care system, even tests to detect—or rule out—the existence of life-threatening diseases often went awry, delaying diagnoses and creating anxiety. Such was the case on September 13, 2000, at the Artesia Clinic on South Pioneer Boulevard in Los Angeles County. Dr. Saeed Yadegar, chief of radiology for several KPC clinics, was preparing to do more tests on a woman whose mammogram showed two groups of microcalcifications in one breast.

Microcalcifications are minute flecks of calcium, less than 1/50 of an inch in size, that appear as little white dots on the film. Usually they are harmless, but some are an early indicator of breast cancer. While a skilled radiologist can often distinguish between the two by their size, shape, and arrangement, sometimes a biopsy is required to rule out cancer.

In this case, Dr. Yadegar deemed that a biopsy was needed. Before the minuscule deposits could be removed for examination, it was necessary to pinpoint their precise location. Dr. Yadegar began by inserting two needles into the breast to place two small wires that would mark the location of the calcifications. The procedure required clear, high-contrast radiographic images. While the two needles were in the breast and the radiologist was trying to localize the microcalcifications, the "chemicals used to process the mammograms ran out." The films turned gray, and the radiologist could no longer read the image. Since the clinic had run out of the chemicals, and the vendor refused to deliver any more until he was paid for prior shipments, Dr. Yadegar had no choice. He removed the needles and sent the patient home without completing the test.

Is this what health care in America has become? A woman being tested for breast cancer is sent home without completing the exam when the clinic runs out of chemicals. A man dies after physicians debate for two days about who should or would perform emergency surgery, based on who would or would not get paid. X-ray laboratories shut down for lack of supplies. Another patient cannot obtain a diagnostic test in time to predict the likelihood of a heart attack—so he waits for the heart attack to occur. A man with serious lung disease dies before he is seen by a specialist because the specialists have not been paid or will not work for a certain system.

Does all of this really reflect medical care delivery in a country that spends $1.7 trillion a year on health care?

The plight of the KPC clinics, although extreme, wasn't an aberration, an outbreak of random events in an otherwise healthy system. The only difference between KPC and countless other managed-care operations across America is one of degree. Increasingly, all the problems faced by KPC's patients are confronting patients elsewhere, although in many instances they may be unaware of what's taking place. That it happened in California is understandable. The state has experimented more fully with managed care than any other. Since many social and economic trends of the last half-century, for good and ill, began in California, what happened there may soon be coming to your doctor's office or a hospital near you—if it's not already there. This is why the story of KPC deserves a closer look.

A BAD BUSINESS MODEL

The chaos that engulfed the California clinics had its origins in the 1970s, when Congress began encouraging the growth of health maintenance organizations. All through that decade and the years that followed, HMOs were touted as the way to bring health care costs under control. Lawmakers embraced the idea that the free market was the best way to achieve savings and promote efficiency, without sacrificing quality care. Successive administrations and Congresses engineered a system built around that philosophy, in the belief that Wall Street knows what's best for you, that competition is the road to low-cost quality health care—an oxymoron if ever there was one. In fact, free-market medicine and competition have produced a lower quality of care than you would ever knowingly accept.

While there were flaws in the free-market medicine theory from the start, HMOs flourished, making many investors and executives rich. They even seemed to work; just by limiting hospital stays, they shaved billions of dollars off the nation's medical bills. But those were one-time savings. To keep paring costs, they began micromanaging the daily decisions of individual physicians. Doctors who had spent their professional lives dictating patient care suddenly were on the receiving end. Insurers now told them which treatments they could use with their patients and which they couldn't; which drugs they could prescribe and which ones they couldn't; which tests they could administer and which they couldn't. And they were told what they would be paid for their services.

As noted earlier, it was in part to counter the growing power of HMOs and hospitals that the physician practice management (PPM) idea took off, and nowhere was it greeted more enthusiastically than in California. The state had long been a fertile ground for large group practices and neighborhood clinics and appeared to be an ideal setting for the national PPM chains to penetrate the region.

Among those acquiring a segment of the California market was MedPartners Inc., the Larry House–run PPM, you will recall from our earlier discussion, that was a Wall Street favorite in the 1990s. In 1995, Alabama-based MedPartners bought a large, privately held physician practice management company headquartered in Long Beach, California, Mullikin Medical Enterprise L.P., and changed its name to MedPartners/Mullikin Inc.

Serving 350,000 HMO enrollees at fifty-eight clinics, Mullikin had been a fixture of California health care for decades. MedPartners/Mullikin was launched with high hopes and big promises, telling investors: "[The company] enhances clinic operations by centralizing administrative functions and introducing management tools, such as clinical guidelines, utilization review and outcomes measurement."

The company struggled from the start, due to flaws in the PPM concept and the special nature of California health care. Under the California model, which was being adopted by other states, HMOs and insurers like Blue Cross of California and PacifiCare Health Systems negotiated a fixed fee, or capitation payment, for each patient under the care of a physician management company. The HMOs mailed the checks to the management company, which in turn subcontracted with doctors and specialists who provided the care. If the patients covered under the plan were healthy and spent little time in the doctor's office, the system worked splendidly. But once someone was sick and had to be treated or hospitalized, the doctors began to lose money, in effect, forced to pay for the care they provided out of their own pockets.

In some instances, even routine care was a money loser. A California Medical Association (CMA) study found that the state's pediatricians on average lost $270.96 for each child treated. The capitation rates did not even cover the cost of preventive care, including immunizations and office visits, and physicians were expected to lose $157.99 a year on each child. "Given these numbers," the CMA said, "it is no surprise that experts who have studied this issue have concluded that children with chronic conditions would probably remain at risk if they receive their health care through a competitive health care market, such as the one in California."

With HMO reimbursements not covering costs, MedPartners soon hemorrhaged red ink, and by 1998 it was losing $16 million a month.

Meanwhile, the MedPartners parent company in Alabama was crumbling, creating all sorts of problems in southern California. Doctors and hospitals there were owed tens of millions of dollars, and patient care was suffering. Treatments were delayed, and patients in need of mammograms, MRIs, X-rays, and ultrasounds were turned away because no one was getting paid. Oncologists themselves paid for chemotherapy drugs. In the meantime, the MedPartners holding company in Alabama had begun to sell off some of its California assets, leaving doctors uncertain about "assignment of patients, whom to bill, and whom to call for prior authorizations." Finally, MedPartners notified its California doctors that it would no longer turn over the capitation payments. Instead, it would pay for services actually rendered. Exactly how much was unclear. The doctors never received a rate schedule, so they had no idea what they would be paid for an office visit or specific procedure.

Even by the chaotic standards of California health care, the MedPartners catastrophe was breathtaking. Profit-driven, free-market medicine had been creating untold financial carnage among California physician management groups for years. More than one hundred PPMs had collapsed, leaving patients to scramble for doctors and doctors to scramble for new associations with ties to the HMOs. Many of the failures were small; some involved huge enterprises.

The state had been stunned in July 1998 by the crash of San Diego–based FPA Medical Management, another publicly held physician practice management company, with 7,900 doctors and 1.4 million patients in some two dozen states, including 300,000 in California. The company's sudden trek to Bankruptcy Court created havoc among physicians and patients in California and left the state struggling to arrange doctor coverage for thousands of insured patients. The state didn't want to be surprised again. On March 11, 1999, the state Department of Corporations seized control of the

MedPartners Provider Network, which had grown to include 4,000 physicians and 1.3 million patients in California, and forced the firm into Bankruptcy Court.

But that is hardly the place to run a medical practice. The court excels at untangling complex financial arrangements, deciphering contracts, following money trails, and unearthing hidden assets. It was never intended to deal with life-and-death medical issues. With that in mind, state officials and physicians began looking for someone to take over MedPartners. Seemingly out of nowhere, a candidate emerged, and health care in southern California would never be the same.

DOCTOR C'S EMPIRE

It is safe to say that few MedPartners patients had ever heard the name Kali P. Chaudhuri when state and bankruptcy officials began grappling with the thorny question of what to do with the collapsed provider. A pathologist by training and an orthopedic surgeon by trade, Dr. Chaudhuri was an American success story. According to published accounts and medical professional records, he was born to a wealthy family in India, earned a medical degree in Calcutta, emigrated to the United States by way of Newfoundland, worked at a small hospital in Coudersport, Pennsylvania, and in 1984 settled in the Riverside County town of Hemet, about ninety miles southeast of Los Angeles. With a population that would nearly triple to more than 60,000 by 2000, Hemet was becoming a magnet for immigrants from India, Taiwan, and other Asian countries, as well as home to a growing Hispanic population.

At first glance, Dr. Chaudhuri, or "Dr. C" as some called him, appeared to be a worthy successor to MedPartners. Starting from scratch, he had built a thriving orthopedic practice and served as chief of staff for Hemet Valley Medical Center. He taught orthopedic surgery at nearby Loma Linda University Medical School. The California State

Senate cited him for his exceptional fund-raising efforts on behalf of a local hospital. He hosted political fund-raisers at his home. He was a pillar of the community.

Along the way, Dr. Chaudhuri evolved into a medical entrepreneur. He organized a physician management company serving thousands of Hemet-area patients. By 1999, he had built a miniconglomerate, called KPC Global Care, that managed physician practices and served 200,000 patients in the Inland Empire, the rich agricultural basin in Riverside and San Bernardino counties. He also had become a million-aire many times over.

If those state officials searching for a successor to MedPartners had looked more closely, they might have realized they were replacing one smooth operator with another. By all accounts, Dr. Chaudhuri was a charismatic figure, far more so than Larry House. Like House, he gave the impression that he understood the business of health care. He said all the things doctors wanted to hear, although many never seemed to notice that he practiced what he preached against—"for the last ten years, doctors have been bought and sold in the market like chickens." Like House, his self-professed mission was to free doctors from the drudgery of paperwork and the health care bureaucracy so they could do what they do best—practice medicine. "I don't want to sound like Mother Teresa," Dr. Chaudhuri told a local newspaper. "I believe that if you do what is right, success and money will follow."

It sounded good. Except at the very same time state officials were supporting Dr. Chaudhuri's bid in Bankruptcy Court to take over the MedPartners practices, a management company he co-owned, Valley Health Care Management Services LLC in Hemet, was engaged in some serious cost-cutting at the Hemet Valley Medical Center, a 240-bed, full-service, acute-care hospital.

The Chaudhuri company froze the longtime pension plan and replaced it with a far less favorable one that required employees to wait six years to be vested—no matter how long they had worked there. It slashed sick days from eight to five. It canceled pay for jury duty and eliminated a bonus plan. Not surprisingly, the changes triggered an all-out labor war, with nurses staging repeated walkouts. During demonstrations, they carried signs singling out Dr. Chaudhuri for his role in the cutbacks: "Please don't let the hospital go down the drain like most of KPC's enterprises."

Many of the hospital's nurses quit at the worst of all possible times. The dispute coincided with a severe nursing shortage, and those nurses who left had to be replaced by temporary workers. Ultimately, they would cost more than the savings from the cutbacks. Looming on the horizon were conflicts of interest involving Dr. Chaudhuri's growing private medical organization and the publicly owned hospital.

Nonetheless, in September 1999 Dr. Chaudhuri orchestrated the biggest deal of his life. A large piece of the MedPartners California branch was transferred out of Bankruptcy Court and into his KPC health care empire. Dr. Chaudhuri's initials or name were stamped on many of the corporate entities, from the umbrella company, KPC Medical Management Inc., to individual clinics, like the Chaudhuri Medical Group of Long Beach/Artesia Inc. Dr. Chaudhuri was the sole shareholder and chief executive officer of most of the businesses. In some cases, he was the only member of the board of directors. In addition to the medical practices, his health care conglomerate also included companies that owned real estate, like TROL Realty LLC, MFH Realty LLC, and Montclair Realty LLC. Later, there would be talk that money moved mysteriously among the many businesses. For the time being, he was quite simply California's most imposing medical entrepreneur.

The empire that Dr. Chaudhuri presided over was indeed huge. Nearly one million patients and one thousand doctors were covered by clinics under his control across four southern California counties. It was the largest physician practice management company in California, and one of the largest in the country. Annual revenue was close to a billion dollars. Some wondered how a man who only a few years earlier had overseen a modest orthopedic practice could manage such a vast system. Dr. Chaudhuri sought to dismiss the doubters. "I am a positive guy," he would say later. Plus no less an authority than Merrill Lynch certified that Dr. Chaudhuri had the wherewithal to bring off the deal. "Dr. Chaudhuri is a man of considerable resources," his lawyer, Bill Thomas, told the press. "All of his finances have been verified by Merrill Lynch [MedPartners's banker]."

Dr. Chaudhuri launched his new enterprise by closing clinics and firing doctors and staff members. By year's end, some two dozen facilities had been shuttered, and seventy doctors and 500 staff members were let go. The drastic cutbacks did not translate into a smooth-running operation as 2000 began.

The Cerritos clinic on East 183rd Street, on the Los Angeles County–Orange County line, ran short of supplies, from photocopier paper to toilet tissue. With too few employees, the clinic's telephones rang constantly as patients sought in vain to schedule appointments. At the South Gate clinic on Tweedy Boulevard twelve miles south of downtown Los Angeles, most of the nursing and office staff resigned. So, too, did several physicians. In March, the water company shut off service for one day due to nonpayment. And by April, patients were feeling the impact of KPC's management style.

That month Dr. German Zermeno, a family practitioner, examined an elderly woman who had blood in her stool, which suggested the possibility of cancer in her gastrointestinal tract. He referred her to a KPC specialist, but the appointment was later canceled; her insurer had terminated its relationship with KPC. Next, the patient switched insurers and made another appointment. That failed also. The GI specialist canceled all appointments with KPC patients because of nonpayment. Finally, an appointment was scheduled with a specialist who had just transferred into the KPC network. Overwhelmed by a backlog of appointments, he was unable to see the woman for months. When Dr. Chaudhuri had taken over the former MedPartners practices, he had pledged to make sure specialists were paid. That promise was proving hollow.

Dr. Chaudhuri either remained unaware of or chose to ignore what was happening at the clinics. As problems multiplied, physicians would later remember a staff meeting at corporate headquarters in Anaheim in January 2000 when many voiced their concerns. They talked about the deplorable state of the telephone network, among other things. Doctors were unable to communicate with other offices. Pharmacists seeking to refill prescriptions could not reach doctors for days, sometimes weeks. Patients couldn't get through to make appointments, and they were forced to come into the office to get lab and X-ray results, as well as referrals. The unreliable telephone network meant that fax machines, the lifeblood of modern medicine, were equally unreliable.

But KPC's chief had a vision. And telephones were not a part of it. According to physicians who were present, Dr. Chaudhuri made it clear that he had no plans to upgrade the phones in the immediate future. Instead, he intended to spend millions to build a state-of-the-art computer system and employ the latest information technology that would track quality control and patient satisfaction. KPC would even have its own Web site so patients could make their appointments over the Internet. Never mind that many had no access to the Internet. When doctors continued to complain about the phones and general working conditions, he seemed annoyed. One recalled Dr. Chaudhuri saying: "Why do you only give me bad news?"

KPC continued to unravel. In March, a ninety-year-old nursing-home patient under KPC's care was unable to eat or drink. A request for a gastroenterologist to insert a feeding tube went unanswered. Four weeks later, still waiting for the specialist, the patient began bleeding in her lower gastrointestinal tract. She lost weight and became severely dehydrated. Finally, a KPC employee called 911 to take the woman to a non-KPC emergency room to have the tube inserted. The hospital found a tumor in her esophagus. In May, at KPC's Long Beach clinic, Dr. Joseph A. Lombardo, a family practitioner, saw a young man in his twenties who needed "a biopsy of a probable malignant lesion on his face." He sent the patient home when the staff was unable to find the "medical instruments necessary to perform the biopsy."

A medical clinic without instruments? No specialists to treat KPC patients? It was happening throughout the system because KPC wasn't paying its bills. The company had run up $12 million in unpaid claims. The staff went through the motions of paying bills. They would write checks but then sit on them. Donald B. Smallwood, KPC president, conceded that they often cut checks with no intention of mailing them. Instead, they stashed them in locked filing cabinets in the Anaheim office.

KPC tried to create the impression that it was turning things around. Smallwood announced in May 2000 that Dr. Chaudhuri had negotiated a $12 million loan that would enable "the company to pay down claims and vendor invoices to a point that we are current with our obligations. Due to the large volume of invoices, it is anticipated that it will take approximately two weeks to get all of the checks out."

Even so, KPC remained in arrears on its bills. They continued to pile up along with the dunning letters. On July 21, Quest Diagnostics wrote that if it did not receive the "full account balance in the amount of $127,656.81" by August 4, it would terminate all laboratory services. "Your account will then be turned over to a collection agency or attorney," Quest's credit administrator said. Quest would have to stand in line. By August, the unpaid bills had soared to more than $18 million. Once again, a fresh batch of unmailed checks accumulated in file cabinets. Finally, KPC even halted that pretense and stopped cutting checks.

Across Dr. Chaudhuri's empire, specialists willing to look at a KPC patient were about as rare as a Californian who didn't drive. Dr. Daniel Scaff, a pediatrician at the Cerritos clinic, was treating a ten-year-old girl who had headaches and was bleeding in the whites of her eyes "as a result of being improperly restrained at a dental office." The headaches increased in frequency and severity, and she developed vision problems. Dr. Scaff requested a referral to a child neurologist—the only one still accepting KPC patients. Some days later, the little girl's mother returned to his office, referral in hand, and said that when she called for an appointment she was told that the neurologist was not accepting any KPC patients.

Elsewhere within the system, anesthesiologists refused to tend to KPC patients, so surgeries were delayed. Infectious-disease specialists were unavailable for AIDS patients. And although psychiatrists were supposed to meet patients with schizophrenia, depression, hallucinations, and other psychoses at least once before prescribing psychotropic drugs, one staff member reported that only two of her forty KPC patients on such medicines ever saw a psychiatrist. Some KPC physicians advised their patients that if they needed immediate medical attention and were unable to see a specialist, they should go to a hospital emergency room for treatment.

Health plan enrollees who tried to ensure good health for family members also fared poorly with KPC. Parents seeking immunizations required by law for their children to attend school played the health care lottery daily, without knowing it. Sometimes KPC had the vaccines. Sometimes it didn't. Many standard vaccines were in short supply, and Dr. Scaff recalled that there were acute shortages of hepatitis and polio vaccines at the Cerritos clinic. When parents arrived with children for their hepatitis shots, they often were told to return at a later date. "For each child who could not be vaccinated," Dr. Scaff said, "I had to write a note to the school officials so that the child would be allowed to attend school."

Even some of the basics that patients have long taken for granted when seeing a doctor—their charts, mammograms, and X-rays—were often not available to KPC doctors when they examined patients. Dr. Jerry Floro, a cardiologist at KPC's Artesia clinic, recalled: "I saw approximately half of my patients on any given day without charts. Often the charts couldn't be located at all. This meant that I had to treat patients on whom I had no medical history."

At the Long Beach clinic, Dr. Shahla Heshmati, a pediatrician, said she often had charts for only one out of five patients. "When I saw a child in the clinic, I usually did not have any records of the patient's prior visit, my previous evaluations of his or her health and medical conditions, immunizations, or laboratory tests," she said. "I did not even have a record of the medications that I had prescribed previously, or whether the patient was allergic to any medications."

Dr. Joseph Lombardo, the family practitioner, said he "often had no medical records for the patient, even if they had been my patient for seventeen years." Sometimes the records were missing because of KPC's failure to pay its bills to storage centers that maintained and retrieved the records. Sometimes it was because of KPC's inability to perform the most basic tasks. Part of Catherine Babington's job as regional administrator was to check on the status of records at the Downey Clinic on Firestone Boulevard. In March 2000, she measured the volume of paperwork waiting to be placed in patient files. The result, according to Babington's tally, was astonishing: "twenty-four feet of unfiled lab, radiology, and hospital reports," including the most recent reports on the medical conditions of clinic patients.

MELTDOWN

Nowhere was the situation more out of control than at the Artesia clinic in southern Los Angeles County. In March, a patient who had

been diagnosed with a kidney stone endured a prolonged and unnecessary delay. Dr. Ernesto Cortez had referred the patient to a KPC-con-
tracted urologist. When the patient arrived for the appointment, he
was told the urologist was no longer seeing KPC patients. Not to
worry. Dr. Cortez asked the KPC referral department for another specialist. The news was not good. In an area with scores of urologists,
there was not one who would take a KPC patient. The best they could
do was send him to a specialist in Burbank—a sixty-mile round-trip.

The clinic's resident obstetrical ultrasound technician resigned in
July. "She had been with the clinic for over ten years, had special training and skill in evaluating pregnancies, and excelled in detecting fetal
abnormalities," according to Dr. Eric Kaplan, chairman of the obstet-
rics-gynecology department for the Artesia–Long Beach area. She was
replaced by technicians from a temp service. Within two months, even
that arrangement stopped. The service wasn't being paid. Left with no
alternative, Dr. Kaplan said, the doctors began relying on technicians
from the clinic's radiology department "who had no particular training
or skills in obstetrical ultrasounds."

Because of inexperience, one technician failed to detect early in a
pregnancy a case of anencephaly, a condition in which the skull, scalp,
and part of the brain are missing. Although some babies may survive
for a short time, the condition is always fatal. It wasn't until sixteen
weeks into the pregnancy that the birth defect was detected. "Pregnancy termination at sixteen weeks is a prolonged and painful procedure," said Dr. Kaplan, "and is riskier than the short and relatively
painless procedure which could have been done at twelve weeks."

Since KPC wasn't paying the Artesia clinic's bills, suppliers refused
to deliver certain medications, such as those needed to treat fibroid
tumors of the uterus and endometriosis, both painful and potentially
serious conditions. They also stopped shipment of mechanical devices
used in cases of uterine and vaginal prolapse. On April 17, a desperate

e-mail went out from a clinic staff member to a supervisor: "Artesia will be out of chemicals to process films by noon today, [mammogram] is already out and is sharing the main processor, which will not last through mid day. Patients are being rescheduled now."

The company that furnished lab coats for the staff repossessed them during office hours, while doctors were seeing patients. As Dr. Kaplan recalled: "I was approached by a vendor representative in the clinic hallway, in the presence of clinic patients, and was told to surrender my lab coats. I literally had to take my lab coat off of my back."

As the year wore on, even the most basic services collapsed. By July 2000, according to Dr. Angelyn Moultrie-Lizana, an osteopathic physician, "trash in offices and exam rooms was overflowing. Outside the clinic, trash accumulated in the shrubbery." The air-conditioning in her first-floor suite stopped working. When KPC made it clear the air-conditioning would not be fixed, she moved her offices to the second floor.

In August, Dr. Moultrie-Lizana was treating a breast cancer patient who had undergone multiple surgeries for removal of the cancer and reconstruction. Her oncologist wanted a bone scan to determine if the cancer had spread. Dr. Moultrie-Lizana secured a referral and advised the patient to contact her if she did not receive the paperwork in ten days. In mid-September, the patient called back, seeking a referral to another clinic. The Artesia clinic had been out of certain chemicals to conduct a bone scan for at least a month. "There is no telling what effect the month's delay in assessing any spread of her cancer may have on this patient's prognosis and life expectancy," said Dr. Moultrie-Lizana.

An e-mail the following month from Dr. Yadegar, the radiology chief, to KPC's medical director and other staff physicians underscored how its imaging services—just one phase of the clinic's operations—were being overwhelmed by the company's financial and management misfortunes:

Computerized tomography: Our unit has been out of operation. Picker Corp. has put us on credit hold and are refusing to service the unit. As an alternative, we had been using Los Coyota Imaging Center, but last week I had a phone call from the president of Radnet, informing me that as of last Thursday they will stop seeing all KPC patients throughout Southern California.

MRIs: Radnet is refusing to see our patients. I had Devin call MRI center of Long Beach to see whether we could send our patients there. We were informed that they will not accept our patients . . . The only facility left is DICI in Inglewood which is way too far for the majority of our patients.

Nuclear Medicine/Nuclear Cardiology: As of the end of last week we were placed on credit hold by Syncore. We have cancelled all of our studies including patients that are being worked up for coronary disease . . . Some of these patients have been cancelled twice.

The folks who provide ultrasound techs for our OB work pulled their techi out of our facility as of the end of last week . . . There are a lot of angry and frustrated patients out there and I assume that some of them are high risk OBs . . .

Time was running out for Dr. Chaudhuri. Nevertheless, he continued to put a positive spin on KPC, just as he had done from the beginning. Profitability was always just around the corner—a result predicated on the time-honored managed-care formula of delay and deny. Although in KPC's case the practice had the added twist of approving care by a specialist and then not paying the person for months. The company called it "cash conservation."

A national medical publication reported in January that Dr. Chaudhuri expected "to break even between March and June of this year." By May, the situation was so dire that the health plans and Tenet had to come up with a $30 million cash infusion, prompting Dr. Chaudhuri to promise solvency by July. Within weeks KPC had reverted to form, which meant stiffing the specialists and stringing out patients. Instead of moving into the black, KPC remained mired in the red, and Dr. Chaudhuri was looking for another bailout. The situation became more grim when Blue Cross canceled its contract with KPC, and CIGNA, concerned about the quality of care and nonpayment of specialists, said it would begin moving many of its 70,000 enrollees into another system.

The decisions sounded alarm bells in Governor Gray Davis's office. A representative of the governor brought the health plans together to negotiate yet another financial aid deal. If KPC folded without warning, hundreds of thousands of patients would be dumped into other, already overtaxed practices. The wait to see a doctor could stretch into months. Critically ill patients would be forced into hospital emergency rooms. Other medical practices already were grumbling about the 100,000 KPC patients they were forced to pick up from insurers, complaining that many were sick and costing too much money to treat.

After several weeks of talks, the parties came up with a $30 million package on August 11, mostly in the form of a loan guaranteed by KPC real estate. Dr. Chaudhuri pledged to invest more money in the business, and the HMOs agreed to raise the monthly fees they paid for each patient. Once again, Dr. Chaudhuri foresaw good times. "If everyone keeps their promise," he said, "not only will we break even, we will do very well."

Still, every time KPC seemed to take a step forward, it went back two steps. Just before the $30 million deal was structured, Drs. Barrientos, Yadegar, Floro, Lombardo, Kaplan, and fifty others all resigned en masse over the quality of care. According to their employment agreements, they were required to remain on the job for two months after submitting their resignations. After that, they established a new practice called Pioneer Medical Group Inc. Dr. Chaudhuri would blame the defecting doctors for the collapse of his empire, but the available evidence suggested otherwise.

Within weeks of the relief package patched together in August, KPC faced another cash crunch. As usual, the bills weren't paid. This time Quest Diagnostics skipped the threatening letter and told KPC it would "terminate all laboratory services effective November 14." The HMOs withheld a portion of their November payment. Dr. Chaudhuri failed to come through with his share of the bailout. Even though KPC was obviously disintegrating, state officials believed there was little likelihood that its patients would be unloaded, severing long-standing doctor-patient ties. Daniel Zingale, director of California's Department of Managed Care, told the *Orange County Register* on November 9: "It seems to me that everyone understands that an abrupt disruption of many patients' care would not meet our standards."

On Friday, November 17, the HMOs announced that they would begin transferring their enrollees—about a quarter-million in all—to new doctors. Some insurers intended to do it at once; others over a period of weeks. State officials still promised it would be an orderly process.

Dr. Chaudhuri's health care empire had become a bottomless money pit. It began life with nearly one million patients. A little more than a year later, it was down to about 300,000. After clinic closings, layoffs, denial of services by specialists, and millions in financial aid, KPC was still hemorrhaging red ink, still not paying its health care providers, and hurtling toward a $40 million loss for the year.

Over the weekend, Dr. Chaudhuri reacted to the insurers' decision by setting in motion plans to close all KPC facilities abruptly and dismiss nearly all its employees—physicians, nurses, technicians, secretaries, and other staff members. All told, more than three dozen clinics across the Los Angeles metropolitan area would be shut down, disrupting health care for 300,000 patients and throwing 2,000 health care workers, including doctors, out on the street. Adding insult to injury, employees were told not to cash their last paychecks. The company did not have enough money to cover them. Some employees also lost health insurance coverage for themselves and their families when KPC failed to pay the premiums. The orderly transition state officials had promised quickly turned into something entirely different.

VANISHING HISTORIES

That Monday morning, November 20, Marcia Marcinko arrived at KPC's Friendly Hills Medical Center at Tustin in Orange County for a much-anticipated appointment. The medical center looks a lot like doctors' offices you see all across suburbia. It's a plain two-story stucco building, nicely landscaped, with plenty of parking spaces out front, just off busy Newport Avenue. Over the years, Marcinko had been there more times than she could remember, mostly for routine check-ups. A lot of those visits blur together, but she will never forget the last one.

She had just stepped out of her car when she knew that something was wrong. People were standing around in front of the clinic, and some were leaning over makeshift tables set up on the sidewalk. They looked worried. When she walked through the double doors into the usually bustling waiting room, all was quiet. A lone receptionist sat at the front desk. "The clinic's closed," she said. "We don't have jobs anymore. The doctors are all gone."

Marcinko couldn't believe it. The familiar place where she had been coming for so long was suddenly out of business. This appointment was especially important to her. For months she had been plagued by a mysterious ailment. It had started with a strange tingling in her left cheek; then she began to feel little twinges elsewhere on her left side. Always healthy and rarely missing a day of work from her job as director of volunteer services for Jewish Family Services in Orange County, Marcinko was mystified. Initial tests were inconclusive, but eventually doctors began to suspect that she might be in an early stage of multiple sclerosis, a difficult-to-diagnose disease that wreaks havoc with the nervous system. She had come to Friendly Hills to see a new neurologist who planned to review the results of a recent MRI.

Instead, she was directed back outside, where health-plan representatives were trying to help anxious patients find new physicians. When she passed back through the double doors, Marcinko put aside her own worries. There she came face-to-face with groups of older women and men who were confused and upset. They had come to the clinic for a variety of reasons, and now they didn't know what to do. "They didn't have their medicine and they didn't know where they could get it," she said. "They were lost."

Scenes like this unfolded across southern California that day—in La Habra, Yorba Linda, Temecula, and more than thirty other towns where clinics had also closed suddenly. Patients who kept appointments to be treated for infections, diabetes, heart ailments, and high blood pressure, who arrived to pick up X-rays, lab results, and prescriptions, all had the same bewildering experience. In Westminster, patients found the front door of the clinic padlocked and a sign reading: "No appointments will be seen today. For medical emergencies, call 911." Patients who called and asked the whereabouts of their doctors were told: "That's your problem. Call your insurance company."

Later in the week, KPC Medical Management and fifteen related companies filed for protection in Bankruptcy Court, merely a formality before going out of business. Debts exceeded assets by $200 million. Specialists who had treated KPC patients were stuck with millions in unpaid bills. So, too, were community hospitals, including Loma Linda University, where Dr. Chaudhuri had taught. And then there were all the suppliers holding unpaid bills, from MRI clinics to testing laboratories.

Desperate creditors billed patients directly. Some doctors sent strongly worded letters. One physicians group sent a heart-attack patient a $2,000 bill with this note: "Please understand that insurance coverage does not relieve you of your liability for these services and we are under no obligation to wait for your insurance carrier to pay." An anesthesiologist owed $1,330 threatened the same patient: "If we have not heard from your insurance within 30 days we will assume this to be your responsibility." It wasn't, of course, and this tactic prompted insurers to fire off letters warning health care providers that attempts to collect directly from patients violated state law.

The KPC collapse roiled the already unstable California health care system with an unprecedented jolt. Even in the best of circumstances, the system is hardly a well-oiled machine. With so many individual parts, it's easy for something to go wrong: Test results don't arrive for a patient appointment. A referral is delayed. The lab temporarily misplaces paperwork. A backlog of MRI tests slows down a diagnosis. The slightest delay or misstep can throw off the order, and when a company involving hundreds of thousands of patients comes crashing down with nothing to fill the void, the result is anarchy.

In addition to the immediate upheaval on patients and doctors, the shutdown triggered a long-term catastrophe. It cast into limbo millions of patient records. Years of individual medical histories—blood-pressure readings, cholesterol tests, EKG results, cytology slides, pathology reports, surgical records, biopsies, AIDS screens, mammograms, MRIs—all the cumulative data and information tracking patients' health was suddenly inaccessible, locked up in abandoned clinics with no one to retrieve them.

Marcia Marcinko was not even thinking about her medical records when she arrived at Friendly Hills that day. She just wanted to meet her new neurologist, become acquainted, and map out a course of action to diagnose once and for all the cause of her illness. As for her medical records, she would recall later, she simply took them for granted. She just assumed they would always be there.

After she and other patients recovered from the initial shock of learning they no longer had doctors, they met with representatives of various health plans standing by outside the clinic. Her insurer, CIGNA, got her started on finding a new primary-care physician. As for her medical records, no one seemed to know just how she could obtain them. She knew that her new physician would need the old records, especially the MRIs, which can be the single most valuable tool in identifying multiple sclerosis. They can show the condition of the myelin, the insulation encasing nerves, indicating whether it has deteriorated and is thus affecting the nervous system. For Marcinko, it was worrisome enough to have to find a new doctor, but at least her records would give whoever it turned out to be a start in assessing her condition.

She remembered feeling powerless that day. There she stood, outside the medical clinic, knowing that just a few feet away, inside the file room beyond the reception desk, were her records. "And I couldn't get them," she said. She was given a form and a telephone number to call and told to work through her insurance company. Maybe they could help. Puzzled but not yet alarmed, she went back to work.

Within a few days, Marcinko filled out the form and sent it to an address in Anaheim that Bankruptcy Court had designated as a clearinghouse for retrieving and distributing the medical records. Thousands of other KPC patients did the same thing. They all assumed that shortly they would receive their medical files and that the disruption in their lives, however inconvenient, was only temporary.

What they didn't know—and what almost no one else realized at the time—was that the whole system for keeping track of their medical records had collapsed along with the clinics. When the KPC offices closed, the files were removed, ostensibly for safekeeping and in some cases to make way for new tenants. Most of the files were trucked to a former KPC building in La Habra in Orange County.

At all hours, truckloads of patient records poured in from Brea, Hemet, Long Beach, Sun City, Rancho Cucamonga, Chatsworth, Westminster, and dozens of other clinics and offices, to be deposited in the vast facility that KPC had used for remote storage. Attempts to keep them in order failed. Files from one clinic became commingled with those of another. There was so much paper that even La Habra couldn't handle it all, and some records wound up at sites miles away. Andy's Transfer & Storage, an Allied Van Lines affiliate in Glendale in the San Fernando Valley, became the custodian of more than 3,000 boxes, some dating from the 1970s. Overall, the volume was staggering—enough to fill a hundred tractor-trailer trucks.

Adding to the confusion was the jumbled state of the original files. Many came from doctors' offices that had undergone multiple mergers, acquisitions, and bankruptcies over the years. KPC had gone out of business before it had time to even attempt to impose any order on them.

When Marcinko heard nothing after filing the first request for her records, she filed a second. And then another. Her new neurologist also requested the records. Still no answer. Then she began calling. Each time, after interminable waits and difficulty navigating endless voice-mails, she finally got through to a human. For weeks and weeks, she repeated her request.

"It was a horrendous process," she recalled. "I kept talking to ten different people every time I would call, and nobody knew anything." They would tell her that the request was being processed but provide no details. They would try to assure her, "'We're taking care of you. You'll get your records.' They were just snowing [me]."

After months of frustration, she phoned the local newspaper, the *Orange County Register*, and spoke with Bernard Wolfson, a reporter who had been covering the KPC debacle. "I just thought it was important to get this message out to people that this can happen," she said.

Wolfson wrote a story about her travails and those of other KPC patients. The next day, Marcinko received a call from a former KPC clinic telling her they had found her records: "Come pick them up."

By then her new neurologist was piecing together bits of her medical history from her own meticulously kept diary to chart out treatment. Still it was important to have the records providing a benchmark from the past.

Not everyone's story turned out as well as Marcinko's. Thousands of KPC patients never would see their medical histories again. In all, an estimated 11.7 million records—nearly a half-million cubic feet of paperwork—were stored at three different locations in the Los Angeles area. Add to that an estimated one million physical items—mammograms, X-rays, MRIs, Pap smears, bone marrow, pathology slides, cytology slides, laboratory workups for HIV and hepatitis, blood samples, CT scans, biopsy material, and tests for other diseases. Some of the results had not been interpreted; no one will ever know how many. Women who had mammograms wouldn't know if cancer lurked. Patients who had blood tests for a particularly virulent strain of venereal disease that was spreading across the region wouldn't know if they had contracted it. Men and women would be blissfully unaware if they had HIV. And all the other abnormalities evident in MRIs, blood work, and other tests would go undiagnosed.

To be sure, most of the patient histories were not the product of KPC physicians. In fact, the KPC records were combined with the MedPartners records, which were combined with the records of Med-Partners's predecessors and their predecessors before them. Incredibly, there was no master index identifying the records by patient names, notwithstanding Dr. Chaudhuri's talk of a sophisticated computer network. Sorting it all out was a task worthy of an Indiana Jones in *Raiders of the Lost Ark.* But there was no Professor Jones in the ranks of KPC or Bankruptcy Court.

In the beginning, former KPC employees and health plan workers struggled to return records to patients like Marcinko who had submitted requests early on and then persevered until they got them. But between January 2001 and March 2001, about 21,000 individual requests came in that were never answered. As the amateur archivists worked their way through the backlog, they began sending out files at the rate of 150 a day. At that pace, it would take ten years just to return the records to former KPC patients. To return all the files would take 300 years. Obviously, a new plan was in order.

The records processing had become such a nightmare for Judge James N. Barr, who was overseeing the bankruptcy, that he appointed a special representative, giving him the novel title "Responsible Person," to sort it all out. Franklin B. Stevens, the Los Angeles lawyer named to the post, quickly assessed the situation: "To obtain addresses they would need to open each of the records and search for an address," Stevens informed the court. The cost of the search would be astronomical. In fact, the postage alone would run $3 million.

Stevens reasoned that the best approach was a hasty exit. Or, as it was phrased in appropriate courtroom legalese, his efforts were "devoted primarily to trying to find the best long-term solution for the records consistent with the resources to which debtors may have access and consistent with the public good."

To that end, Stevens launched a search for a document-management firm that would take control of the Mount Everest of records, index them, and return those that patients sought. He didn't have far to look. The scope of the project overwhelmed nearly all companies—most didn't even want to bid because of the high up-front costs—save one: Iron Mountain.

A Boston-based business with revenue of $1.3 billion, Iron Mountain was the world's largest records manager, with 650 facilities across the United States, Canada, Latin America, and Europe. The company's clients ranged from government and entertainment organizations to "more than half of the Fortune 500." Even better, it offered another critical service. If it was unable to return all the records, Iron Mountain had state-of-the-art document-destruction equipment, "industrial-grade shredders and pulverizers" that could "completely destroy all materials—whether stapled, clipped, or bound."

For $2.4 million, Iron Mountain agreed to index the files and fulfill requests—at least until August 30, 2002, after which it would be free to destroy the remaining records. The company began by consolidating all the files at its central storage facility. Then it separated the records of patients who saw a doctor between 1997 and November 2000 and compiled an electronic database with the patient's name, birth date, medical record number, and file location number. That left about 11 million patient histories that would be unaccounted for.

The company also set up a Web site so patients and doctors could complete the paperwork to retrieve the documents. The news media, notably the *Orange County Register* and the *Riverside Press-Enterprise,* published articles warning people that the records eventually would be destroyed. Even so, by the time the deadline arrived, millions of records had still not found their way to patients, their families, or doctors. State regulators stepped in and ordered that the records be kept available for cancer patients and others undergoing treatment. Insurance companies contributed $2 million toward storage and distribution.

By the spring of 2003 the money had run out, and the stage was set for the last act in the saga of the KPC medical records. With its contract to store and process the files expired—it would cost the company $350,000 a year to keep them—Iron Mountain was free to begin destroying them. But the company seemed reluctant to do so, perhaps correctly sensing the potential for a public relations nightmare. As the summer of 2003 gave way to the summer of 2004, the KPC records remained in storage, and patients could attempt to retrieve them for a fee.

Still, it is only a matter of time until Iron Mountain readies its fleet of industrial shredders. The files—all the paper, the film, the slides, everything—eventually will be ground into tiny particles. Afterward some material will be recycled, according to a spokesperson for Iron Mountain. Into what?

All kinds of things, she said with a laugh, including "something we all need"—toilet paper.

In the end, no one knows where all the money went. No one knows how much the HMOs and insurers shortchanged KPC with inadequate reimbursements because they were taking care of their shareholders or themselves. No one knows how many side deals were cut among some of the players—under MedPartners and KPC—and how much money was siphoned off and spent for purposes other than health care. Although doctors, hospitals, and other providers were left holding IOUs for millions in unpaid medical bills, a few people picked up checks. On the eve of bankruptcy, KPC paid a $500,000 retainer to one of its law firms and $150,000 to another. And bankruptcy judge Barr wondered why a failed company wanted to pay its president, Donald Smallwood, $480,000.

The mechanics of free-market medicine are so Byzantine that even officials in Bankruptcy Court—the court that specializes in overseeing the complex finances of America's largest corporations—eventually threw up their hands over KPC. The court agreed to accept $1.5 million from Dr. Chaudhuri to settle claims against him after it was decided that it would take too many years and cost too much to follow the meandering money trails through sixteen bankrupt companies.

As for Dr. Chaudhuri personally, he pulled in millions during his little more than one-year tenure at KPC and then slipped out of the spotlight that had tracked his rise as a medical entrepreneur. He went back to seeing patients and being the power behind the scenes at Hemet's lone hospital, the Hemet Valley Medical Center, one of his remaining operations. Most of Dr. C's empire had vaporized, even his pre-KPC miniconglomerate. In the spring of 2001, he sold a financially ailing Corona Medical Group, and in September 2002, his Inland Global Medical Group in Upland shut down suddenly, stranding nearly 50,000 patients and leaving 240 physicians with $6 million in unpaid bills. It, too, was eventually forced into Bankruptcy Court. Even the Hemet hospital had fallen on hard times under his management. A $20 million surplus had disappeared over five years, labor relations continued to be strained, and diagnostic equipment was so poorly maintained that patients had to be dispatched to other hospitals for routine radiology procedures. But none of this seemed to have any visible effect on Dr. Chaudhuri's way of life.

Throughout it all, he continued to live in the same comfortable gated home on a Hemet street, appropriately called Chaudhuri Circle, near lush orange groves that have long made the San Jacinto Valley's citrus crops famous. Despite the bankruptcy of KPC and Inland Global, despite numerous lawsuits and unpaid bills, his homestead was as secure as ever. Long before trouble enveloped his health care businesses, disrupting the lives of patients, doctors, and vendors alike, Dr. Chaudhuri had had the foresight to place his home in trust.

As for all of KPC's patients, they provided damning evidence that free-market medicine and quality health care are incompatible. Corporate decisions at a manufacturing plant may have economic consequences affecting the paychecks, dividends, or stock options of workers, executives, and investors. The same decisions in a health care company are matters of life and death.

The Labyrinth of Care

Margaret Utterback had just come out of the bathroom of her home in San Leandro, California, on the morning of January 26, 1996, when the pain hit—a sharp stab in the back, radiating along the right side toward her abdomen. Utterback wondered if she had hurt her back the day before when she sat in a hard chair. Or was it the shellfish she had eaten the night before? She was seventy-four years old and in reasonably good health, but the pain was intense, so when it persisted, she called her daughter, Barbara Winnie, at 8:15 A.M., and asked if she would come over. Utterback then placed a call to her primary-care doctor at a Kaiser Permanente clinic in nearby Hayward, California, to seek an appointment.

A Kaiser patient for fifty years, Utterback had been dealing with the health plan's clinics for decades. However, the call she made that morning did not go to the clinic she had used for years. It was automatically forwarded to another location—a Kaiser call center that had taken over the task of scheduling doctors' appointments and dealing with other medical matters that were previously handled by the clinics. Utterback got a recorded message and was placed on hold. When no one answered for what seemed like an interminable time, she hung up.

Her daughter Barbara arrived at 9.30 A.M. and found her mother in bed, still wearing her pajamas, and in pain. At 9:45 A.M., they placed a second call to Kaiser, this time getting through to a person. Utterback told of her symptoms and asked for an appointment. The woman at the call center said her doctor was booked that day and could not see her. Utterback again explained that she was in pain and asked if she could at least be put through to her doctor to discuss it. The woman said she "could not do that" and suggested that Utterback call back at 3 P.M. and request an "urgent care appointment for that evening."

Frustrated, the two women considered what to do next. Utterback attempted one more time to get an appointment. She placed a third call to Kaiser and again described her symptoms to a new clerk. After being transferred, she found herself talking with a woman at 10:15 A.M. who at least seemed sympathetic, and who offered to send an e-mail message to Utterback's physician to ask if she could be seen that day. In the meantime, Utterback was to wait for a call back.

Utterback and her daughter did just that. They waited through the lunch hour, certain they would hear any minute from her doctor. When they didn't, and the pain intensified, Utterback could wait no longer. At 1:45 P.M., she telephoned the Kaiser call center to check on her status. Again she explained to yet one more anonymous voice at the other end why she was calling—that she was in intense pain, that for hours she had tried repeatedly to make an appointment with her doctor, and that she was distressed because she couldn't get in to see someone. As before, she was transferred several times until she was referred to a unit called "Patient Assistance." When that turned out to be another voicemail recording, Utterback hung up in despair.

She called back—her fifth call of the day. She was connected to a new clerk, and again she told her story. She was shuttled back and forth on the phone among various clerks until finally someone arranged an appointment for 4:15 P.M. with her doctor at the Point Eden clinic in Hayward.

Utterback and her daughter didn't wait. They left for the clinic at once, arriving at 2:45 P.M., where they sat until 4:30 P.M. According to California records, once her physician, Dr. Rod Perry, finally examined Utterback, he immediately diagnosed the cause of her pain: an abdominal aortic aneurysm. The condition, which kills some 15,000 people a year, is brought on by a weakness in the wall of the aortic artery that causes the vessel to swell. If the artery ruptures, the patient can quickly bleed to death. In Utterback's case, the doctor concluded that the blood vessel already was splitting apart. Even so, it was an hour before the clinic managed to get the endangered patient transferred by ambulance to nearby Hayward hospital. By then she was so racked by pain that she was thrashing about on the gurney.

Minutes after she was wheeled into the emergency room at 5:31 P.M., nine hours after she first sought medical help, her abdominal aorta ruptured. Utterback's blood pressure "crashed" as blood gushed out of the artery and emptied into her body. She was rushed to surgery, and for the next five hours doctors attempted to repair the damage. She was bleeding so badly that doctors gave her twenty-four pints of blood. Afterward, in grave condition, she was moved to the critical care unit and hooked up to a heart-lung machine while physicians and nurses frantically tried to raise her blood pressure. She never fully regained consciousness. In the hours that followed, her only communication with her stunned family was when she gently squeezed the hands of two of her daughters. At 5:45 on the morning of January 28, thirty-six hours after she underwent surgery, Margaret Utterback died.

When the California Department of Managed Health Care investigated her death, the agency concluded that Kaiser had failed Margaret Utterback at every stage—starting with the call center and ending in the physician's office. Calling it a "systemic breakdown," the department levied a $1 million fine against the Kaiser Foundation Health Plan for neglecting to provide "basic health care services including preventive care and emergency services." Kaiser said it would vigorously contest the finding. But in 2002, after a court ruled against it, Kaiser agreed to pay the fine, the largest ever assessed by the California managed-care agency. In 2003, the health plan paid $1.1 million into California's general fund.

THE NEW BUREAUCRATS

Every day thousands of Americans pick up a phone and become entangled in the faceless bureaucracy of health care. They deal with endless voicemail options. They get passed from person to person. They wait. They're advised to call back. They're told that the people they need to speak with are unavailable. Often the calls are about simple matters—a doctor's appointment, a bill, a question about insurance coverage, requests for referrals. But woven through these basic queries are the life-and-death calls from the Margaret Utterbacks. How many of the critical pleas for help are processed with the same indifference as a request for a new insurance card, no one knows. Nor has any government agency or regulatory body sought to find out. The mistakes are buried in the bureaucracy, which excels at consuming the time of callers while delaying and denying requests for treatment.

Since the 1980s, America's health care bureaucracy has mushroomed into one of the nation's fastest-growing industries. But this new industry is not designed to serve consumers or to improve the delivery of medical services. Rather, it's driven solely by the need to manage the process of referrals, billing, and reimbursements among the nation's thousands of health plans. To do so, it uses an army of call-center clerical workers, claims-processing agents, software developers, private contractors who manage medical back offices, and on-site accounting personnel who track claims for doctors' offices and hospitals. Hundreds of thousands of people are part of the bureaucracy that has evolved from insurers' efforts to deny, discourage, or postpone care, and to shift more of the expense to consumers. At best, it's a costly and wasteful system that siphons off precious health care dollars. At worst, it causes injury and death.

It wasn't supposed to be this way. For-profit health care wasn't sold to the American public on this basis. When market-based medicine began to take hold in the 1980s, the idea was that it would modernize the field and reduce spending. Introducing businesslike practices, the theory went, would streamline health care and contain costs.

But defying the collective wisdom of America's business schools, just the opposite happened: A massive bureaucracy has grown up to administer an ever-more-intricate matrix of health plans and their myriad provisions, wasting an ever-larger share of health care dollars in a paperwork factory that would be the dream of a 1950s Soviet bureaucrat.

Members of this new bureaucracy have job descriptions and professional organizations that didn't exist twenty years ago, when patients were on a first-name basis with the person who answered the doctor's telephone. The American Academy of Professional Coders is a national organization dedicated to training medical coders to help doctors and hospitals obtain proper reimbursement for their services. When its 35,000 members are invited to the annual convention, thousands come, like those who flocked to Hawaii in 2003. In the past, before battles between doctors and insurers over fees and reimbursements reached epidemic proportions, there was little need for such a group. The Professional Association of Healthcare Reimbursement Specialists is another new group; its theme at a recent convention was "The Reimbursement Jungle." Neither was there a National Association for Claims Assistance Professionals, or an American Medical Billing Association, or a Professional Association of Health Care Office Management.

"Medical billing in the United States has become a regulatory, policy guideline nightmare," observed one Canadian health care writer, Henry Sporn. "It's impossible for any single individual to keep up with all the guidelines and policies and payment practices that pertain to an individual specialty."

Adding to the cost is the structure of the industry. While everyone recognizes the names Aetna and Humana, these are only two of more than a thousand health plans. Each has its own guidelines covering what it will pay for, how long a patient may be hospitalized, what medical conditions require referrals, and how much time a doctor may devote to a patient. Because most physicians participate in multiple plans, their employees must know the requirements of each, thereby adding additional layers to the administrative labyrinth. What's more, every health insurer offers multiple plans, with varying deductibles and options. Medical researchers in Seattle found that insurers in that area alone offered some 755 different health insurance products.

In any other industry, such a variety of choices would be great for consumers. Competition in automobiles, electronics, and apparel has worked wonders to provide good quality and low prices. But in health care, the multiplicity of plans hasn't helped consumers at all, because most people actually have few choices. Those who have health coverage usually must join one of the handful of plans selected by their employer or dictated by where they happen to live. Unlike buying a car, you can't shop around for the best deal on the model of your choice.

In the end, while every plan follows a unique set of guidelines and procedures, each does pretty much the same thing. All major plans have their own call centers, claims operations, and reimbursement formulas. So the bureaucracy isn't able to take advantage of economies of scale. Rather than becoming efficient, it has instead created vast overlap, duplication, and waste.

Though the United States pioneered the information revolution, the multitude of health plans—excess competition, if you will—has created one other bizarre phenomenon. Most computers within the industry are unable to talk with one another. Think of an elementary school classroom with twenty-four students, each speaking a distinct language, unable to understand what the other twenty-three are saying—and the teacher insisting on keeping it that way.

"Currently, health care institutions that wish to communicate electronically have no standard way of doing so," according to the Massachusetts Health Data Consortium. "Hundreds of thousands of health care providers and payers use their own systems, many of which are based on proprietary data sets that are confusing to other organizations." A white paper by the Information Technology Association of America (ITAA) says that "[Health care] industry fragmentation represents a significant barrier to the widespread adoption of IT networks. The diversity of participants in the health care industry and the complexity of their relationships with each other have frustrated the voluntary adoption of industry standards."

Doctors and hospitals deal with the consequences of this every day. For them, it means spending more time and money on administration and paperwork, and less time on patients. It also markedly increases the risk of patient mistakes.

OVERRULING THE PHYSICIANS

Musette Batas was six months pregnant when she suddenly felt an all-too-familiar pain. For years, she had suffered periodic attacks of Crohn's disease, an often debilitating inflammation of the intestine. Sometimes medication brought it under control, but occasionally the attacks were so severe that she required hospitalization. This was one of those times. On March 19, 1996, in agony and worried over how the flare-up might affect her unborn child, Batas was rushed to Winthrop University Hospital in Mineola, New York, near her Long Island home.

After being admitted, she was told that her health insurer, Prudential, would authorize only a one-night stay. The next day, when her symptoms persisted, her doctor recommended that she remain in the hospital until the attack subsided. But two days later, Batas, still in pain, was told that a Prudential nurse, without consulting her doctor, had reviewed her chart and concluded that further hospitalization was "not medically necessary." Batas was told that she would either have to leave the hospital immediately or pay for subsequent days out of her own pocket. For her there was really no option. "I could not afford the hospitalization," she said later. Still suffering, and frightened about the health of her baby, Batas checked herself out of the hospital. Soon she would be back, more scared and sicker than ever.

These days, the person who determines how long you stay in a hospital may not be your doctor. Your health insurer usually has the last word. To make that decision, many insurers rely on a set of little-known but widely used manuals that spell out in detail how many days a patient with a particular condition should be hospitalized: double-bypass heart surgery, four days; pneumonia, two days; gallbladder removal, one day; stroke, one day.

Insurers also use these guidelines to decide whether a specialist should be called in; whether to approve a physician's request to perform surgery; whether hospitalization is needed for a procedure, and for how long; and even whether the procedure should be performed at all. The guidelines have been translated into computer programs so that a health plan's employees, in deciding whether a patient's hospital stay should be extended, can quickly access the information and cut off payment if the patient exceeds the specified norm.

With the rise of free-market medicine, this kind of control became inevitable. As health care has been converted into just another profit-making enterprise, insurers have sought to impose more rigorous controls on doctors and hospitals to reduce the time patients spend in hospitals. Decisions that once were left solely in the hands of physicians—evaluating a patient's condition, determining the need for surgery, and deciding how long a patient should be hospitalized— became opportunities to shave costs. By setting strict targets that restrict hospital stays, and keeping pressure on doctors and nurses to abide by them, insurers hold down costs and fatten their own bottom lines.

The drafting and implementing of these guidelines, as well as appeals from them by physicians and hospitals, involve hundreds of millions of health care dollars each year—money that could and should go into patient care. Instead, that money now feeds the burgeoning health care bureaucracy, one that was spawned, ironically, to control costs.

So exactly who wrote the guidelines that led to Musette Batas's discharge from the hospital while she was still in pain and sent her home? A Seattle-based actuarial and employee benefits consulting firm, Milliman USA.

Milliman is the dominant player in this little-known guidelines field and is typical of many private companies that have capitalized on opportunities to profit from the chaos that has enveloped health care. Milliman's guidelines are now used by health plans that cover more than 100 million Americans. In the company's own words: "Few areas of American life have changed as much as health care delivery. Milliman has been at the center of that upheaval."

For much of its half-century-plus history, Milliman had little more than a passing interest in health care. The company developed actuarial tables for pension funds and calculated risk for life and property insurers. It wasn't until 1990 that the company, then known as Milliman & Robertson, moved into health care in a big way with "Inpatient and Surgical Care," the first of a series of pathbreaking volumes that showed insurers how to enforce shorter hospital stays. As health insurers sought to justify their cost-cutting, the guidelines were, as one Milliman executive put it, "the right idea at the right time."

Seven guidebooks followed on other subjects, including outpatient care, case management, and pediatrics. Every one has been controversial. Doctors call Milliman's guidelines "cookbook medicine" for what they consider a simplistic view of patient care that doesn't reflect the real world. Their chief complaint is that Milliman calls for much shorter hospital stays than many doctors believe are necessary to treat certain conditions.

Milliman recommended that mastectomies be performed on an outpatient basis and that congestive heart failure patients be hospitalized for one day or less. For vaginal births, twenty-four hours in the hospital was their standard. And for a cesarean, forty-eight hours. Both the American College of Obstetricians and Gynecologists and the American Pediatric Society strongly disagreed, saying that the minimum hospitalization for both types of births should be doubled.

The company's most infamous recommendation—though few in the public connected it to Milliman's name—also involved childbirth. That was the so-called "drive-through deliveries," in which Milliman advocated same-day delivery and discharge for mothers and newborns. Eventually, forty-one states and the federal government passed laws to ban outpatient deliveries. Milliman also once proposed that elderly people with cataracts receive surgery in only one eye because seeing in both eyes wasn't essential. A public outcry forced the company to backtrack on that cost-cutting ploy.

Many doctors don't object to the idea of guidelines; they just believe that Milliman's are too stringent. They say the company's suggested stays are unrealistic because they reflect best-case scenarios, relatively simple cases with no complications. For its part, Milliman insists the guidelines are based on reviews of scientific literature, medical charts, consultations with physicians, and up-to-date evidence. But study after study by physicians, medical schools, and researchers has concluded otherwise.

A surgeon in Durham, North Carolina, Dr. Robert Rutledge, reviewed North Carolina hospital discharge records for adults who underwent surgery in twenty-five categories and concluded that Milliman guidelines were "at wide variance from the actual length of stay of patients treated for these diseases." Dr. Rutledge warned that the guidelines, if enforced across the board, "may hurt some patients."

Similarly, a national study of trauma patients by the Wake Forest University School of Medicine showed that Milliman's hospital stays bore little relationship to the length of time trauma patients actually spent in hospitals. Using data from 85,000 patients in the National Trauma Data Bank (NTDB), the researchers found that Milliman "grossly underestimates the LOS [length of stay] observed in patients from the NTDB. Patients in the NTDB who actually met [Milliman] guidelines had a significantly higher mortality than did those whose LOS was over [Milliman's] specified LOS." In other words, a considerable percentage of the patients who left the hospital on Milliman's abbreviated timetable were those who died.

Milliman says its guidelines are only tools in medical decision making, to help hospitals and physicians identify the norm in tracking a patient's progress. Yet Milliman also asserts that quality care can be achieved by what it calls "minimizing variation," and when variation is reduced, "patients are diagnosed and treated quickly and effectively." The company maintains that its goal is to improve patient care and reduce waste, not to supplant the doctors' decisions with generic guidelines: "In no situation are [the guidelines] intended to be a substitute for sound clinical judgment based on an individual patient's condition." And in a statement that has helped insulate Milliman from the legal wrath of physicians and patients alike, the company claims that any HMO or other provider that uses the guidelines as the "sole basis for denying authorization for treatment without proper consideration of the unique characteristics of each patient or as the sole basis for denying payment for treatment received is using our Care Guidelines inappropriately."

Nice words. But that isn't what is happening. In fact, insurers and HMOs invoke the guidelines inflexibly to save money and maximize profits. Rather than serving as a guide, the manuals have become the bible for insurers to exert strong pressure on doctors and hospitals to adhere to them. As one New Jersey doctor told the *New York Times*: "The trouble is that rather than becoming a guide it becomes a crucifix, a cross of gold."

In December 1998, Milliman issued its eighth and most controversial set of hospital-stay guidelines, *Pediatric Health Status Improvement and Management.* These guidelines for infants and children outraged many pediatricians for much the same reason earlier Milliman manuals had provoked an outcry—the suggested length of stays proposed for childhood illnesses and diseases were much too short in their opinion. A California pediatrician, Gary F. Krieger, told the *AMA News* that the guidelines were "totally irrational for day-to-day use . . . these guidelines talk about the ideal, and the ideal is not the real."

Writing in *Pediatrics*, three medical doctors at the Boston University School of Medicine—Howard Bauchner, Robert Vinci, and John Chessare—contended that "the use of Milliman and Robertson as a way to judge appropriate length of stay and to benchmark and compare institutions has no basis in fact, is not justified and may lead to suboptimal care."

A Baltimore-based health care consultant, HCIA-Sachs Institute, reviewed 3.5 million pediatric cases and found that more than two-thirds of the children were hospitalized longer than Milliman recommended for the same illnesses. Overall, HCIA found a substantial gap between Milliman's suggested stays and how long children actually remained in hospitals. For asthma, Milliman allotted one day; nationally, the median was two days, according to HCIA. For bronchiolitis, a lung infection, Milliman also recommended one day; the national median was two. For bacterial meningitis, Milliman suggested three days of hospitalization; HCIA said the median was 8.5 days.

The 55,000-member American Academy of Pediatrics called the pediatric guidelines "beyond the realm of reality." Of the Milliman recommendation that children in a coma could be released after three days, the Academy noted: "It boggles the mind that a patient would be discharged in three days after having been in a coma forty-eight hours before with seizures."

The pediatrician perhaps most upset by Milliman's guidelines for children was Dr. Thomas G. Cleary, head of pediatric infectious diseases at the University of Texas–Houston Medical School. When the guidelines were published, Dr. Cleary was listed as a contributing author. But he wasn't. Not only had he not contributed, he considered some guidelines dangerous. He would later tell the *Houston Chronicle* that Milliman's pediatric guidelines were the "most outrageous thing" he'd seen in twenty-eight years of practicing medicine.

Dr. Cleary had become entangled in the controversy by default. In an attempt to make the guidelines more palatable and give them wider acceptance, Milliman formed an alliance with the large, well-established pediatrics department of the University of Texas–Houston. Milliman gave the department a grant of $100,000 and hired one of its faculty members, Dr. Robert Yetman, to oversee compilation and drafting of the guidelines. In early 1998, Yetman sent Cleary a list of recommendations for pediatric hospital stays that he planned to include in the upcoming guidebook. Cleary said later he was appalled at their brevity: "Kids might die from these guidelines." He jotted down some concerns and sent them back to Yetman.

When Milliman formally released its 400-page pediatric manual in December 1998, Cleary was stunned to see that he was listed as a contributor, together with other members of his department. In the preface, Millman sought to give the impression the book had been a joint project with the university's pediatrics department. It read: "Milliman & Robertson Inc. and the University of Texas–Houston Medical School Department of Pediatrics are pleased to present *Pediatric Health Status Improvement and Management (HSIM)*, a comprehensive set of health management guidelines created to assist clinicians in the management of pediatric disorders."

After reviewing the manual, Cleary concluded that every page contained at least one risky recommendation. Most distressing were the very brief hospital stays suggested for children with major illnesses. For a case of bacterial infection (neonatal sepsis), Milliman recommended three days. Cleary thought two to three weeks was closer to the norm. For osteomyelitis, a bone infection that Cleary said often required four to six weeks of hospitalization, Milliman recommended two days. "In two days you may not have the organism isolated, you don't know if it's sensitive to antibiotics, you don't have a clue where you are," Cleary said.

Cleary demanded that his name be dropped from the manual, as did three other faculty members, and that Milliman withdraw the manual. Milliman sent out a corrected list of contributors, omitting the names of Cleary and the other department members who had protested. Eventually, the pediatrics department itself asked to be disassociated from the guidelines. Milliman agreed to comply in future editions, but in the meantime it continued to market the published manual to health insurers and hospitals.

Cleary and his colleagues subsequently filed a lawsuit seeking to recall the manual. They charged that their reputations had been harmed by linking them to guidelines for which "there is no accepted authoritative medical or scientific basis." Their real aim was to force withdrawal of the guidelines. If the court should agree with them, Cleary said that any award he received would be donated to charity. "Doctors get sued, we don't sue," he told the *Houston Chronicle*. "But in this case I felt I had no choice. If this lawsuit makes me any money, I'll have to figure out which charity to give it to. I don't want money with blood on it."

Musette Batas, the expectant mother who was discharged from the New York hospital over the objections of her physician when her health insurer invoked the Milliman guidelines, returned to her home in hopes that the stubborn attack of Crohn's disease would subside so she could enjoy the last three months of her pregnancy. But just a week later, Batas was experiencing crippling pain and running a high fever. Her mother rushed her back to the hospital, this time to the emergency room.

The attending physician wanted to perform exploratory surgery to determine the cause of the pain and contacted Prudential for authorization. Doctors felt that Batas was "extremely ill" and that both her life and that of her baby were "at risk." When her physician heard nothing from Prudential the next day, he called the insurer, only to be told the request was still "pending."

Two days later, the authorization to operate still pending, Batas's intestine burst. Without immediate surgery, she would bleed to death. Her physicians could delay no longer. Before moving her to the operating room, they felt obligated to tell Batas and her husband that there was only a slim chance the baby would survive. Batas was in the OR for hours, where surgeons removed part of her colon. Miraculously, both she and her unborn baby survived. But her relief was soon tempered by a grim warning from doctors: During the traumatic emergency surgery, the baby might have suffered brain damage. Only time would tell.

Four days after the lifesaving operation, Prudential, not to be influenced by Batas's experience, insisted that she be discharged. Her physician was outraged. When he pointed out that his patient "was barely out of surgery, was pregnant and was seriously ill," the insurer backed down—temporarily. A week later, the company ruled that further hospitalization was "not medically necessary." Batas was discharged. A little more than two months later, she returned to the hospital and, to the relief and wonder of all, gave birth to a healthy baby girl.

One of her doctors, Patrick F. Vetere, believed that Batas had been extremely fortunate. But that didn't temper his deep dissatisfaction with a system that had endangered his patient's life and that of her baby. In Dr. Vetere's opinion, relying on "third-party guidelines" to save money on hospitalization, as the insurer had done, violated "acceptable standards of care in the medical community." Had he acted as the insurer did, Dr. Vetere said, "I would have committed an act of medical malpractice."

THE WRONG JOBS

Nearly one of every three dollars now spent on health care goes for administration, from processing the voluminous paperwork of billing to enforcing the length-of-stay guidelines that brought grief to Musette Batas. A generation after introducing business practices to health care, the United States spends a higher percentage of its health care dollars just to administer the system than any other country. A study published in the *New England Journal of Medicine* in 2003 comparing administrative costs in the United States and Canada concluded that U.S. costs are three times higher: $1,059 per capita in the United States in 1999; $307 per capita in Canada.

Administrators, clerks, and other members of the bureaucracy comprise an ever-expanding share of the health care workforce, at the expense of nurses, doctors, and other caregivers. "Between 1969 and 1999, the share of the U.S. health care labor force accounted for by administrative workers grew from 18.2 percent to 27.3 percent," according to the *NEJM* study. In Canada, the increase during the period was 3.1 percent.

What is most remarkable about the *NEJM* findings is that the study didn't include *all* the administrative jobs. The computations intentionally excluded a key sector of the industry—"926,000 employees in life insurance or health insurance firms, 724,000 in insurance brokerages, and employees of consulting firms." These workers weren't included for two reasons: to give a more accurate comparison with the Canadian health care system, where private insurers are bit players; and because it was impossible to pinpoint how many insurance, consulting, and brokerage employees are specifically engaged in health care rather than other types of insurance. Thus the total number of administrative jobs was greatly understated, since the study did not count thousands of employees who answer calls or process claims, the very heart of the insurers' bureaucracy.

The study's authors—Dr. Steffie Woolhandler; Terry Campbell, M.H.A.; and Dr. David U. Himmelstein—did not attribute the high administrative costs to any one factor, but noted the "growth coincided with the expansion of managed care and market-based competition, which fostered the adoption of complex accounting and auditing practices long standard in the business world." They also pointed out that "a system with multiple insurers is intrinsically costlier than a single-payer system," noting that "Canadian physicians send virtually all bills to a single insurer." Through Canada's national health program, Canadian hospitals have an annual budget and receive lump-sum payments from provincial governments, thereby eliminating the cumbersome billing structure of U.S. hospitals. "The existence of global budgets in Canada has eliminated most billing and minimized internal cost accounting, since charges do not need to be attributed to individual patients and insurers," they concluded.

While Washington continues to encourage this private bureaucracy by championing the misguided belief that competition in health care will control costs, some states are beginning to see things differently. In 2001, the Maine legislature, worried about soaring outlays and the growing numbers of uninsured residents, authorized a study by the Mathematica Policy Research Inc. of Princeton to evaluate whether Maine could implement a single-payer system. In December 2002, Mathematica concluded that it could be done, largely through savings derived by consolidating operations of the state's numerous health plans:

> Such a system would centralize the processing of claims and decrease or eliminate costs related to activities such as billing and the adjudication of claims. It would increase economies of scale by covering all Maine citizens under a single program and eliminating the complexities associated with the participation of multiple insurers with multiple benefit designs.

And ultimately eliminate a lot of the bureaucracy.

In the meantime, that bureaucracy will only grow. In an effort to extract their own profits from health care delivery, insurers will do everything they can to hold down their costs by delaying, reducing, or denying claims filed by doctors and hospitals. That in turn compels physicians and hospitals to work even harder to obtain reimbursements. The *NEJM* study estimated that physicians' administrative costs were $72.6 billion in 1999—or 27 percent of their gross income.

THE INSURERS' SECRET CODES

Next time you leave your doctor's office, look at the invoice you're asked to drop off on your way out. It probably will be a legal-sized form filled with rows of boxes. Whether your exam was brief or comprehensive, and whether you were given tests or evaluated for a specific ailment, there seems to be a box for just about every medical condition and procedure. Next to each is a five-digit number: 90658 (a flu shot), 95115 (an allergy injection), or 81002 (a urinalysis). The single most common number is 99213—a routine office visit. Depending on what was done during the visit, your doctor will check one or more of the boxes.

Most patients pay no attention to the maze of numbers. But to many doctors the five digits are their financial lifeblood. The codes determine how much they earn, how quickly they get paid by insurers, and whether they will be reimbursed if they perform two procedures during one visit, or if they must require a patient to return for the second one.

The five-digit numbers, called CPT codes—short for current procedural terminology—date from 1966, when the American Medical Association devised them to bring some order to billing following the enactment of Medicare. For the first time, a number was used to describe a procedure and service, with the aim of making clearer and more precise the actual nature of the services physicians rendered. Doctors weren't all that crazy about the idea of using a number rather than words to classify a patient visit, but over time they grudgingly accepted the codes as a way to streamline billing.

Through the years, as new medical technologies and procedures developed, the AMA steadily added codes, with the total building to more than 7,800. Every year the process of adding or subtracting codes is intensely lobbied and debated in the medical community. An entrepreneurial company that develops a new device seeks an AMA code for its product. Obtaining one can mean all the difference.

Cambridge Heart Inc., a Bedford, Massachusetts, company specializing in products to diagnose cardiac disease, developed a sophisticated test to identify heart patients at risk. Its Microvolt T-Wave Alternans Test measures extremely subtle fluctuations in a person's heartbeat. These tiny variations—counted at one-millionth of a volt—are detected using proprietary sensors. Like most small health-technology firms, Cambridge Heart struggled. It wasn't until the AMA established a CPT code covering the T-Wave Alternans Test that Cambridge began to see hope. Hailing the AMA action, the company's CEO and president, David Chazanovitz, said the CPT code "should greatly improve our customers' ability to submit claims efficiently and be paid quickly."

Overseeing the codes is one of the AMA's most important, yet obscure divisions, the CPT department, a multimillion-dollar operation. The department and its sixteen-member editorial panel, which includes eleven physicians, approve new codes and modify existing ones. In addition to its role in medicine, the division underpins the AMA's financial health. The AMA has trademarked CPTs, so every insurer and any other party that uses the codes must pay the association a royalty. That brings the organization about $70 million a year. "Without those royalties," says one medical consultant, "the AMA would be out of business."

With the shift toward managed care, CPT codes became even more important, but for an entirely different reason. As insurers looked for ways to bolster profits, the CPT classifications rapidly evolved into a battleground. Here was a way to squeeze doctors: By disregarding or combining certain categories and lumping multiple procedures or services into one category, insurers could reimburse physicians for only a percentage of the care they had provided.

What happened to Dr. Manual Porth is fairly typical. An orthopedic surgeon in bustling Broward County north of Miami, Porth has practiced medicine more than twenty years. Once, billing wasn't such a hassle, but over time Porth observed a trend: Insurers would be late with payments or refuse to reimburse at all for certain services. Often he would submit a bill for five separate procedures and be reimbursed for only one. Even when he supplied extensive backup documentation, he explained in a deposition, "you get slapped in the face with a check for $950 for $8,000 worth of services."

Porth was a victim of what is known in the medical world as "downcoding" and "bundling," two practices that health insurers use to drastically reduce their payments to doctors. Bundling occurs when a physician submits a claim for two or more procedures or services to a patient during one office visit and the insurer bundles them together and reimburses for just one, typically the one that pays the least.

Downcoding takes place when an insurer unilaterally changes the CPT code a physician has submitted to a code that reimburses at a lower rate. One of the most common downcodes involves new patients. For a first-time visit, many physicians seek reimbursement under CPT code 99204 (a so-called level 4), meaning that the doctor spent more than the usual amount of time. This would seem only natural. After all, any good doctor would spend a disproportionate amount of time compiling a detailed history, reviewing medications, interviewing the patient, and getting to know that person, all to provide appropriate care in the future and avoid potential mistakes. Nonetheless, many insurers automatically downcode the visit to 99203 (level 3), which assumes shorter visits and pays less. In other cases, health plans reject CPT codes for more than one service, depriving doctors of full reimbursement. Doctors can contest the denials, but the process is costly and time-consuming—and often fruitless.

To Barbara J. Cobuzzi, president of a New Jersey company that represents doctors who challenge these adverse decisions, it's a constant battle. She illustrates the experiences of many doctors with this analogy: Imagine that you take your car to a mechanic to have its transmission repaired. To do the work, the mechanic has to pull the engine. In doing so he finds a problem in the engine that he repairs. Then he fixes the transmission and charges for the time he spent working on both the engine and the transmission. If he were a doctor, Cobuzzi says, "he wouldn't get paid for working on the engine because he had to pull that anyway to get to the transmission."

Doctors rarely receive an explanation for a lower payment, and all too often they don't realize until later what has happened and how much income they have lost. Furthermore, the CPT codes selected for bundling and downcoding are always changing, and some codes may be accepted by an insurer one month, then rejected the next. To make matters worse, most doctors deal with several health plans, and a CPT code accepted by one insurer may be rejected by another. The recoding is done in secret, with little or no notification to doctors. The result is uncertainty and mass confusion.

Dr. John Hansen-Flaschen, chief of Pulmonary, Allergy and Critical Care at the Hospital of the University of Pennsylvania in Philadelphia, had just that experience. After hearing about downcoding from other doctors, Dr. Hansen-Flaschen began reviewing claims filed by his practice for reimbursements from Pennsylvania Blue Shield. In case after case, he discovered that Blue Shield was replacing certain CPT codes with ones that paid less—even though the level of care being provided by physicians hadn't changed. As he explained to a medical journalist:

"If an individual experiences serious complications of major surgery and has a critical illness lasting six or seven days, three or four days [of care] would be systematically downcoded at the end of that illness. If that individual subsequently recovers a little bit, only to return to the ICU one or two weeks later for a second critical illness, all of the days in that second critical illness would be downcoded."

Downcoding not only affects doctors' incomes, Dr. Hansen-Flaschen maintains, but it also has the potential to harm patients. Every patient who needs critical care is "experiencing a tragedy of a lifetime," he said. Such problems require an immediate response by a physician. "If physicians after a long day are worrying whether they are to be paid or how much they are to be paid, I worry that they will not provide the best level of services they know how to provide under those circumstances," he continued. "I think, in a more general sense, quality of care is eroding when physicians cannot trust insurance carriers to pay them fairly and honestly for the services they provide."

While ostensibly used to save money, downcoding and bundling actually consume millions of dollars in unnecessary administrative expenses that otherwise might go for patient care. Talk to doctors, nurses, office managers, technicians, bookkeepers, and other personnel in physicians' offices and they will tell you about the time they waste on the phone with insurers, the long stretches spent waiting on hold, and their frustration over not being able to get through to someone who can explain why a code was changed or rejected.

The experience of Dr. Glenn Kelly, a Colorado vascular surgeon, mirrors that of many physicians. In a court deposition, Kelly said that health insurers refuse to call back about rejected claims, that it is common to make three or four phone calls before getting through to a person in an insurer's call center, and that even when someone is reached the person has little or no knowledge of medical terminology—all of which has imposed an enormous workload on his office, diverting time away from patient care. "I think there was an intent to complicate the system and make it unresponsive to the physician so that we were unable to obtain payments or unable to obtain them in a timely fashion," he said.

Kelly grew especially frustrated by rejections and slow payments from one insurer, CIGNA, and after he reported difficulties with the company to the Colorado State Insurance Commissioner's Office and the Colorado State Medical Society, CIGNA canceled its contract with him. Kelly believed that because the delays and denials happened so often they "were intentional maneuvers to prevent us from getting paid." On that score, he and other physicians are hardly alone. Patients encounter a similar practice in their dealings with insurers and call centers. Hospital and insurance bills are needlessly obscure, seemingly designed to confuse the recipients and secure a payment, especially from the elderly and less knowledgeable, when in fact no money is owed. Even worse, insurers play off patients (their customers) against doctors. They send a partial negotiated payment for services to the physicians and then suggest to patients they are obligated to pay the difference. The sophisticated know otherwise. But to wade through the billing morass, patients may spend several hours complying with voicemail options, grilling call-center clerks, and assembling and forwarding paperwork before successfully resolving an erroneous claim.

Often the first statement from an insurer will show no payments to the health care provider, or a notification that the patient owes a large portion or the entire bill without any explanation. For example, an insurer's bill for physical therapy shows a therapist charge of $375 and a network rate of $192.33. Actual benefits paid: zero. Patient's portion due: $192.33. That prompts the first in a series of dealings with call-center clerks and, when they feign ignorance, their supervisors, and then their supervisor. If the clerk insists there is no record of a prescription for the treatment, the patient must root through his or her records to find a copy of the prescription, assuming a copy was made, and fax it to the call center. More conversations with call-center clerks follow before the patient receives another version of the statement showing paid in full. Depending on the size of the bill, many patients are simply worn down by the process or don't have the time to devote to the issue, and forward a payment they do not owe. And that's but one of many different ways in which insurers trick patients into paying bills the insurers themselves are obligated to pay. Their dealings with the elderly are even more egregious. For their part, insurers will insist that these are just errors. But as is the case with insurers' treatment of doctors, the frequency of such "errors" suggests otherwise.

In the case of physicians, a profession of individualists where consensus is hard to come by, the billing nightmares resonate with everyone from primary-care doctors to surgeons. An AMA survey in 2001 found that doctors regarded downcoding and bundling as impacting more on their practices than all but one other issue, insurers' delays, or denials of claims.

For more than twenty years, Dr. Michael Burgess delivered babies in Lewisville, Texas, twenty miles north of Dallas. All through the 1990s, his reimbursement rates "eroded significantly" while his overhead soared. Burgess said he found it increasingly difficult to keep his office open and his staff paid. But hardest of all to take was what was happening to his profession. "The anxiety level, the frustration level of practicing medicine has—has gone through the roof," Burgess said in a court proceeding. "If a young person came to me today and said, 'Boy, I'd like to be a doctor, I'd like to be just like you,' I'd say, 'I'm flattered. Go talk to a stockbroker or a lawyer.'"

In 2002, Burgess took some of his own advice: He quit medicine, ran for Congress, and became a congressman representing the twenty-sixth district of Texas.

Battles between physicians and insurance companies over reimbursements are an old story, but in recent years the advantage has shifted overwhelmingly to the insurers, largely made possible by development of sophisticated computer programs that can automatically downcode, bundle, and otherwise reduce doctors' fees.

The most widely used medical claims software is ClaimCheck of McKesson Corporation, the health care giant that had 24,500 employees and revenue of $57 billion in 2003. The corporation has offices around the world, but few with more impact on physicians than a modern three-story brick building in the western suburbs of Philadelphia. It was in a leafy office park in Malvern, Pennsylvania, that Claim-Check was born twenty years ago, and from there it continues to exercise ever-greater influence on physician income.

McKesson licenses ClaimCheck to health insurers who modify the program to fit their own claims-paying policies. Every year, it saves health insurers billions—money that comes straight out of the pockets of doctors. Mention "ClaimCheck" to a physician and you are likely to get an earful. To many it embodies everything that has gone wrong in medicine: a computer program that overrides medical decisions and dictates how much doctors can earn. McKesson says that ClaimCheck only corrects coding errors and collars cheating doctors. Physicians see it differently. "I call it fraud against doctors," says Texas gynecologist Dr. David E. Rogers.

Ironically, the software that has made doctors miserable was inspired by a doctor. Elmer R. Gabrieli, a Buffalo pathologist with an interest in computers, began tinkering with programming in the 1970s to translate doctors' notes into computer terms. In 1984, Dr. Gabrieli and his son Christopher founded GMIS Inc. (Gabrieli Medical Information Systems). The company soon became a pacesetter in the emerging field known as automated medical management. The Gabrielis quickly realized there wasn't much money to be made peddling software to doctors. So they switched to what one Wall Street analyst called "the payer side of the health care equation," the insurance companies.

The breakthrough year was 1989, when GMIS introduced Claim-Check, a revolutionary new product that "automatically identifies and corrects billing errors that can inflate physician payments." With insurers increasingly intent on cutting costs, ClaimCheck seemed heaven-sent, a way to systematically reduce payments to doctors.

GMIS saw itself as an agent to control health care spending, albeit at the expense of doctors. In annual reports, the company spoke of "preventing unnecessary care, eliminating inappropriate payments and identifying patterns of inefficiency" as well as "eliminating inefficient providers" and "preventing physicians from providing expensive, unwarranted procedures."

ClaimCheck was an immediate success. GMIS turned a profit the year it came on the market and recorded progressively higher earnings. Within three years, the company had licensed the software to more than a hundred health insurers, including some of the nation's largest—Aetna, Humana, and CIGNA. The rewards were awesome. For an annual licensing fee of $325,000, Aetna said it reaped $24 million in yearly savings.

In 1991, GMIS went public, and investors snapped up the shares, marking the beginning of a rapid rise in the company's stock price. Wall Street was enthusiastic. "Fundamentally, we like GMIS," wrote an analyst for Robinson-Humphrey Company Inc. in 1993. "GMIS' focus on the health care market has clearly paid off. Revenues have risen at a rate of 55 percent since 1989, and operating income growth has exceeded 43 percent each year . . . we believe that GMIS is clearly well-situated to continue its rapid growth." GMIS was sold in 1996 to a larger public company—HBO & Co., an Atlanta-based vendor of computer systems for hospitals and doctors—for $220 million. Two years later, HBO & Co. was acquired by McKesson.

Except for doctors, just about everyone involved with GMIS has done well. The original investors profited; the GMIS acquisition helped make HBO & Co. an inviting takeover target for a larger company; and ClaimCheck solidified McKesson's position in the health care technology field.

As for the Gabrielis, the family earned millions from the software. Christopher Gabrieli became a successful venture capitalist in Boston as a partner in one of the nation's oldest private venture capital firms, Bessemer Venture Partners. With some of the money he made from

GMIS and other companies, he dabbled in politics. In 1998, while seeking the Democratic nomination for the Boston congressional seat being vacated by Joseph P. Kennedy II, Gabrieli latched on to a hot issue with voters—anger toward HMOs.

In a series of slick advertisements and campaign speeches, Gabrieli pounded away at HMO abuses. "See to it that you and your doctors, not HMO accountants, decide what's best," urged one ad. Gabrieli said his polling showed that voters liked the idea that he could "help them fight medical bureaucracies." The *Boston Herald* called him the "poster boy for HMO hatred."

Gabrieli seemed untroubled that his former company, GMIS, had done much to foster practices that were now stirring that hatred. When a *Boston Globe* reporter asked if he saw any conflict between his stance attacking HMOs and the role his entrepreneurial company had played in empowering their billing practices, Gabrieli answered that the charge was "baseless." The software behind the current controversial billing practices of HMOs, he insisted, was different from that developed when he was associated with GMIS. Gabrieli eventually spent an estimated $5 million of his own money before his bid for Congress failed.

LONG-DISTANCE DIAGNOSIS

A generation ago, your personal health care decisions—a medical appointment, a prescription, a test, a recommendation for a specialist—flowed through your doctor's office. Your physician decided whether you would have a procedure, whether you would be admitted to a hospital, and how long you would stay. To cut costs, the insurers took much of that power away from doctors and gave it to the health care call center. Here, in their lexicon, was a way to "manage" care, which really meant to restrict and deny care. The length-of-stay guidelines and coding schemes were but tools to achieve that end. The call center became the command post to carry it all out.

Since then, hundreds of call centers have popped up across the country, employing thousands of workers. A few are located in or near big cities, but most are in medium-sized communities or small towns. Often they are in areas where jobs are hard to come by, thereby enabling owners to hold down wages and still attract grateful workers. Bismarck, North Dakota, hosts some of the health care industry's largest centers. In towns like Visalia in central California, the call center is the largest employer.

For many Americans, the centers are perhaps the most infuriating symbol of U.S. health care. The chief function of the faceless people who answer the phones seems to be to see how long callers can be kept on hold or how many times they can be compelled to call again and again before securing a satisfactory answer to a question. Housed in warehouse-like buildings, the centers sit anonymously alongside interstate highways or sequestered in featureless office parks. The interiors of these places don't look like they have anything to do with medicine, and the workforce could just as easily be filling orders for L.L.Bean.

Imagine an empty Wal-Mart, lined with row after row of cubicles, each separated by a low partition, stretching in every direction as far as you can see. Inside each pod is a compact workspace with a computer terminal and an operator, usually a woman, wearing a telephone headset. Rising above this vast grid of squares is the constant sound of phones ringing, people talking, and computer keys clicking. In some centers, the sound goes on twenty-four hours a day. As calls stream in, they are randomly routed to operators. If a caller complains of a medical problem, the operator asks a series of questions: Where is the pain or discomfort? When did it start? How intense is it? Have you had it before? Who is your primary-care physician? The questions may give callers the impression that they are speaking with someone who is well versed in medicine. But most operators are simply reading questions that appear on their computer screens and keying in the answers.

The operators rely on software programs called scripts that offer up standardized queries about various ailments and injuries, allowing people with no medical training to diagnose conditions that were once solely the responsibility of medical professionals. In theory, a caller who has a serious problem will be turned over to a nurse or physician. But that decision rests largely with the operator, often a low-paid worker who is new to the job.

For many call-center employees, their only training is mechanical and rudimentary—how to answer the phone, how to use the computer, how to access the scripts, how to input the caller's answers, and how to make a referral. A good telephone manner is a plus, but it's not essential. What the industry requires most is bodies to answer an ever-growing tidal wave of calls. Although these workers have become crucial cogs in the health care bureaucracy, they rank at the bottom of the industry's hierarchy. When insurers cut their budgets, they are among the first to go. People hired one month are often laid off a few months later, and sometimes long-standing employees are terminated only to see their jobs filled by new hires at lower pay.

The call centers are essentially factories, today's equivalent of yesterday's assembly lines. Tethered to telephones all day and fielding an endless stream of inquiries, appeals for help, billing questions, and requests for referrals, prescription refills, and doctors' appointments—all the while under pressure to move on quickly to a waiting call—workers are much like their predecessors in textile mills at the dawn of industrialization. The surroundings may be cleaner, better lighted, and less noisy, but they are every bit as regimented and stressful.

The work is intense. On any given day, an operator handles dozens of calls from worried and angry patients and physicians asking why a referral didn't come through, or why a patient had to pay such a large percentage of a medical bill, or why a physician wasn't reimbursed in full for a procedure. Doctors become livid when they talk about the amount of time they waste on the phone with clerks who, after consulting their computer screens, refuse to grant a referral or authorize a test because they deem the physician's request to be medically unnecessary.

Call-center workers are the health plans' gatekeepers who restrict and ration care by saying "no" to patients and physicians alike. Technically, they are customer-service representatives, but usually their work is just the opposite—to discourage care, tests, or procedures, and reduce or delay reimbursements.

Operators are under enormous pressure to minimize the time they spend talking on the phone or processing claims. Those who take longer than average are reprimanded and threatened with dismissal. Says an employee at one California operation: "They will say, 'Now what is the problem here? You know how long you are supposed to be on the phone.'" In this job, she says, the fear of spending too much time with a patient is "always hanging over your head." The briefer the calls, of course, the more calls that can be fielded, which means fewer employees and more for the bottom line. One health care consultant says, "If you measure this by the number of calls they have to take, these are sweatshops."

Unlike the chronic repetition of assembly-line work, health care calls are anything but predictable. Rarely is one exactly like the one that preceded it. Many require individual attention, and some cannot be swiftly resolved. "What happens if you get stuck with calls that are difficult, that take the most time?" asks the consultant. "All of a sudden, you say to the caller, 'I have to get off now. I'm taking too much time. Call back later. Bye.'"

Health care companies deny that they have quotas, but there isn't much doubt that they impose performance targets on their employees. Indianapolis-based Anthem Inc., the fourth-largest publicly traded health benefits company with revenue of $13 billion in 2002, implemented one such program in the late 1990s. Formerly a privately held mutual insurer in Indiana, Anthem went national in the 1990s and acquired nonprofit Blue Cross and Blue Shield affiliates, converting them to profit-making enterprises. Today its Blues provide health insurance for more than 12.5 million Americans in nine states—Colorado, Connecticut, Indiana, Kentucky, Maine, Nevada, New Hampshire, Ohio, and Virginia. When a planned merger with Wellpoint Health Networks is completed, Anthem will be the nation's largest health benefits company, providing coverage for about 28 million Americans in thirteen states.

While positioning itself to go public, Anthem sought to make the company more attractive to investors by cutting costs and promoting efficiencies. To reduce payments to doctors, the company rigorously tracked the work of its call-center claims agents. As later spelled out in a lawsuit filed by Connecticut physicians, with information provided by whistle-blowers inside the company: "Utilization and claims personnel were instructed by Anthem that certain targets and goals were established for utilization of healthcare services. . . . If a specific target was not met, [a] supervisor responsible for overseeing the particular claims personnel would be reprimanded by senior management and warned that there would be serious ramifications if a particular target was not met the following month." Conversely, call-center workers who met their targets were rewarded, reportedly with bonuses of up to 25 percent of their salaries. Connecticut doctors later sued, charging that Anthem was interested in "financial benchmarks without regard for individual medical needs."

In northern California, Kaiser Permanente dangled similar incentive bonuses before clerks to keep calls brief. In a plan implemented at three large centers in Sacramento, San Jose, and Vallejo in 2000, Kaiser promised, according to the *Los Angeles Times,* to reward clerks with upward of a 10 percent salary bonus if they accomplished three of four objectives:

- Handle regular calls in less than three minutes and forty-five seconds.
- Schedule or request appointments for patients in no more than 15 percent to 35 percent of cases.
- Transfer fewer than 50 percent of calls to nurses for additional help.
- Spend an average of 75 percent or more of the workday answering calls.

In a year's time, an aggressive clerk could earn a bonus of $2,500 by keeping talk to a minimum and referring fewer callers to physicians and nurses. Kaiser maintained that the program was to promote good service, but it sparked outrage among Kaiser's call-center nurses, who believed that it encouraged untrained clerks to make medical decisions that might harm patients. After two years, Kaiser abandoned the experiment, saying that it "wasn't working." But Kaiser's long-range strategy, like that of most HMOs and insurers, is still to shift more work to lower-paid clerks with no specialized medical knowledge.

Such is the case at Kaiser's Vallejo call center in San Francisco's East Bay. Off I-80 in a nondescript building that resembles a warehouse, several hundred call-center representatives answer phones around the clock. More than half have no medical training. The rest are registered nurses with years of experience treating patients. Many of the calls that stream in are routine—requests for the name of a specialist, the location of a clinic, or a duplicate health care card. Yet even some calls that might appear routine can require a medical decision.

Catherine Elsdon has seen this firsthand. An "advice nurse" at Vallejo, Elsdon has been a registered nurse for nearly three decades, working primarily with oncology patients. In 1999, feeling burned out because she could no longer provide good care in understaffed hospitals, she went to work at Kaiser's recently opened Vallejo center. Outgoing and gregarious, Elsdon felt the call center would let her stay in touch with patients, which she enjoyed, in a setting much less stressful than the hospital floor.

But at Vallejo she and other nurses have encountered a different kind of stress. All incoming calls first go to clerks who decide whether they should be transferred to one of the registered nurses for further evaluation. As they follow the queries on their computer screens, the clerks attempt to assess each caller's condition. But in the minds of Kaiser's nurses, this is risky business. Clerks unable to recognize the nuances of a caller's symptoms may miss a serious health problem that a nurse would be more likely to pick up. "This is where I am most anxious about what they do," said Elsdon. "Patients don't always know how serious their condition is, when they should see a doctor right away."

She cited an example of a woman concerned about a burning sensation during urination. The clerk sends a routine message to the patient's doctor. Because the clerk considers the query "non-urgent," the physician's office has forty-eight hours to return the call.

"But in the meantime, the patient is getting sicker and sicker," said Elsdon. "And twenty-four hours later, she still hasn't heard from her doctor because it was a non-urgent message. And now the patient calls back and she has severe pain in her kidneys—fevers, chills, blood in the urine—and now she has to go to the emergency room because it's after hours. There is no other choice; this patient is too sick to wait until the next day to be seen. The patient should have had an appointment that day."

Elsdon and other nurses fear that instances like that are bound to become more common. (Remember Margaret Utterback?) When the Vallejo call center first opened, the clerks and nurses were grouped together in the same sections. Then Kaiser separated them, putting the operators on one side, nurses on the other, making any substantive contact between the two nearly impossible.

"Personally, I liked being intermingled," said Elsdon. "I think it helped more with the team approach. The operators could turn to us if they had a question. Also, I could overhear them, and if someone was saying something that was inaccurate to a caller, I was right there to straighten it out. Now I don't hear those calls."

Nurses believe that Kaiser mandated the new seating arrangement to give clerks more power and encourage them to be more aggressive in denying care. Ella Sangco, another Kaiser registered nurse at Vallejo, believes the company is playing off one group against the other. "But who loses here?" she asks. Of course, it's the patient. To be fair, Kaiser at least hires nurses for its call centers. Many other insurers don't even bother.

Companies add to the oppressive environment by monitoring employees' every move. Sophisticated computer software tracks how many minutes workers spend on each call, how many calls they handle, how many they refer to nurses, and how much time they spend away from workstations. If an operator leaves her desk to use the bathroom or stops to chat with another employee, the center knows she isn't working because an incoming call goes unanswered.

As might be expected, given the low pay and unsatisfying nature of the job, workers are constantly leaving. Says one health care consultant: "They don't pay them. They work them like dogs. They measure them wrong. The people get disenchanted. They can't handle the stress. [Companies] don't get the productivity they want and out the door they go." The turnover, which reaches 100 percent a year in some centers, creates a perpetual cycle of recruiting and training. "It's a huge waste," says the consultant, "and they don't want to fix it."

ONLINE AND OFFSHORE

Today, when you phone your health care company, you have no idea who's answering the call or where that person is located. Not so many years ago, companies tried to place centers in the same region as their enrollees. But that effort gave way to pressures to consolidate into ever-larger facilities, to cut costs, and to save money. If you place a call to your health provider from your home in Ohio, you might just as easily wind up talking to someone in New Jersey or North Dakota or California; the whole process is so anonymous, so remote. Courtesy of fiber-optic cables and satellites, it's about to get even more remote. Before long, your call will connect you to someone so polite, so well spoken, and so American-sounding that you won't know that you're speaking to a person halfway around the globe—in India.

This new stage in the evolving world of American health care got under way quietly in late 2000 when Aetna, one of the nation's largest health insurers, embarked on a little-known pilot project in the heart of India's Silicon Valley. Starting with twenty-three employees, Aetna established a claims-processing operation in the southern Indian city of Bangalore to transfer information from personal health claims filed by Aetna subscribers in the United States into the company's database. Previously, such claims had been processed at an Aetna call center in Allentown, Pennsylvania.

Earlier that year, Aetna instructed its Allentown workers to bundle up paper claims and ship them to a company in Texas, where they were electronically scanned into portable document files (PDF). The images were e-mailed to two Aetna offshore sites, one in Ireland and a newer one in Bangalore. Workers at each then input the data from the imaged claims.

Over the next two years, Aetna, lured by wage rates that averaged 80 percent less than in the States, shifted more of its claims processing to India. In Allentown, where the offshore processing was reviewed, claims agents noticed errors in the data coming back. "The only time you could have any communication was by e-mail, and it was difficult to explain to them what they were doing wrong," said one former employee who asked not to be identified. "For the consumer it is a shame. The average person has no idea this is going on."

Aetna was so pleased with its Bangalore venture that it added more workers there and opened another claims center in New Delhi. Aetna employees from Allentown were dispatched to train their Indian counterparts. By the end of 2002, Aetna had more than five hundred agents in India processing American health claims. As the hiring continued in India, the layoffs began in Allentown.

Although Aetna kept a low profile about its Indian operation, word spread rapidly among health care companies. For years there had been talk about tapping the low-wage, English-speaking Indian market to take over some of the administrative expenses incurred by call centers in the States, but this was the first sign that it might be feasible on a wide scale. "Aetna was absolutely the groundbreaker on this," said one Indian consultant, "the big kahuna."

Others soon followed, and still others planned to do the same. UnitedHealthcare, the nation's second-largest insurer, launched plans for a 300-person call center and claims operation in Mumbai (Bombay) and let it be known it hoped to have as many as 4,000 agents in India in coming years. Consultants who track the industry say that more insurers and health plans, including Wellpoint, Coventry, Horizon Blue Cross & Blue Shield, Humana, and Blue Cross & Blue Shield of Michigan, are actively trying to establish Indian call centers.

Industry observers believe that it's only a matter of time before a substantial number of American patients who phone their health care plans will reach someone in India. And most of them won't even know it's happened. The sophistication and technical expertise of the Indian call-center industry is such that connecting an American health care consumer to an Indian worker in a call center halfway around the globe is virtually seamless. Technology is only part of the reason. Young, college-educated Indian call-center employees undergo training to Americanize their voices and become familiar with contemporary American culture.

Schools have sprouted across the subcontinent to train workers to sound like Americans when they answer phone calls from the United States. At Call Center College in Bangalore, students receive four weeks of intensive instruction in which they are "immersed in the American sound," says Julian P. Gurupatham, vice president of training. The goal, he says, is to produce an accent "any American can understand." Equally important is cultural immersion. Trainees watch hours of American television shows and movies to soak up pop culture. *Friends, Ally McBeal, The Simpsons, Whose Line Is It Anyway?,* and *Sabrina The Teenage Witch* are popular TV serials. Among movies, *The Truman Show, Volcano,* and *Jurassic Park* are big hits. After this training, says Prakash Gurbaxani, former CEO of an Indian high-tech company, "it's very rare that anyone will figure out that their 1-800 call is actually being answered in India."

Inside the call centers, to remind workers of their American state of mind, walls are plastered with American flags and slogans, and each clerk's phone flashes a message indicating the city and state of the incoming call. At the most sophisticated centers, clerks even get up-to-the-minute information on weather conditions and the latest sports scores in the caller's hometown. To make American callers believe they are speaking to someone in the States, workers in many Indian centers adopt American names and, when asked, give their location as a city or state in the United States. "At work I am Candy," one Mumbai call-center employee told an Indian online journal. "Outside I am Rehka. That's how I see it. There's nothing more to it. It is like with actors. They play a part every time." But the deception troubles some: "Can a company genuinely argue that they are offering excellent . . . 'customer service' if the first thing they tell their agents to do is lie about their name and then their geographic location?" asked a worker in an Internet chat room.

Less than a decade ago, India's international call-center industry got its start by setting up offshore operations for U.S. credit-card companies.

It has since expanded into computer services, online sales, software technical support, banking, tax returns, travel services, and more. Everyone agrees that the American health care market is the next big frontier, the one offering the greatest potential of all. The vast number of administrative jobs and constant pressure on insurers to maximize profits are expected to produce a steady migration of call-center and other health-industry jobs to India. Ravi Shah, a Wisconsin-based consultant who is working to facilitate the transfer, thinks it will be huge: "Given the right approach, successful execution, offshore [business processing] is likely to become an integral part of [the health care] industry. . . . What we have seen so far is not even the tip of the iceberg, with the best yet to come."

Shah and other consultants see a process unfolding: Most of the health care giants will start with claims processing, as Aetna did. Then they will move on to more direct call-center services such as telephone inquiries. Eventually, offshore call centers will take on most of the tasks now performed in U.S.-based centers, including claims adjudication, membership enrollment, and policy changes, in which India-based agents will converse with American health care consumers. Ultimately, the centers could provide medical advice as well. "There are tons of doctors and nurses in India today who don't have jobs," observes Julian Gurupatham of Bangalore's Call Center College.

American health insurers are keeping quiet about the move. Says one consultant: "Most of these companies don't want to make a lot of this information public because it creates a lot of problems for them, like a backlash from consumers, who wouldn't be thrilled to know that somebody in India is reading their medical records."

And for good reason. Any call-center worker in the United States who made public a patient's medical records could be charged with violating privacy laws and fined for divulging confidential personal medical information. But what recourse is there if a clerk in India, Pakistan, or elsewhere in Asia decides to do just that?

In late 2003, a low-paid medical transcriber in Pakistan, processing paperwork from the prestigious University of California, San Francisco, Medical Center threatened, during a pay dispute, to post patient records on the Internet. Like most medical centers, UCSF outsources medical transcriptions, the detailed dictation doctors give to record all aspects of patient treatment, from physical examinations to surgical procedures. It's a $20-billion-a-year business, and it's estimated that at least 10 percent of the work is now done offshore, much of it in India, where 75 medical transcription companies already in operation are expected to swell to 400.

One of UCSF's sub-subcontractors turned out to be a Pakistani woman embroiled in a dispute with a UCSF subcontractor. When the transcriber felt no one was paying attention to her pay demands, she sent this e-mail to UCSF: "Your patient records are out in the open to be exposed, so you better track that person and make him pay my dues or otherwise I will expose all the voice files and patient records of UCSF Parnassus and Mt. Zion campuses on the Internet." The *San Francisco Chronicle* reported that medical records of two patients contained in dictation from UCSF doctors were attached to the e-mail. The transcriber withdrew the threat when she was paid, but the incident illustrates the vulnerability of patient information once it leaves the United States.

Despite potential hazards to patients, the offshore health care bureaucracy will continue to grow, for the same reason that consumers buy dresses, shirts, trousers, shoes, and other clothing made anywhere from the northern Mariana Islands to China: cheap labor. But don't look for the savings to show up in your health insurance premiums. Instead, the money will flow to the insurers' bottom line, and your premiums, co-pays, and deductibles will continue to spiral upward.

As for the insurers, it's going to get even better, thanks to the information technology revolution. The next health care work expected to move offshore, notably, again, to India: the reading of mammograms, X-rays, and MRIs.

Madison Avenue Medicine

E ach year, the U.S. Department of Health and Human Services conducts a nationwide survey on the medical well-being of the American people. The 2003 study, like the ones before it, showed that most of us think we are in good health. In fact, 35.5 percent of those questioned assessed their health as "excellent," and another 31.9 percent labeled it "very good." Similar findings a year earlier buttressed the underlying health statistics that prompted Surgeon General David Satcher to sound a positive note. "In many ways," Satcher said, "Americans of all ages and in every racial and ethnic group have better health today."

But if two-thirds of the population rates their health as excellent or very good, how is it that so many of us are sick? In fact, by some accounts we may be the sickest people on the face of the planet. At least that's what we're being told by television and radio reports and commercials, newspaper and magazine articles and advertisements, medical foundations, universities, and the health care community itself. The numbers are breathtaking.

"Approximately one hundred million Americans have excessive levels of total cholesterol," the American Heart Association warns. "More than sixty million American adults experience GERD [gastroesophageal reflux disease]," according to *FDA Consumer*. "Ten million individuals are estimated to already have [osteoporosis] and almost thirty-four million more are estimated to have low bone mass," the National Osteoporosis Foundation claims. "About 3.8 million kids have Attention Deficit Hyperactivity Disorder (ADHD)," the American Academy of Pediatrics reports. "More than nineteen million Americans suffer from some kind of anxiety disorder," the Anxiety Disorders Association of America contends. "Somewhere between forty-five million and sixty million Americans now have the genital form of [herpes]," maintains *Drug Topics*. "An estimated twenty-five million adults have incontinence . . . significant enough to make it difficult for them to maintain good hygiene and carry on ordinary social and work lives," the Harvard Medical School reports.

There's more: The Johns Hopkins Medical Institutions say thirty-five million people have irritable bowel syndrome. The American Association of Clinical Endocrinologists says thirteen million Americans have thyroid disease. *Medical Devices & Surgical Technology Week* says nine million men suffer from benign prostatic hyperplasia (BPH), a noncancerous enlargement of the prostate gland. The CDC says nearly seventy million adults suffer from chronic joint pain. *Biotech Business Week* says more than two million Americans have atrial fibrillation, a common arrhythmia that can result in an abnormally fast heart rate. The American Liver Foundation says twenty-five million people have a liver disease. NBC's *Today Show* says two million people have hyperhidrosis, a genetic problem that causes abnormal sweating. The National Institutes of Health says twelve million people have chronic obstructive pulmonary disease and twenty-four million have impaired lung function.

Then there's latent tuberculosis infection, ten to fifteen million people; male impotence, thirty million men; rosacea, fourteen million people; eating disorders, eleven million; fibromyalgia (chronic pain in muscles and tissues around joints), six million; obesity, sixty million;

Alzheimer's, four million; chronic headaches, forty-five million; psoria-
sis, seven million; peripheral arterial disease, thirty-four million; hypertension, fifty million; clinical depression, eighteen million; peptic ulcers,
twenty-five million; chronic kidney disease, twenty million; allergies,
forty million; sleep disorders, seventy million; restless legs syndrome,
twelve million; and excessive menstrual bleeding, ten million women.

To be sure, this litany overlaps in certain areas. Some of the 58.4
million with high blood pressure most likely are among the sixty million with cardiovascular disease. On the other hand, this list is far from
complete, omitting scores of diseases, disorders, and conditions from
cancer to chronic fatigue syndrome. If all those said to be suffering
from some ailment are taken into account, it's estimated there are more
than 1.5 billion sick people in the United States—or five times the
population. Assuming one-third are in the "excellent" health they
claim, then two out of every three people you pass on the street are
walking around with at least eight different maladies.

Are Americans really that sick? Of course not. So what's going on
here? Simply put, it's in the best interest of a market-driven medical
system to make you think you are sick, or soon will be, or worry you
over the possibility. The grossly exaggerated numbers are in the best
interest of everyone—everyone except the public. For drug companies
that offer multiple pills for every affliction, real or imagined, they
mean billions of dollars for the bottom line, which helps explain why
they are the country's most profitable businesses year in and year out.
For doctors and hospitals, those inflated numbers mean more billions
in revenue. For Madison Avenue, newspapers, magazines, television,
and radio, they mean billions in advertising revenue and commissions,
as well as increased ratings and sales. For testing laboratories and manufacturers of expensive diagnostic equipment, such as MRI machines,
they mean more billions in revenue. For special-interest groups, they
mean billions in permanent funding for a bloated health care bureau-

cracy. For members of Congress, they mean campaign contributions and positive headlines as lawmakers wage a perpetual crusade on behalf of the sick. For celebrities raising funds for their favorite disease, they mean endless publicity and generous fees.

As more individuals are encouraged to ask their doctors to examine them for conditions they don't have and treat them for nonspecific ailments, they become an ever-growing drain on public and private funds. The United States already wastes tens of billions of dollars on needless visits to doctors' offices, unnecessary or excessive medical tests, over-diagnosis, over-treatment, needless surgical procedures, and the unwarranted dispensing of prescription drugs on a titanic scale, thereby turning the country into the world's pill capital.

The personal price tag for all this is staggering. The paychecks of workers continue to shrink as they are compelled to pick up a larger share of health insurance premiums and co-pays. People with serious diseases are priced out of the insurance market. Companies tired of relentless health care cost increases are scaling back or canceling coverage for their employees and retirees. Saddest of all, the truly sick, the aged, the infirm, and families dealing with catastrophic illnesses are forced into poverty and bankruptcy.

A lot of money is being made by striking fear in the hearts of Americans that they will die prematurely unless they rush out and buy the latest medication. Few are profiting more from this tactic than the pharmaceutical companies, which hold the patent on profitability. New York–based Pfizer Inc., the world's largest pharmaceutical company, posted a 28.4 percent return on revenue in 2002. That was some four times better than ExxonMobil Corporation, nearly nine times better than Wal-Mart Stores, and more than thirty-one times better than General Motors Corporation.

On a scale no one could have foreseen, the drug companies have enlisted the expertise of Madison Avenue to sell you their wares. Using techniques advertising has perfected over decades to entice consumers to buy soap, cereal, beer, perfume, and dog food, the drug companies are transforming the way we look at medicines and fattening their own profits in the process.

From 1994 to 2000, spending for consumer drug advertising rocketed from $266 million to $2.5 billion—a whopping 840 percent increase. Sales of prescription drugs shot up from $79 billion in 1997 to $164 billion in 2002. At the present pace, sales will reach a quarter-trillion dollars by 2007. As a result of this runaway spending, overpriced prescription drugs are driving up health care costs for everyone. While drugs account for just 10 percent of the nation's total health care bill, they are the fastest-growing component. Between 1993 and 2002, spending for hospital care went up 52 percent and outlays for physician services increased 69 percent. But prescription-drug spending climbed three to four times faster—spiraling to 217 percent. This trend is likely to accelerate as the Medicare drug benefit takes effect fully in 2006, and Congress refuses to abandon a legislative policy that makes American consumers pay the highest prices in the world for prescription drugs.

BLAME IT ON BAD BREATH

Today's prescription-drug ads on television owe their origins to a revolutionary change on Madison Avenue that occurred nearly a century ago. The slick commercials with the appealing personal stories that play on everyone's fantasies and fears and urge all to buy the latest—and most expensive—drug on the market, originated in the 1920s, when the stakes were considerably lower. It all began with the marketing campaign for a product peddled as a cure for bad breath.

In 1879, Dr. Joseph J. Lawrence, a St. Louis physician, hit upon an idea for an antiseptic solution. Two years later, he sold the formula to

Jordan Wheat Lambert, also of St. Louis, who established the Lambert
Pharmacal Company—that's the Lambert in what would become
Warner-Lambert, the giant pharmaceutical company—to sell the new
product as "a multi-purpose antiseptic." They named it Listerine in
honor of Sir Joseph Lister, the Glasgow and London surgeon who in
1865 had first demonstrated the use of a disinfectant (carbolic acid)
during surgery. That simple innovation eventually reduced surgical
deaths from more than 50 percent to 3 percent. Within a decade,
Lambert's company was selling Listerine to dentists as an oral antiseptic. Soon it was used for everything from "filling the cavity during
ovariotomy"—an incision into or removal of the ovaries—to a cure for
gonorrhea. The latter should not be surprising, since Listerine also is
touted today in Internet chat rooms as a way to avoid sexually trans-
mitted diseases during oral sex; prostitutes are urged to carry Listerine
"and rinse out after each client."

Listerine sales were lackluster until the early 1920s, when Lambert
Pharmacal Company mounted an advertising campaign that would
transform it into a mass-market consumer item. The breakthrough
concept would eventually have wide-ranging ramifications in our own
time in the marketing of prescription drugs.

In Listerine's time, the economic retrenchment of the war years gave
way to the Roaring '20s and sweeping changes in lifestyle and work
rolled across the country. The explosive growth of modern appliances
like electric refrigerators and gas stoves, along with the introduction of
the automobile and new forms of entertainment—radio and motion
pictures—transformed daily life. It was the dawn of the culture of con-
sumerism.

Installment credit was introduced to fuel buying power, encouraged
by advertising that portrayed debt as a virtue instead of the biblical
vice it had been since the country's founding. New industries with
their mass-produced products led to a glut of consumer goods. This in

turn led to a new mission for the advertising industry: Make people buy more goods. "The American citizen's first importance to his country is no longer that of a citizen," editorialized Middletown's favorite paper, "but that of a consumer. Consumption is a new necessity."

To pull it off required an original advertising philosophy, one that keyed ads to emotions. As one adman put it: "It may be necessary to fool people for their own good. Doctors, and even preachers, know that and practice it. Average intelligence is surprisingly low. It is so much more effectively guided by its subconscious impulses and instincts than by its reason." With that in mind, admen began to sell neither soap nor perfume, "but youth, beauty, sex, romance. Not automobiles, but manly dominance and social prestige." And fear—fear that if people did not buy Listerine, women would never find a husband, men would forever live alone, workers would never advance in their jobs, and everyone would be terminally sick.

Unhappy with sales of its three-decade-old mouthwash, the president of the St. Louis–based Lambert Pharmacal Company, Gerard B. Lambert, the son of the founder, invited a pair of advertising copywriters, Milton Feasley and Gordon Seagrove, to come up with a new campaign. To help with the project, Lambert asked the company's chief chemist to provide Feasley and Seagrove with background on Listerine. At one point in his conversation, the chemist dropped the word *halitosis,* an old medical term derived from a combination of Latin (*halitus* for "breath") and Greek (*osis* for "condition"). That was all the imaginative admen needed. With a single word, one that had a scientific ring to it, they launched a campaign that "frightened the continent, not because bad breath was a fatal malady but because it was a social disaster."

In the campaign they devised, one advertisement featured the face of a man portrayed as a kindly doctor, over a headline "What I know about *nice* women." It began: "Listen to a doctor whose practice includes hundreds of the better class. 'It is simply unbelievable,' he says, 'how many women—supposedly *nice, fastidious* women—are suffering from halitosis and utterly ignorant of the fact. No wonder their husbands no longer kiss them, or that women friends avoid them.'" The ad promised that women could keep themselves "on the popular side by gargling with full strength Listerine morning and night, and before meeting others." What's more, Listerine was so powerful that "it kills even Staphylococcus Aureus (pus) and Bacillus Typhosus (typhoid) germs in fifteen seconds." In large type across the bottom, the ad pronounced: "Halitosis is a *daily threat* . . . end it with THE SAFE ANTISEPTIC Listerine."

Perhaps the most popular ad in the series played to women's fear of failing to find a husband. One version depicted a bride at the top of a spiral staircase, throwing her bouquet to her bridesmaids with outstretched hands below, with the words: "Milly caught the bride's bouquet but everybody present knew that nothing would come of it . . . that she wouldn't be the next to marry by a long ways . . . and they knew the reason why, too. People with halitosis (unpleasant breath) simply don't get by. It is the unforgivable social fault."

Another ad pictured a dejected young woman in a bridesmaid's dress, clutching the bouquet, resting her face on her hand pressed against a wall, illustrated with a phrase that would become one of the most successful slogans of all time: "Often a bridesmaid . . . never a bride!"

The ads introduced the concept of storytelling to sell a product, imitating the personal-interest stories and advice-to-the-lovelorn columns in the tabloid newspapers. As the advertising industry's journal *Printers' Ink* reflected in a tribute to Feasley: "He dealt more with humanity than with merchandise. He wrote advertising dramas rather than business announcements—dramas so common to everyday experience that every reader could easily fit himself into the plot as the hero or culprit of its action." The ads were a stunning success: Lambert's sales and profits soared. Listerine sales were so strong that they caught the attention of Wall Street. In 1926, Goldman, Sachs & Company and another Wall Street firm "acquired a large interest" in Lambert Pharmacal, with plans to take it public.

In the years to come, Lambert constantly sought to expand the market by advancing new uses for Listerine, or reintroducing old ones, each promoted in a fresh series of advertisements. For women at a certain time of the month, with a condition that could not be mentioned by name at the time, Lambert promoted Listerine "for feminine hygiene." A stark headline warned: "*The Harm that* WOMEN DO *Themselves*. Intimate use of harsh antiseptics *leads to untold damage*. Women now hail a gentle, *safe* means." The text began: "The use of harsh, powerful antiseptics in connection with feminine hygiene often results in illness that may lead to an operation. Women suffering thus crowd the hospitals. Will you sooner or later be one of them? Are you going to let half truths or ignorance of proper measures rob you of vitality, health, and peace of mind?"

Madison Avenue had crafted a winning formula to get people to buy products based on their anxieties, fears, and hopes. No industry ultimately would embrace the concept more eagerly or with more stellar results than the pharmaceutical industry.

THE TV AD BLITZ

Hard as it may be to believe, amid the current barrage of drug ads, advertising of prescription drugs to consumers is a fairly recent development. In the first half of the twentieth century, doctors wrote out on a prescription pad the various ingredients to treat a cold, fever, infection, or some other condition. A neighborhood pharmacist would then compound, or combine, all the substances to create the medication. Compounding declined through the 1930s and 1940s as manufacturing of specific medicines increased. Penicillin, other antibiotics, and antihistamines were produced by pharmaceutical companies from World War II on. Drugs for high blood pressure and antidepressants arrived in the 1950s. Hence there was little product advertising beyond the over-the-counter market.

With some exceptions, the health and medical ads the public saw tended to be informational. Typical was one in a July 1947 *Saturday Evening Post* by Parke, Davis & Company. Illustrated by a Norman Rockwell–style drawing of laughing girls leaving a redbrick schoolhouse, the headline read: "Some things you should know about epilepsy." With supporting statistics, the ad began: "Epilepsy is one of the most widely misunderstood of all diseases. Many people believe that there's no effective treatment for it, that it's a kind of feeble-mindedness, that it always becomes worse as the patient grows older, and that he has no chance of leading a normal life. *Your doctor, however, will tell you these ideas are false.*" The ad then went to the punch line: "In most cases, modern drugs are the doctor's chief weapon. *Only the doctor knows which drug or drugs should be used, and in what dosage.*"

From the 1950s to the 1970s, most advertising was restricted to specialty journals aimed at doctors. Ads that actually named the drugs for treatment of select diseases or conditions were reserved for medical publications such as the *Journal of Obstetrics and Gynecology* and the *Journal of the American Medical Association*. Physicians, it was reasoned, would have the knowledge and understanding to weed out the hype and determine which drugs would be best for their patients. In the pages of those esoteric periodicals, pharmaceutical companies promoted their wares to physicians and other health care professionals, hopeful that they would generate sales of new and existing drugs.

By the 1980s, drug companies, in search of a larger market, began advertising in general-circulation newspapers and magazines. But television, the medium that would one day revolutionize drug selling, was still largely off-limits to anything other than so-called informational commercials. The FDA required that commercials pitching prescription drugs for treatment of a specific condition list the potentially harmful side effects. In other words, recite the fine print on the insert that accompanies the medication. That requirement made TV advertising impractical.

All that changed in 1997, when, under pressure from drug-industry lobbyists and their friends in Congress, the FDA opened the door wide to advertising direct to consumers (DTC) on television. It allowed commercials to extol a drug as long as they mentioned the major side effects and referred viewers and listeners to more detailed print advertisements that contained complete prescribing information. Drug companies selling a product that might cure—or harm—could reach millions of people with a single message. The profit potential was dazzling, and Madison Avenue—at the behest of the pharmaceutical industry—responded accordingly.

In the early months of the changeover, a then more vigilant FDA advised several drug makers that their commercials were misleading, failed to adequately explain possible side effects, or neglected to advise consumers how to obtain complete information. Among those cited: Merck & Co.'s Zocor ad for cholesterol, Zeneca Pharmaceutical's (now AstraZeneca) Accolate ad for asthma, and Schering-Plough's Claritin ad for allergies. The companies all pulled the questionable commercials.

But within a few years, an understaffed FDA was unable to keep up as the volume of television advertising skyrocketed and the drug companies pushed the envelope on their claims. Then a change in the regulatory process ordered by the U.S. Department of Health and Human Services in November 2001 dragged out the notification period on misleading ads, so that by the time the FDA could issue a warning to a drug company the offending commercial had disappeared.

Even in the rare cases when a warning is issued, months, sometimes years, go by before the public is advised that they were watching and reading false claims. In March 2001 and again in December that year, the FDA sent warning letters to Bristol-Myers Squibb Company objecting to the drug maker's "unsubstantiated efficacy claims" for Pravachol, a cholesterol drug. Nothing happened. So on August 7, 2003, the FDA sent a third letter complaining about the company's "false or misleading" promotional materials for its big-selling drug. More months went by. Finally, on February 20, 2004, Bristol-Myers published full-page advertisements in newspapers that carried this headline: "Important Correction of Information about Pravachol (pravastatin sodium) tablets." The "correction," written with an obscurity unknown in commercials promoting drug usage, continued:

> Bristol-Myers Squibb Company, maker of Pravachol, ran ads for Pravachol that the FDA determined were misleading. The statement they determined misleading was 'Pravachol is the only cholesterol lowering drug proven to help prevent first and second heart attack and stroke in people with high cholesterol or heart disease.' This statement suggested that Pravachol has been proven to help prevent stroke in people without heart disease. Please note, Pravachol has not been proven to help prevent stroke in people without heart disease. Pravachol is proven to help prevent stroke only in people with coronary heart disease (CHD) . . .

A study by *Consumer Reports* showed that in 2002 "the number of regulatory letters [the FDA] sent manufacturers about false or misleading drug ads has dropped precipitously, from more than one hundred per year in the late 1990s to just twenty-four as of November 2002."

Most disturbing, according to the *Consumer Reports* study,

> [the letters] revealed a broad and disconcerting range of misleading messages: ads that minimized the product's risks, for example;

exaggerated its efficacy; made false claims of superiority over competing products; promoted unapproved uses for an approved drug; or promoted use of a drug still in the experimental stage.

Worse, many people appear to believe that drug advertising is meticulously regulated. A study by researchers at the University of California at Los Angeles and Davis, involving 329 randomly selected Sacramento residents, found that half of the respondents wrongly believed that drug ads are pre-approved by the FDA, and 43 percent wrongly believed that only "completely safe" drugs can be advertised.

Prescription drug ads—few of them screened for accuracy—are as prevalent as commercials for toothpaste and laundry detergent. Turn on the television set any time and you will see a drug commercial. Begin with one of the morning shows, *Good Morning America,* and Pfizer's Lipitor. A female announcer says: "For millions of adults with high cholesterol, diet and exercise aren't always enough. But adding Lipitor can help lower your total cholesterol 29 percent to 45 percent. . . . So take the next step—ask your doctor if Lipitor is right for you."

On the afternoon soaps, Novartis Pharmaceuticals pushes its Zelnorm for irritable bowel syndrome with constipation. On the evening news at CBS, it's Merck's Fosamax for osteoporosis in postmenopausal women. On the repeat of the *Larry King Live* show on CNN at 12:30 A.M., it's Plavix. Bristol-Myers Squibb and Sanofi Pharmaceuticals sell Plavix to keep clots from forming and help protect against a heart attack or stroke.

Where necessary, Madison Avenue takes a page out of the Listerine sales manual to make a condition more appealing for treatment. That's what it did with "erectile dysfunction," another brilliant success story in manipulating popular thought. Before Madison Avenue, erectile dysfunction was called impotence. But one doesn't ask a Mike Ditka to help mass-market a Levitra for a condition called "impotence," a word with a much different connotation.

From 1970 to 1990, the words "erectile dysfunction" appeared in newspapers little more than a dozen times, about once every six months. The phrase instead was reserved for medical journals. That changed when the admen arrived and the FDA erased its prohibitions on pill advertising on television. In January 2004 alone, the words appeared in newspaper articles more than 200 times. And that doesn't count television commercials.

The pharmaceutical industry likes to present this kind of approach as a public service. "DTC must be understood as something more than mere advertising," says J. Patrick Kelly, president of Pfizer U.S. Pharmaceuticals. "We provide information that helps patients understand their conditions and their treatment options—information that helps them have more mutually rewarding interactions with their physicians and helps them get diagnosed and receive appropriate treatment."

Actually, what it has done is change prescription drugs from a needs-based product to a demand-driven product, just like Eggo French Toaster Sticks, Trix Yogurt, and Apple Jacks. Advertisements and commercials that persuade people they will live a longer and healthier life if only they take daily medication to lower cholesterol and ease stress are out of the same advertising sales manual that suggests your social relationships will suffer unless you use a certain mouthwash.

The commercials are powerful, convincing, and, most of all, manipulative. If you're feeling perfectly healthy at the crack of dawn, by day's end you will certainly wonder if you might be suffering from one or more of the many maladies that are the subject of ads appealing to people's insecurities. Remember those Listerine ads? It isn't likely that millions of people were walking around with breath so bad that even their best friends were reluctant to talk about it. Nonetheless, they purchased Listerine.

Madison Avenue counts on the basic instincts of Americans to look for a quick fix, hoping that after taking in a couple of commercials you will begin gulping multiple pills so that you can enhance your sex life, calm your anxieties, postpone the aging process, reduce your blood pressure, heighten your concentration, build thicker bones, improve your blood flow, sleep more restfully, dull the pain in your shoulder, and slash your cholesterol to prevent heart disease—even though one-third of all people who die of heart disease actually have low cholesterol.

To increase the chances you will succumb to the ads, Madison Avenue offers the lure that reels in buyers of laundry detergent and specialty coffees—free samples and trial offers. AstraZeneca's commercials pitching Nexium, the purple pill for heartburn and acid reflux, end with the announcer saying: "Call this number for more information and a Nexium free trial offer. Don't let acid reflux eat at you." Not to be outdone, commercials for a Nexium competitor, TAP Pharmaceuticals' Prevacid, make the same offer. "A friend told me about Prevacid," says a middle-aged female, "so I called the number and they sent me a certificate for a week's worth free." A helpful announcer follows: "Call today for a Prevacid free trial offer."

Eli Lilly and ICOS did the same when they introduced Cialis, the latest entry in the crowded erectile dysfunction field, during the 2004 Super Bowl, which more aptly might have been called the Sex Bowl, what with a halftime show highlighted by Janet Jackson's breast-baring and commercials pushing Cialis competitors. But Cialis, also an "official partner of the PGA Tour," offered something extra for users: It was good for thirty-six hours. Lilly and ICOS expected the difference (Cialis already was known in Europe as the weekend drug) to appeal to their target audience—45 percent of the men watching the game.

Scenes in the commercial showed a man and a woman in a bathtub, a couple holding hands, a couple at a coffee bar, a couple in a car going away on a trip, and a man with his hand over a woman's eyes, with the words "thirty-six hours" on the screen, while the velvety-voiced announcer intones: "If a relaxing moment turns into the right moment, will you be ready? Introducing Cialis, the first tablet for erectile dysfunction that gives you up to thirty-six hours to choose the moment that's right for you and your partner." After reciting the obligatory warning—"Cialis is not for everyone"—the announcer ticked off possible side effects, "most common" and "rare," including: "Erections lasting longer than four hours, though rare, require immediate medical help." And finally the offer: "Ask your doctor if a free sample of prescription Cialis is right for you."

Pharmaceutical companies defend their commercials by insisting the advertisements "raise awareness of conditions and diseases that often go undiagnosed and untreated." An industry spokesman told Congress that "by informing people about the symptoms of diseases and the availability of effective, noninvasive treatments, direct-to-consumer advertising can improve public health." But it also creates a demand for which there is no medical need. Among the users of erectile dysfunction drugs: young males who want to drink heavily and have sex. The drugs offset the downside of alcohol.

"ASK YOUR DOCTOR"

The medical mantra "Ask your doctor" has become one of Madison Avenue's most successful catchphrases ever. "Ask your doctor about Imitrex." Or "Ask your doctor about adding Plavix." Or "Ask your doctor about getting relief with Zelnorm." Or "Ask your doctor about Celebrex." Or "Ask your doctor about Zocor." Or "Ask your doctor if prescription Prevacid is right for you." Or "Ask your doctor about new once-a-day Wellbutrin XL." The unrelenting commercials pitching pills for the treatment of everything from arthritis to high cholesterol end with the ubiquitous phrase. The commercials play on the trust that patients have in their doctors. Many doctors, in turn, say that when patients ask for a certain medicine by name, they feel pressured to prescribe it.

Truth to tell, doctors sometimes have little more independent understanding than you do about a particular drug. They derive their knowledge largely from advertisements similar to the ones that you see and from information supplied by the drug companies directly. An army of sales representatives, carrying armloads of samples, descend on doctors' offices daily. In addition, the companies hold seminars, take doctors to dinners, and distribute lucrative fees for serving as "advisors." The purpose of the ads and the personal contact is to sell a product, not to discourage its use by dwelling on what could go wrong. The drug companies spend many more billions of dollars on this marketing effort than on advertising.

While physicians read many of the reports on clinical trials or studies in medical journals, no one can read and absorb them all. There are not enough hours in the day to keep abreast of all the studies involving all the drugs that are available—and also see patients.

That's why doctors are as susceptible to advertising as you are. And always have been, even during an earlier era when ads were confined to technical journals. Such was the case back in the 1950s with a widely touted drug called desPLEX, originally marketed to prevent abortion, miscarriage, and premature births. A 1957 ad from the Grant Chemical Company of Brooklyn depicted a smiling baby with her finger inserted in her mouth and the word, in large type, "Really?" The ad, published in a medical journal, went on to say that the drug was "Recommended for routine prophylaxis in ALL pregnancies . . . 96 per cent live delivery with desPLEX in one series of 1200 patients—bigger and stronger babies, too. No gastric or other side effects with desPLEX—in either high or low dosage."

DesPLEX was one version of the synthetic estrogen diethylstilbestrol (DES), formulated in 1938 and prescribed for millions of American women from the 1940s to the 1960s. As so often happens when a wonder drug is introduced, physicians also used it to treat a variety of other conditions. It was, they said, good to ease hot flashes and other symptoms of menopause, an early-day hormone-replacement therapy. They said it was good for acne and prostate cancer. They used it to stunt the growth of teenage girls who, it was feared for social reasons, were growing too tall, and they handed it out as a morning-after birth control pill. They even prescribed it for "women without a history of pregnancy-related problems because of the belief that it would make for healthier babies"—a sort of superbaby vitamin. Another ad promoting desPLEX, illustrated with a laughing infant, read "live healthy babies." And in large block letters: "EFFECTIVE. SAFE."

DES turned out to be anything but safe. In 1971, the *New England Journal of Medicine* published a study documenting a rare form of vaginal cancer that was turning up in adolescent girls exposed to DES in utero. The numbers were small but unmistakable. Sales of the drug tracked the rise in the number of women who had taken DES and whose daughters two decades later developed cancer and other reproductive tract abnormalities. Within months of the study, the FDA, which had approved the use of DES more than thirty years before, warned physicians to stop prescribing it during pregnancy. Other medical researchers concluded that not only did the drug fail in its stated purpose of preventing miscarriages—it actually increased the risk. There also was a greater likelihood of breast cancer. And for DES daughters, there was a greater chance of preterm births, ectopic pregnancies, and infertility.

Betsy W. Wood, the daughter of a Jacksonville, Florida, surgeon and his wife, was among those. Betsy's mother had taken DES during each of her three pregnancies. In June 1977, at age twenty, Betsy was examined by Dr. Robert C. Nuss, a Jacksonville gynecologic oncologist, who concluded that she had certain "cervical changes compatible with diethylstilbestrol exposure." But there was no evidence of cancer. To be safe, Nuss recommended yearly checkups. His advice proved sound. The following year a biopsy showed "clear cell adenocarcinoma." Betsy, who was twenty-one years old, had part of her vagina cut out, and she was added to the national registry of patients exposed to DES. Subsequent biopsies showed no recurrence of tumors. But in 1984, the cancer was back. Seven years later, she died at the age of thirty-four.

Those who approved and sold DES for widespread use ignored early studies from the 1930s and 1940s that showed it led to cancer in laboratory animals, and the FDA did no tests. The DES ads aimed at doctors carried not a hint of the unfavorable animal studies. In fact, the ads promoted the effectiveness and safety of DES. Years later, researchers are following not only DES daughters, and sons to a lesser extent, but also grandchildren to determine if disease and abnormalities will continue into a third generation, as has been the case with mice. What's more, many of the five to ten million women and men who were exposed to DES don't even know it, their cancers and birth defects forever buried in anonymous health statistics.

While the dangerous side effects of drugs often take years to appear, the power of the "ask your doctor" ads has shown up right away on the income statements of the drug companies. Tell people to ask their doctor for a drug and they do just that. That's why companies spent up to $2 million for thirty seconds on the Super Bowl. It's why Madison Avenue jilted newspapers and magazines for television. From 1997 to 2001, TV's share of total drug advertising shot up from 25 percent to 64 percent, and the print media's share went down accordingly.

The shift paid off. A study by the General Accounting Office, the investigative arm of Congress, found that between 1999 and 2000 "the number of prescriptions dispensed for the most heavily advertised drugs rose 25 percent, but increased only 4 percent for drugs that were not heavily advertised." In 2000, three oral antihistamines, Allegra, Claritin, and Zyrtec, "accounted for 86 percent of all oral antihistamine sales, and all three of them were among the fifteen most heavily advertised drugs," the GAO reported. The makers of the three drugs also collected a record twenty-two letters from the FDA citing them for violating the agency's advertising regulations.

Nonetheless, advertising, whether truthful or not, has proven amazingly successful. Every dollar the companies spend on advertising yields additional sales of more than four dollars. An analysis of prescription data between 1997 and 2001 found that almost half the spending growth was attributable solely to an increase in the number of prescriptions written.

In 2001, doctors prescribed 146 drugs for every 100 office visits, compared with only 109 drugs per 100 office visits in 1985. Watch for those figures to jump off the charts over the next decade for three reasons. The most imminent push will come as a result of decisions by the federal government and health care industry to lower thresholds at which drugs are prescribed. The decisions, often based on less-than-conclusive research, are worth billions to the pharmaceutical industry. In one such instance, health officials recommended in July 2004 that patients whose cholesterol levels had been deemed safe should begin taking cholesterol-lowering drugs, and many of those already on medication should increase their dosages. The *Washington Post* reported: "Millions of Americans should consider trying to drive their cholesterol levels lower than had been previously recommended, the government said yesterday, endorsing a more aggressive strategy for fighting heart disease, the nation's leading killer." The Medicare drug provision will pump up sales in 2006, and when the Baby Boomers begin to retire in 2011, drug companies can look forward to an even bigger market, since older Americans consume ever-larger numbers of pills.

RISKY BUSINESS

Mounting pressure to introduce new drugs as fast as new soups and soaps will pose ever-greater health risks, let alone costs, as doctors prescribe medicines without fully knowing or understanding the long-term consequences. It often takes years for a drug's truly serious side effects to show up. The same will be true for dangerous interactions between drugs, as people consume more kinds of pills for longer periods. All that's certain is people will die. How many remains to be seen.

Medical ethicists and pharmaceutical industry executives, to get around what is often portrayed as the first rule of medicine—"to help, or at least *do no harm*"—have come up with their own justification for the bad luck that will befall some people from taking new drugs. They reason that if one million people take a certain drug, and that drug helps some, has no effect on others, harms a small number, and kills a few, they have satisfied the Hippocratic oath.

The medical community's interpretation of "do no harm" certainly has merit in treating fatal diseases and possibly even in treating diseases that might one day become fatal. But it's questionable in situations that are not immediately life-threatening. More important, the theory is indefensible unless it is explained clearly by the prescribing doctor, and unless the label on the medicine bottle states unequivocally the potential outcome, no matter how small the risk. We all know when we get in a car that we take a chance we will be injured or die in an accident. Most of us do not know we are taking a risk with medicine. We assume it will make us better, or at least not worsen our condition. We do not expect to die.

Mary J. Linnen, a thirty-year-old Hingham, Massachusetts, woman planned to get married. In the spring of 1996, about twenty-five pounds overweight, Linnen obtained a prescription for two widely touted diet drugs. At the time they were all the rage of the news media, talk shows, Wall Street, and morning news programs. The popular name was "fen-phen." The "fen" half was shorthand for fenfluramine, a cousin of the antidepressant Prozac. Fen was marketed under the brand name Pondimin by Wyeth. The "phen" half was phentermine, sold under its generic name. Together the two drugs altered the brain's chemistry to curb the craving for food. Linnen took the medications for less than a month. Then her health began to deteriorate. She suffered heart palpitations and shortness of breath, began to lose her vision, and was hospitalized more than a half-dozen times. By February 1997 she was dead. The official cause: pulmonary hypertension associated with fenfluramine and phentermine therapy.

Fen-phen's sudden popularity followed the arc of so many medications. In May 1992, the journal *Clinical Pharmacology and Therapeutics* published the results of a diet drug study conducted by Dr. Michael Weintraub, a researcher at the University of Rochester School of Medicine. Weintraub's four-year clinical trial, funded by the National Heart, Lung and Blood Institute, showed substantial weight loss by people who took the two drugs. Although each had been independently approved for weight loss years earlier by the FDA, the agency had never given its OK for their use in combination—meaning they were prescribed together off-label.

The news media, as it is given to do upon publication of a study in a medical journal, rushed to proclaim the latest miracle drug. Never mind that such articles sometimes have all the depth of a *National Enquirer* takeout on astrology. Mere publication in a scientific journal is sufficient to warrant a few minutes on national news or the morning shows, and prominent headlines in newspapers everywhere. "Drugs Found to Keep Lost Flab Off," asserted the headline over a *New York Times* article on July 5, 1992.

The *Times* reported:

Some experts on weight loss hailed the study . . . saying [it] could mark a pronounced shift in the way obesity is studied and treated. These experts said the results showed obesity could be treated the way chronic diseases like high blood pressure or arthritis are. In those diseases, drugs can be taken indefinitely to keep symptoms in check.

One day later, the *CBS Morning News* weighed in: "For years the top diet researchers predicted that in the future, we would treat weight control with medications. Well, that future may be here today." After reviewing the study findings, CBS's medical reporter said: "These are just the first medications, and we're expected to see better and better ones. What I suspect is going to happen is this: That just like with high blood pressure and high cholesterol, you're expected to do a little something, get on a diet, begin an exercise program. But once you've done your part, doctors are going to give you medications."

For overweight people, the answer seemed clear: Take some pills and lose weight. To be sure, the blizzard of stories often contained caveats about possible side effects and the unknown consequences of long-term usage. Sometimes the cautionary advice was limited to a phrase or sentence or two. But even the lengthier warnings were drowned out by the testimonials from those who lost weight taking the drugs as well as from the physicians who prescribed them.

The upbeat stories led to the opening of weight-loss clinics that dispensed the drugs, which in turn led to ever-more-positive publicity, which in turn prompted ever-more-promising reports from physicians specializing in weight loss. Dr. Weintraub, whose article sparked the diet pill revolution, joined the FDA in Washington, from where he offered advice to budding fen-phen entrepreneurs.

The positive publicity seemed to be never-ending. Three years later, in February 1995, the ABC News program *20/20* opened a show this way: "Well, now a medical breakthrough that is changing the lives and the images of thousands of Americans. They are people with a serious problem—they are obese—and that description now applies to more of us than ever before. Obese people often say that they can't help it, that they feel driven to eat beyond control. Well, now there is research that backs them up and, even more exciting, a new treatment that seems to do for obese people what they can't do all by themselves. . . ."

The drumroll continued through 1995. At one point, Wyeth-Ayerst Pharmaceuticals was unable to turn out enough fenfluramine to meet demand, and a nationwide shortage developed. By year's end, *Fortune* magazine had joined the frenzy, at least from a financial standpoint, taking note of the billions that could be made in the diet business. "The potential for the pharmaceutical industry is enormous," declared *Fortune*. "Consider: About fifty-eight million adults carry enough extra weight to put them at some health risk. Not all of them will want—or qualify for—drug treatment, but enough will so that Wall Street is smelling the bacon."

Wall Street's enthusiasm only grew when the FDA approved its first new weight-loss drug in more than twenty years. Never mind that the vote was by the narrowest of margins and under curious circumstances. The drug, called Redux, was a cousin of Pondimin, one of the fen-phen pair. It was developed by Interneuron Pharmaceuticals Inc., a high-flying biotech company in Lexington, Massachusetts, and marketed, once more, by Wyeth.

Citing safety concerns, an FDA panel originally rejected Redux in September 1995 by a narrow vote of five to three. A highly unusual second meeting was called in November. With some of the original dissenters absent, the panel this time approved Redux by a six-to-five vote. Politics won over patient safety, and the FDA subsequently authorized sale of the new drug.

As *Fortune* had predicted, Wall Street greeted Redux enthusiastically. "What we have here is probably the fastest launch of any drug in the history of the pharmaceutical industry," said one securities analyst. "Our projection is that this product will hit one billion dollars in sales in five years." Wyeth was ecstatic. At the end of 1996, the company told stockholders that "the introduction of Redux was one of the most successful U.S. drug launches ever."

Physicians that year wrote eighteen million prescriptions for Redux, Pondimin, and phentermine. No one wrote them faster than Dr. Pietr Hitzig, who dispensed the drugs from his office in Timonium, Maryland, a Baltimore suburb, as well as over the Internet. Traffic was so heavy at times that patients began popping the pills while still in the waiting room. In time, he would brag on his Web site that he had "successfully treated over 8,000 patients" with fen-phen—and not just for obesity, but for other conditions from alcoholism to Gulf War Syndrome.

In addition to individual entrepreneurs like Hitzig, clinics also handed out fen-phen like candy. In the Los Angeles area, an estimated 10,000 people visited the offices of California Medical Weight Loss Associates. Said Aaron Baumann, the group's administrator: "This is L.A. People tend to want to be thinner than in the rest of the country." Allowing that he personally took fen-phen, Baumann said the drugs "work like magic."

The country's weight-loss programs, large and small, were swept up by the diet drug craze. Nutri-System Inc., one of the biggest and best known, converted nine of its Philadelphia-area offices to Nutri-RX Clinics that offered the fen-phen regimen and advertised two free months of the pills for dieters who switched from competitor Jenny Craig. Said Nutri-System's vice president of scientific affairs: "I don't believe it's another fad. I think you're seeing a new direction in the treatment of obesity." In Chestnut Hill, Massachusetts, a Boston suburb, the Medical Weight Loss Center advertised: "Hot New Diet Pills! Fen/Phen & Redux. Lose 20 lbs in 4 weeks."

As it turned out, the FDA, diet doctors, family practitioners, Wall Street analysts, and the news media that promoted fen-phen had made a mistake. Throughout the country, patients who had taken the two drugs developed defects in their heart valves. Even as reports surfaced about the drugs' adverse side effects, the FDA was slow to respond. It wasn't until July 1997, five months after the death of Mary Linnen, that the agency issued a warning to physicians that patients taking the drugs should be closely monitored. The agency did so after doctors at two separate clinics in North Dakota and Minnesota independently discovered that twenty-four previously healthy women taking fen-phen had developed primary pulmonary hypertension, a rare disorder in which blood pressure rises far above normal in the artery carrying blood to the lungs, making the heart work harder. Some patients may need round-the-clock oxygen, some a heart-lung transplant. Some may die.

The FDA should have been more vigilant. The diet-pill fad had taken hold in France several years earlier and had led to illness and death. France's FDA-equivalent estimated that twenty to forty people were dying each year from primary pulmonary hypertension. Two months after its warning notice, citing new evidence of serious side effects, the FDA asked for the withdrawal of Pondimin and Redux. The FDA made its decision after doctors prescribing the drugs found that 30 percent of patients had abnormal echocardiograms, a much higher than expected percentage. The "findings call for prompt action," said Dr. Michael A. Friedman, FDA deputy commissioner, adding: "The data we have obtained indicate that fenfluramine, and the chemically closely related dexfenfluramine (Redux), present an unacceptable risk at this time to patients who take them."

To dispose of lawsuits filed by women and men who suffered heart valve damage, Wyeth set aside more than $16 billion by 2003. As for Dr. Hitzig, he surrendered his medical license and in July 1999 was indicted on thirty-four counts of illegal drug distribution. He subsequently was convicted and sent to prison.

Fen-phen's phenomenal sales were fueled by the media, word of mouth, print advertising, and, more significant, by a diet industry that employed the same promotional practices that drug companies use in their direct-to-consumer marketing. That is, they exaggerated the benefits, downplayed the risks, and in the process encouraged use of the drugs by people who didn't need them.

For several reasons, the fen-phen story portends more disquieting news for people popping pills in coming years, with even more harmful or deadly consequences. One reason is the runaway growth in the practice of prescribing drugs for conditions not originally intended—so-called off-label prescriptions. The FDA approves drugs for treatment of a specific condition. Through trial and error, doctors often find a drug is effective for treating other illnesses and are free to write prescriptions for that purpose. In the case of fen-phen, the individual drugs were FDA-approved, but not their use in combination.

Overlying this are two other relatively recent phenomena. First, the number of individual patients taking multiple drugs is growing daily. And they are taking more different kinds of drugs than ever before. Many over the age of sixty-five take six or more different drugs, in addition to over-the-counter medications. Some patients see several physicians for their prescriptions and fill them at different pharmacies so that no one tracks their total usage. Baby Boomers who grew up mixing antidepressants, antibiotics, antihistamines, and other assorted medications will up the ante as they age. So, too, will their children, at least those in metropolitan areas, who have elevated prescription drugs to a new level best described by a twenty-five-year-old female graduate student in *New York* magazine: "I take an antidepressant called Celexa and I take Ambien [for sleep disorders]. And then I stay up an extra half-hour just so I can feel kind of looped—I call it my little Ambien party for one. Also, I sometimes get Ritalin from a friend, because I'm in school now and it's harder to get a prescription for that."

At the same time, the pharmaceutical industry is flooding the market with ever more drugs to increase sales. During the 1970s, the FDA approved 173 new drugs. That jumped to 279 in the 1980s and to 359 in the 1990s. To keep the money rolling in for prescription drugs whose patents are expiring, the industry is beginning to combine two different drugs in a single pill. This adds up to a growing potential for lethal reactions from a deadly mix of drugs that no one understands—until it's too late, as was the case with the heart drug encainide, which killed people during the 1980s, instead of saving them. Making this even harder to track, the honor system for reporting adverse drug reactions is primitive at best. The FDA itself has acknowledged that "it is impossible to accurately quantify adverse event rates because FDA's postmarketing surveillance system receives reports on only a relatively small percentage of all adverse events caused by drugs." In short, the drugs you take ultimately may harm or kill you, but no one may ever notice, or tell if they do.

In many ways it's an old problem the drug industry doesn't want to face. A half century ago the *Journal of the American Medical Association* took the pharmaceutical industry to task in an editorial for the large number of products being introduced each year:

A fundamental requirement to successful treatment is that the physician have the clearest possible understanding of the remedial agents that he prescribes. This is difficult at best, and is rendered increasingly difficult with multiplication of agents that are nearly but not quite equivalent. Each may show minor differences, which may or may not be practically important, but which are difficult to learn if he spreads his experience too widely and therefore too thinly, as he is urged to do when pharmaceutical firms introduce and promote many actual or near duplicates, with the chief purpose of profiting in a presumably lucrative field, rather than with any real consideration for the welfare of the public or of the interest of medical science and practice.

That was in 1949, when the array of medications available for a doctor to prescribe was but a fraction of today's volume.

THE CELEBRITY PITCH

To peddle the new drugs, pharmaceutical companies and Madison Avenue have turned to celebrities. Revered sports figures, entertainers, race car drivers, actresses, television show hosts, children of once-prominent public figures, and models have become pivotal in the incessant campaign to boost sales of drugs and pressure doctors to write prescriptions.

Mike Ditka, the five-time Pro Bowl tight end for the Chicago Bears, who later coached the team to a victory in Super Bowl XX, uses a double entendre to sell Bayer Pharmaceuticals and GlaxoSmith-Kline's Levitra, a Viagra competitor for erectile dysfunction: "Every coach knows the ability to stay in the game is what counts. So, if you want to stay in the game, don't let anything hold you back. Take action to stay in the game. Ask about Levitra."

Erik Lindbergh exploits the achievement of his grandfather, Charles A. Lindbergh, who in 1927 became the first person to fly solo across the Atlantic, to sell Wyeth and Amgen's Enbrel for rheumatoid arthritis (RA): "Even with rheumatoid arthritis, I'm an artist [pictured woodworking], I'm athletic [riding a bicycle], I'm a father [holding a child on the beach], and today I can still be all these things with Enbrel . . . I'm Eric Lindbergh, and even with RA, I was able to fly solo to Paris, just like my grandfather . . . Because of Enbrel, I can be me."

Mark Martin, one of the most successful racers in NASCAR history, drives a Winston Cup car sponsored by Pfizer's Viagra and also promotes the drug in commercials: "I know a little something about making good moves. So if you're thinking about Viagra, one of the best moves you can make is a pit stop to see your doctor."

Penny Marshall, the motion picture producer who began her career as Laverne in the 1970s hit television series *Laverne & Shirley*, promotes Merck's Zocor—although indirectly and never by name. Instead of identifying the drug, Marshall talks about the importance of a new book, also without mentioning the title, *Information About the Heart Protection Study and Zocor*: "Mother. Father. Husband. Grandparent. Or friend. I'm Penny Marshall, and chances are we all know someone who could learn from this book." Then a female announcer says: "The heart protection study is here . . . Get this book that includes information about the study and treatment options." Adds Marshall: "Your physician knows how important this is."

Dorothy Hamill, who won an Olympic Gold Medal for figure skating at the 1976 Olympics in Innsbruck, and was later named Most Trusted Sports Figure in America by *Ladies' Home Journal*, trades on her skating background to sell Merck's Vioxx for osteoarthritis: It's a beautiful morning. "This is my favorite time to skate. I guess it's from all those years of 5 A.M. practices. But it's also the time when the pain and stiffness of osteoarthritis can be at their worst." The Hamill commercial was deemed the second most effective prescription-drug ad for 2002 by the Intermedia Advertising Group.

But no celebrity has done it better than the ageless supermodel Lauren Hutton, living proof that endorsements often are the gift that keeps on giving long after the commercial or ad appears. A onetime Playboy bunny, Hutton began her career as a model and went on to make movies, host her own syndicated television talk show, invent her own beauty products, and finally return to modeling, a symbol of graceful and elegant aging as she approached sixty.

Given her youthful appearance and oft-stated opposition to plastic surgery, Hutton made the perfect pitchwoman for Wyeth's hormone replacement therapy drugs Prempro and Premarin, especially at a time when the oldest Baby Boomers were entering menopause. Women everywhere were intent on finding the Fountain of Youth, and estrogen seemed the answer. Hutton not only looked great, she also came across as a sincere believer in the product. Better still, she didn't have to mention Wyeth by name. All she need do was talk about the miracle of estrogen replacement. The millions of women who rushed to their doctors only had to request estrogen and they were handed prescriptions for Wyeth's products.

Hutton even sang the praises of estrogen in situations seemingly unrelated to Wyeth. In 1999, Yankelovich, the marketing consultancy group that specializes in identifying lifestyle trends and targeting solutions for its customers, surveyed 1,001 women between the ages of fifty and sixty-five on their sex lives, and found that "women taking hormone replacement therapy (HRT) are more sexually active than their counterparts not on HRT."

To underscore the point, the press release, including the poll results on sex and menopause, carried the personal observations of Hutton, the forever model: "As an HRT user for more than nine years, I can attest to its impact on my health and well-being. I feel as alive and sexy at age fifty-five as I did at thirty."

The survey was the first project of Vitality for Life, an "educational campaign" that just happened to be funded by Wyeth. The release was issued at a time when the largest group of American women in history was experiencing, or soon would, the dreaded hot flashes and mood swings. That it was validated by an attractive spokeswoman, already a certified member of the affected generation, led to the predictable television appearances.

In what must have been music to the ears of Wyeth marketing executives, Diane Sawyer introduced the subject on ABC's *Good Morning
America* show: "By the year 2000, about fifty million American women
will be over fifty, leading to the chance to live lives, especially sexual
lives, as they want to. And joining us now is a woman who has been
living her life that way for quite a while, but says it is even better now
at fifty-five than it was when she was thirty. Lauren Hutton joins us
this morning."

With Sawyer leading the way, Hutton didn't disappoint. In response
to a question about the "really nice romantic life" that follows menopause, and the failure of women to talk about it, Hutton said:

"They're not, and they should see their doctor or a clinic, or
Planned Parenthood can help you, tell you about estrogen. I started
taking HRTs, which are hormone replacement therapy, and my doctor
told me if I didn't, I would get old, that I would shrink. And I did
shrink, I shrunk an inch. And I was already short to begin with."

Hutton said her doctor also warned that if she didn't take HRT, "I
was up for colon cancer, eye loss, osteoporosis, shrinkage. Lots of
things." So for eight years, she told Sawyer, she had been taking HRT,
and life had never been better. Hutton sounded a lot like the physicians of the 1920s who prescribed estrogen, then extracted from the
urine of pregnant women at gynecological clinics, with the promise
that it would cure everything from hair loss to schizophrenia.

The Wyeth advertising blitz, accompanied by an avalanche of favorable reports in newspapers and magazines and on TV—including Hutton's unqualified endorsement—helped propel hormone therapy
prescriptions from fifty-eight million in 1995 to ninety million in
1999. They stayed at roughly that level through June 2002, when the
only serious federal study of HRT linked it to an increased risk of heart
disease, stroke, blood clots, and breast cancer. After that, prescriptions
fell steadily, dropping back to fifty-seven million in 2003.

Perhaps the most disturbing aspect of the marketing campaign was that it was the second time that Wyeth had peddled an estrogen product with dubious claims. Thirty years earlier, the company had introduced another generation of women to estrogen. In 1962, the *Journal of the American Medical Association* published an article reporting that estrogen and progesterone given to 304 women between the ages of forty and seventy had proved "prophylactic to breast and genital cancer." The study was authored by Dr. Robert A. Wilson, a Brooklyn, New York, gynecologist whose work was funded in part by the pharmaceutical industry—notably Wyeth.

YOUR NEXT DRUGS

To shorten the time required to bring more drugs to market, the pharmaceutical companies have embarked on a new and decidedly ominous venture, one with potentially grave consequences for future patients. They've enlisted the advertising industry, which has done so well convincing people they need to spend ever more billions of dollars on our current crop of best-selling drugs, to become an integral part of the development of the next generation of drugs. There is nothing comparable in any other Fortune 500 industry. It would be as if Microsoft outsourced the design of its software to an ad agency.

Consider Omnicom Group Inc., one of the world's largest communications firms, which provides advertising, marketing, and a host of other services to over five thousand clients in more than one hundred countries. Headquartered, appropriately, on Madison Avenue, Omnicom actually is a holding company whose subsidiaries include some of advertising's most illustrious names. Among them are two firms that created fifteen of the top 100 campaigns of the last century. Batton, Barton, Durstine & Osborne developed Pepsi Cola's "The Pepsi generation" and Wisk detergent's "Ring around the collar." Doyle Dane

Bernbach conceived Avis's "We try harder" and Chanel's "Share the fantasy."

In October 1999, Omnicom's Diversified Agency Services (DAS) division acquired a minority interest in SCIREX Inc., a drug development company in Horsham, Pennsylvania, a Philadelphia suburb. SCIREX boasts that it leads the world in analgesia research and has pioneered "new pain assessment methodologies." In its relatively brief existence, the company says SCIREX team members have conducted extensive clinical trials, including at least 200 different studies involving well over 21,000 subjects at some 1,500 different locations.

That's an impressive achievement for a company that as recently as 1995 had fewer than a hundred employees. But it reflects the fast pace of drug testing that began to emerge in the late 1980s as pharmaceutical companies, long accustomed to the slow and methodical approach that had been the hallmark of clinical trials conducted by more independent-minded academics, turned to so-called contract research organizations (CROs) like SCIREX.

The pace of this change is accelerating elsewhere. Just as insurers are outsourcing medical records to India, so, too, are researchers outsourcing clinical trials in which participants test new drugs. Moving the trials overseas, of course, could save the drug companies billions of dollars.

The very existence of the CROs depends on delivering research results the drug companies want to hear—and doing so quickly. That's not to say CROs necessarily manipulate the data. But the outcome of new drug tests can be influenced by many variables. If, for example, people recruited for a study group to assess the effectiveness of a pain medicine are especially healthy, the results will be quite different from those of a group composed of more sickly subjects. If there are too few participants, or the duration of a trial is shortened, harmful side effects will go undiscovered.

In an unfettered free-market health care system, the idea is to get drugs to buyers as soon as possible. As Mike Choukas, SCIREX president and chief executive officer, explained: "Omnicom's investment in SCIREX and access to the vast resources of DAS has already accelerated our expansion plans in the UK and Europe and our development of new clinically unique, market-oriented drug development services."

Why would an advertising and marketing firm acquire an interest in a company that tests drugs? Because that's where the money is. Drugs and health care spending represent a massive pool of cash—larger than the gross domestic product of many countries. Thomas L. Harrison, DAS chairman and chief executive officer, said it was Omnicom's desire "to grow its healthcare and pharmaceutical marketing business in a new, strategically sound direction that led [it] to SCIREX.

"What we were searching for was a clinical research firm that would be a strong partner for our marketing companies," Harrison said. "The disciplines of clinical drug development and strategic drug commercialization are converging at an astoundingly rapid pace. With the goal today being faster, smarter, and more efficient commercialization of new drugs, we felt that we needed to get closer to the test tube—to actually work with clinical scientists to develop drugs with a keen eye toward the needs of the marketplace that will exist at the time of the product's launch."

In short, the advertising campaign of the future will begin at the molecule level, long before a product emerges for actual sale, before it has a name, before anyone even knows if it will work safely. At the same time, innovative promotional efforts can find new uses for existing drugs and thereby expand the market through off-label sales.

That's what SCIREX did for Pharmacia and Pfizer's jointly marketed Bextra, originally approved by the FDA in November 2001 for treating pain from arthritis and menstrual cramps. The FDA rejected a plea that

Bextra also be approved for acute pain. To encourage doctors to prescribe off-label for that purpose, the companies retained SCIREX.
What happened next is spelled out in a lawsuit filed by the Congress of
California Seniors: SCIREX recruited patients with impacted molars,
gave them Bextra, and then concluded that "the drug was effective in
treating adults with acute pain." The results were published in a medical journal in May 2002, thereby exploiting a loophole in the off-label
promotion rules that allow drug companies to pass out medical studies
to doctors. Legal papers contend the favorable Bextra article "was not
the result of the type of scientific analysis that the FDA and other scientists would rely upon in proving clinical efficacy." While the off-label
promotional efforts were under way, Pharmacia and Pfizer were forced
in November 2002 to amend Bextra's label when some patients taking
the drug developed "life-threatening" complications.

Off-label prescriptions are so common that it's estimated about half
of all prescriptions are written to treat conditions for which they were
never approved. Most hospital patients receive at least one such prescription. Physicians prescribe antiarrhythmics for neuropathic pain,
corticosteroids for cancer pain, and antidepressants for insomnia.

The industry is even bringing back discredited drugs from the old days.
During the 1950s, doctors in other countries prescribed thalidomide to
treat morning sickness during pregnancy. Unfortunately, thousands of
women gave birth to deformed children. Some babies were born with just
a head and torso, some without arms and legs, some with toes extending
from their hips, some with flippers coming out of their shoulders. Only
the actions of a strong-willed FDA official kept the drug off the U.S. market at the time—a situation not likely to be duplicated today. Instead, the
FDA has approved thalidomide for leprosy patients with this warning:
"Do not take this drug if there is any possibility that you are, or may
become, pregnant. Just one dose can cause severe birth defects."

Although physicians have long been permitted to prescribe drugs to treat conditions for which they were never tested or authorized—often with positive results—it's a practice subject to abuse in the new world of free-market pharmacology. The reason: Selling prescription drugs for off-label uses represents a multibillion-dollar business that requires little up-front investment compared with developing a new drug. Thus, corporate medicine's goal is to expand the market for an existing medicine, blur the appeals for who will benefit from it, and downplay its risks. A medication to alleviate the symptoms of Alzheimer's disease becomes a "memory pill," instantly expanding the potential audience from the eight million patients with the disabling disease or early-stage dementia to millions of otherwise mentally healthy people who believe they need it because they forgot where they put the car keys or can't remember the name of someone they just saw on the street.

Unpleasant side effects get little notice, although the FDA insists upon at least a passing public disclosure. But the details are in the fine print—really fine print—of the circular that accompanies a prescription. On television commercials, the warnings are nearly invisible. In fact, the FDA merely requires the drug companies to refer viewers to the packaging, or to print ads in a magazine or newspaper that include the side effects. It's unlikely that most people rush out to buy a magazine after watching a commercial. As for the packaging warnings, they are so dense and technical that only the most committed patient would ever be able to slog through the text.

A brief commercial on CBS's *The Early Show* hawking GlaxoSmith-Kline's Imitrex for migraine attacks makes no mention of side effects. Instead, the commercial depicts a young mother with children on the beach. An announcer urges in a voice-over: "Now's a great time to try Imitrex, because now you can get your first full prescription free. Call 1-900-Imitrex or visit imitrex.com. Ask your doctor about Imitrex and get your first full prescription for free." To be sure, longer versions include references to side effects. But for the complete listing, a viewer would have to turn to a print ad in a newspaper or magazine, or go to the drug's Web page, which carries a sobering warning that reads in part:

> You should not take IMITREX if you have certain types of heart disease, a history of stroke or TIAs, peripheral vascular disease, Raynaud syndrome, or blood pressure that is uncontrolled. . . . Very rarely, certain people, even some without heart disease, have had serious heart-related problems when taking IMITREX. If you are currently taking other medications or if you are pregnant, nursing, or thinking about becoming pregnant, you should talk to your doctor before taking IMITREX. If your headaches are not migraines, IMITREX is not for you.

What if you fail to seek out the warnings and carefully consider them? What are the possible consequences if you assume pharmaceutical companies would never sell a product that could make one sick rather than healthy? What can possibly go wrong if you believe the FDA, the agency charged with protecting America's health, would never approve a drug that could do harm? A great deal.

After all, this is the industry that, with the FDA's approval, sold Posicor as a safe treatment for high blood pressure until it was determined that the drug was lethal in combination with two dozen other medicines and that people were dying as a result. Posicor's maker, Hoffman-LaRoche, took it off the market in 1998. This is the industry that, with the FDA's approval, sold Lotronex as a safe treatment for irritable bowel syndrome until people began showing up at hospitals with colitis, intestinal damage, and ruptured bowels. At least three patients died. Lotronex's maker, Glaxo Wellcome Inc., took it off the market late in 2000—the same year it was introduced.

This is the industry that, with the FDA's approval, sold Seldane as a safe treatment for allergies until it was determined that in some instances it caused serious and sometimes fatal cardiac arrhythmias. Seldane's maker, Hoescht Marion Roussel and Baker Norton Pharmaceuticals, took it off the market in 1997. This is the industry that, with the FDA's approval, sold Baycol as a safe treatment for lowering cholesterol until it was determined that in some instances it caused rhabdomyolysis, a disease that destroys skeletal muscle and can be fatal. Some two dozen deaths were linked to Baycol and the disease. Baycol's maker, Bayer Pharmaceuticals, took it off the market in 2001.

This is the industry that, with the FDA's approval, sold Rezulin as a treatment for diabetes until it was determined that it led to liver failure in scores of patients and was linked to hundreds of deaths overall. The drug's maker, Parke-Davis and Warner-Lambert, took it off the market in 2000. This is the industry that, with the FDA's approval, sold Propulsid as a safe treatment for nighttime heartburn until it was determined the drug was linked to heart rhythm abnormalities in more than 300 people, eighty of whom died. The FDA not only OK'd the drug, it failed to warn physicians that eight children who took it during clinical trials had died. In the end, twenty-four children under the age of six died. The drug's maker, Johnson & Johnson, took it off the market in 2000.

Think about those results the next time you see a commercial or read a print advertisement touting the latest wonder drug. And then recall one Madison Avenue executive's philosophy from the 1930s: "To tell the naked truth might make no appeal. It may be necessary to fool people for their own good." Then it was only Listerine.

Finally, think about the observations of Harry Loynd, who worked his way up through the ranks during the 1930s and 1940s to take the top job at what then was the world's most powerful pharmaceutical company, Parke-Davis & Company. Loynd's motto was "Pills are to sell, not to take." He had unlimited faith in being able to sell his products—because as he told his sales force: "If we put horse manure in a capsule, we could sell it to 95 percent of these doctors."

6

The Remedy

The D-Day invasion of June 6, 1944, which would turn the tide of World War II for the Allies, was the largest amphibious assault in the history of warfare. Altogether, 5,000 ships, 13,000 aircraft, and 180,000 men took part in the initial landing on the coast of France. While not everything went according to plan, D-Day was both an incredible military success and a spectacular triumph of organization.

But imagine what would have happened if the American, British, and Canadian military units each had gone its own way instead of following a coordinated master plan. Suppose that each of the U.S. Army's twenty divisions had assembled its own list of targets, with the 101st Airborne Division dropping into one part of France, the 82nd Airborne into another. Suppose that each company within each of those divisions had done likewise. Then imagine the same for the British and Canadians: 180,000 troops, each man marching to his own drummer.

That is precisely the picture of the U.S. health care system today, thousands of individual entities heading off in many directions on missions that frequently conflict. It's really no system at all. Rather, it's a stunningly fragmented collection of businesses, government agencies, health care facilities, educational institutions, and other special interests wasting tens of billions of dollars and turning the treatment of disease and sickness into a lottery where some losers pay with their lives.

The United States has 6,000 hospitals and tens of thousands more freestanding medical centers, nursing homes, kidney dialysis centers, laboratories, MRI facilities, pharmacies, and medical schools. Each maintains its own computer system. Some can talk to one another; most can't. Overlying these are hundreds of HMOs, private insurers, and government plans. There's Medicaid for the very poor, Medicare for everyone over sixty-five years of age, TRICARE and the Veterans Administration for the military, and a hodgepodge for everyone else. Each insurer has its own system of co-pays, deductibles, and spending limits. Each produces thousands of pages of impenetrable language setting forth the medical expenses it will pay, the ones it won't, and those that fall somewhere in between.

Then there are thousands of special interests, from the American Cancer Society to the American Medical Association, from the Pharmaceutical Research and Manufacturers of America (PhRMA) to the American Organ Transplant Association, each with its own agenda. Each wages an individual campaign to shape health care policy by manipulating public opinion through TV, newspapers, magazines, and radio. Each seeks to grab a piece of the health care pie. Out of all these thousands of self-interested entities, not one speaks for what's best for American health care overall.

And that explains why U.S. health care is second-rate at the start of the twenty-first century and destined to get a lot worse and much more expensive. It's why some people must hold garage sales to pay their medical bills, why almost no one knows what their health insurance will pay for until it's too late. It's why many Americans are forced to make job choices based not on what they might like to do in life, or what's in their best interest, but on the health insurance packages offered by employers. It's why U.S. corporations are at a disadvantage in a global economy, forced to divert ever more revenue and resources to administering health care plans. It's why some diseases such as colon cancer or attention deficit disorder, which capture the media's attention, get a substantial share of government research and treatment dollars, while other diseases that receive less attention, such as amyotrophic lateral sclerosis (Lou Gehrig's disease) and cystic fibrosis, receive far fewer dollars. It's why millions of Americans are forced to agonize over how to care for aging parents with Alzheimer's disease, or how to pay the bills for children with a catastrophic illness—and do so without depriving siblings of their needs. It's why millions of Americans needlessly consume expensive medications that enrich pharmaceutical companies and Wall Street, but that contribute little or nothing to a longer, healthier life. Finally, it explains why Americans are the most overtreated, undertreated, and mistreated health care patients on earth.

It need not be this way.

The simplest and most cost-effective remedy would be to provide universal coverage and to create one agency to collect medical fees and pay claims. This would eliminate the staggering overlap, duplication, bureaucracy, and waste created by thousands of individual plans, the hidden costs that continue to drive health care out of reach for a steadily growing number of Americans.

Under a single-payer system, all health care providers—doctors, hospitals, clinics—would bill one agency for their services and would be reimbursed by the same agency. Every American would receive basic comprehensive health care, including essential prescription drugs and rehabilitative care. Anyone who needed to be treated or hospitalized could receive medical care without having to wrestle with referrals and without fear of financial ruin. Complex billing procedures and ambiguities over what is covered by insurance would be eliminated.

Radical? We already have universal health care and a single-payer system for everybody aged sixty-five and over: It's called Medicare. For years, researchers, think tanks, citizens' groups, and health care professionals have advocated a similar plan for the rest of the population. Study after study has concluded that the most practical and cost-effective way to provide quality health care and to restrain costs is a single-payer system, but no plan has ever come close to adoption because of fierce opposition by the powerful health care lobby.

To discredit the single-payer idea, insurers, HMOs, for-profit hospitals, and other private interests play on Americans' long-standing fears of big government. This view was summed up by Susan Pisano, a vice president of the American Association of Health Plans, who contended in 2002 that a single-payer system "would lead to the creation of a large federal bureaucracy that would be less responsive and actually raise issues of cost, access and quality more than it would solve them."

In truth, it is the private market that has created a massive bureaucracy, one that dwarfs the size and costs of Medicare, the most efficiently run health insurance program in America in terms of administrative costs. Medicare's overhead averages about 2 percent a year. In a 2002 study for Maine, Mathematica Policy Research Inc. concluded that administrative costs of private insurers in the state ranged from 12 percent to more than 30 percent. Studies of private carriers in other areas have reached similar conclusions. This isn't surprising, because unlike Medicare, which relies on economies of scale and standardized universal coverage, private insurance is built on bewilderingly complex layers of plans and providers that require a costly bureaucracy to administer, much of which is geared toward denying claims.

Some studies have put the price tag for administering the current system at nearly one out of every three health care dollars, much higher than that of any nation with single-payer health care. There is no way of knowing how much the United States could save by adopting such a system, but even with one that covered 100 percent of the population, the savings would be substantial.

What kind of an agency would administer it?

The idea of a single-payer plan run by the U.S. government carries with it far too much political baggage ever to get off the ground. What's needed is a fresh approach, a new organization that is independent and free from politics, one that can focus with laserlike precision on what needs to be done to further the health interests of everyone in a fair manner. For in addition to covering the basic costs of all Americans, a new system needs to institute programs that will improve America's overall health, that will focus on preventing illness and disease as well as treatment, and do so without breaking the bank.

How does the United States come up with such a mechanism?

One possible answer: Loosely copy and then amend and expand on what already exists in another setting—the Federal Reserve System, a quasigovernmental organization that oversees the nation's money and banking policies. The Fed is one of the nation's most ingenious creations, a public agency that is largely independent of politics. The Fed's board members are appointed to staggered fourteen-year terms by the President with the consent of the Senate, meaning that neither the White House nor Congress can substantively influence the Fed's policies.

Call this independent agency the U.S. Council on Health Care (USCHC). Like the Federal Reserve, the council would set an overall policy for health care and influence its direction by controlling federal spending—from managing research grants to providing basic and catastrophic medical coverage for all citizens. Unlike the Federal Reserve, it would be entirely funded by taxpayers. The money could come from just two taxes, a gross-receipts levy on businesses and a flat tax, similar to the current Medicare tax, on all individual income, not just wages.

This would not represent an additional cost to society, but rather replace existing taxes and write-offs. It would cut costs for corporations and raise taxes slightly on individuals at the top of the income ladder. Members of the USCHC board would include both health care professionals and citizens from all walks of life. Its mission: Implement policies that improve health care for everyone, not just those suffering from certain diseases. In short, make the unpopular decisions that the market cannot make.

The council could establish regions similar to those of the Federal Reserve System, which divides the nation into twelve areas. Whatever their number, the geographic subdivisions could take into account cultural and regional differences among Americans. They would allow for health care delivery to be fine-tuned at the local level, and ensure that regulations could take into account the differences between metropolitan and community hospitals.

Although the USCHC could be set up to keep partisan politics out of hospitals and doctors' offices, health care politics, which can be every bit as divisive as the mainstream variety, would still present a challenge. If you have any doubt, just assemble surgeons, radiologists, and internists in a room to discuss the merits of their particular approaches to treatment of a specific disease. But those members of a USCHC board drawn from outside the health care community would at least introduce a moderating influence.

CURING THE ILLS

This is not to suggest that a single-payer system overseen by a Federal Reserve–like board or some other independent organization would instantly correct everything that's wrong with market-driven health care. What it would do is provide the framework to reach that goal. For starters, there are certain basic things it would do:

- Guarantee that all Americans receive a defined level of basic care, including a fixed number of visits to doctors, routine lab work, immunizations for children, coverage for all childhood illnesses, and all hospital charges.

- Establish flexible co-pays for basic care that would vary depending on income as well as usage. Those people who seldom seek medical attention could have their co-pays waived. So, too, could those at the bottom of the income ladder. Those who use the facilities repeatedly without any serious medical reason for doing so could be charged with escalating co-pays.

- Pay all costs to treat any catastrophic illness, such as cancer or any devastating disease. It would pay all doctor bills, hospital charges, and any related costs. There would be no co-pays and no deductibles for the seriously ill.

- Restore freedom of choice by allowing patients to choose their doctors, rather than insurers limiting the selection through their approved lists. They also could choose their hospitals.

- Redirect health care spending by allocating money for disease prevention as well as treatment. It would curtail out-of-control prescription-drug costs. It would rein in those doctors who have never met an expensive drug they didn't like and who practice medicine by prescription.

- Provide critically important drug information to consumers to balance the promotional hype of advertising. The council could insist that the results of all clinical drug trials be made public, so consumers may better assess both the upside and the downside of certain medications.

- Concentrate health care spending on cost-effective areas, such as stemming the growth in diabetes among children, which if allowed to continue unchecked ultimately will cost society more than AIDS, cancer, or other diseases.

- Control costs by getting to the root causes of health care spending, which varies widely among the residents of different states. Even after taking into account disparities in living costs, there is no medical reason that Medicare should spend, as it has, 48 percent more money on seniors in Mississippi than seniors in South Dakota, or 43 percent more on seniors in Florida than seniors in Minnesota, or 31 percent more on seniors in the District of Columbia than seniors in California.

- Halt the existing practice by which insurers, to improve their own bottom lines, squeeze doctors through unrealistically low reimbursement rates. The same for hospitals and nursing homes that squeeze nursing salaries and staffing levels.

- Reverse the costly, but seldom discussed, health care trend of overdiagnosis and overtreatment—something no market system will ever do. While many Americans suffer from a lack of health care, a growing number get too much. They seek out the latest tests, the newest pills, and the most popular screenings regardless of whether they are at risk. The overtreated include middle-income folks with generous insurance, Medicare enrollees, and even lower-income people who qualify for Medicaid. It's the kind of irony that finds some people going to bed hungry while others eat so much they are obese.

Once in place, the scope of the basic care package could be expanded as the system realizes savings derived from standardization, more efficient computer technology, and the end of market-based medicine with its required profits, stock options, and generous executive-compensation deals.

The health council could save money by creating an enforcement agency that would pay for itself by ferreting out fraud, which may run as high as $200 billion a year. One possibility would be to decriminalize health care fraud and make it a civil offense. There would be no perp walk, but the economic penalties could be draconian: Steal from health care and you lose all your personal assets—home, car, savings, retirement accounts, everything—no exceptions.

Individuals could supplement their basic government-supported coverage through private insurance. Wealthier citizens could continue to obtain whatever care they wanted and pay for it. But they would be barred from dropping out of the USCHC and would still be required to pay the earmarked taxes, just as everyone must contribute to Medicare and Social Security. Also, insurers would be barred from offering coverage that competed with the government-backed plan. Similarly, hospitals would be free to accept a certain percentage of cash-paying patients from outside the USCHC.

A unified single-payer system could make it possible to deal with medicine's thorniest issues, ones that the market system has either aggravated or done little to resolve. Three of those are interrelated and have a direct impact on the quality of care patients receive: mistakes, malpractice, and prescription drugs.

To reduce medical errors dramatically, the council could oversee creation and operation of a single information technology system that links all health care players—hospitals, doctors' offices, pharmacies, and nursing homes. Deaths caused by an error in one hospital or nursing home could be identified and corrective steps initiated before the error recurs in other facilities. Patient records would be stored electronically. Prescriptions would be computer-generated. It would help ensure correct dosages and preclude the dispensing of drugs with harmful interactions. Deaths from lethal drug interactions that now go unnoticed could be detected. This will be especially important since such deaths will grow as the population ages and more people take ever more drugs for longer periods. Under the existing fragmented system, no one is assigned the specific task of looking for these deaths. The ones that turn up, in most cases, are discovered by serendipity.

A reduction in medical mistakes also would lead to a fall-off in serious malpractice claims, one of the most contentious aspects of health care. The situation has become so grim under the profit-driven system that many doctors view their patients as potential adversaries and practice medicine accordingly. This is not only bad medicine, but also incredibly expensive. Yet the proposed solution—placing a maximum cap of $250,000 on damage awards—is hardly equitable.

Do you believe it's fair that a woman receive no more than $23 a day over, say, thirty years if both her breasts are removed by mistake? Is it fair for a man to receive the same $23 if a leg is amputated by mistake? Is it fair for an infant with severe birth defects as a result of a delivery mistake to receive no more than $14 a day over fifty years? Would you consider those sums to be fair if the mistakes involved you or members of your family? Yet that's Congress's idea of malpractice equity.

Of course, most doctors also are treated unfairly, compelled to pay exorbitant insurance premiums because of the actions of a few. This has led doctors in some states to go on strike while other physicians uproot their practices and move to less litigious communities.

With fewer errors and thus fewer deaths, lawsuits would decline. Equally important, a national health care database would make it possible for the USCHC to identify those hospitals and health care workers—doctors, nurses, and technicians—who continue to be involved in mistakes and deaths. The most egregious errors could be litigated. For less serious mistakes, a no-fault system could be tested.

In a less hostile environment, doctors could stop practicing defensive medicine. They would no longer feel compelled to order medically unnecessary MRIs, X-rays, laboratory tests, biopsies, stress tests, and specialty consultations, with additional savings the result.

The national patient data archives could provide a treasure trove of information to improve the quality of health care. Researchers would be able to determine with greater accuracy the procedures that work and the ones that don't; which drugs are most effective and which are not. For the first time, the data would allow for large-scale clinical studies that are never done under the existing system. For example, what really is the best treatment for prostate cancer? Is surgery cost-effective? Or is it better to do nothing? While limited studies offer a variety of answers, a unified data bank could provide more solid ones. Similar studies could be carried out for a range of other diseases and conditions: Are colonoscopies cost-effective? What about the Pap smear? The PSA test? The bone-density test? Genetic screening? Or could much of the money for these and other tests be more productively spent to prevent disease and add healthy years to the lifespan of the population at large?

As for prescription drugs, no other segment of health care better illustrates why profit-based medicine and cost containment are mutually exclusive. Drug companies flourish by selling more pills, never fewer. Yet a good health care system would strive to prescribe fewer pills, especially since the effectiveness of many drugs is questionable. Antidepressants, the top-selling category of prescription drugs in 2001, had retail sales of $12.5 billion. But studies show that about two out of every three people who take antidepressants would do equally well on a harmless sugar pill. Furthermore, they wouldn't suffer from, and be treated for, the side effects of many antidepressants, such as sexual dysfunction, anxiety, insomnia, sweating, and nausea.

The USCHC, or some other single payer, could negotiate the best possible drug prices, something that Medicare is forbidden to do by Congress. It also could establish rules for holding down prices in other ways. Barring overwhelming evidence of the effectiveness of a new medication, there would be no mad rush to pay for the latest—and most costly—drug.

The pharmaceutical industry, to be sure, would object strenuously. It would argue, as it always has, that the United States must charge the world's highest prices to fund research for new drugs. Don't believe it. To begin with, taxpayers already have contributed to some drug research through government programs. More significant, companies often do little more than rearrange molecules to create a new version of an existing drug, or promote new uses for old drugs, just to keep the revenue stream flowing. The number of breakthrough drugs introduced in any given year is negligible. During the twelve years from 1989 to 2000, 65 percent of the new-drug applications approved by the FDA involved "active ingredients that were already available in marketed products." Another 11 percent "were identical to products already available on the U.S. market."

Concluded one study: "The increased emphasis on incremental drug development is not surprising. Large brand manufacturers have reached a scale at which they must generate several billion dollars in additional revenue each year in order to meet Wall Street growth targets. Yet only a handful of firms were able to bring ten or more drugs with new active ingredients to market over the past decade, or at least one per year on average."

In addition, pharmaceutical companies have long been sheltered by government policies that have fostered bloated marketing efforts. One-third or more of drug-company revenue is spent on advertising, administration, and marketing, with much of the money going to support the armies of sales representatives who call on doctors to persuade them to write prescriptions.

Policies of a unified health care system could reduce those sales forces, with their dubious medical justification. If you are a professional making life-and-death treatment decisions, do you really need a salesperson to explain why his or her drug is just right for your patients? And if you're a patient, do you want to rely on a doctor who prescribes a pill based on sales pitches? Some physicians already have opted out of the practice by refusing to see drug-company representatives. Of course, these doctors do not get free meals and "consulting" fees, both of which would disappear under a centralized system. Indeed, doctors who overprescribe or misprescribe medications could be identified and penalized.

CRISIS AND OPPORTUNITY

Creating a Federal Reserve–style council to deal with the crisis in health care would be controversial and bitterly opposed, because it would disrupt the powerful health care industrial complex, and because it would challenge many medical myths. Resistance would come from health care providers themselves; from insurers, some of whom would go out of business; from some in the U.S. government bureaucracy who would lose control; from the antitax community; from some physicians and individuals who are content with their personal situations, and most of all, from members of Congress who benefit so handsomely from free-market health care. Many, perhaps most, of these groups and individuals will push instead to solve the crisis by adding on to the existing labyrinth, by expanding coverage to the uninsured through private insurers. That would only delay the inevitable and cost more money, while maintaining all the inequities.

Americans who are skeptical of anything that smacks of big government fear that a universal health plan would restrict personal freedom. But the market system already has done that. Those with health insurance often can go only to physicians or hospitals approved by their plans, unless they are wealthy enough to pay the fees out of their own pockets. Many Americans fear that it would cost too much, even though the market system already has given the United States the world's most expensive health care with little to show for it. They fear the long waits they have heard about in Canada and other countries, even though comparable waiting times for tests and procedures are commonplace in many parts of the United States. Lastly, they fear government-decreed rationing, even though health care is already rationed in the most inequitable of ways, including forty-four million with none at all.

Despite all the fears, change will come. The market system is a devastating failure, and nearly every major public opinion poll finds health care at or near the top of Americans' concerns. While some will always believe that market-driven medicine will work as well as market-driven automobile manufacturing, that attitude is changing, even among those who have long opposed government intervention.

This was confirmed in a study by the Center for Studying Health System Change, a nonpartisan Washington, D.C., think tank. Every two years, the center's researchers survey doctors, insurers, and other professionals in twelve major cities on the state of health care. In its 2004 study, researchers noted a marked shift in opinion among groups that have traditionally opposed a government role: "An insurance broker said, 'The delivery system is a mess. The sectors don't talk. No one wants to change. The government must do something.' A surprised benefit consultant reported: 'There is now a lack of resistance to government involvement.'" As quickly as many offered their opinions, they followed with the caveat, "But we can't say that out loud." The study concluded:

"What is palpable across the twelve communities we studied is the recognition that private market forces are limited in their ability to achieve social objectives in health care services, and a growing sense that a broader conversation about what to do next should begin soon. This conversation may find more willing participants than would have been possible four to six years ago."

Ultimately, the driving forces behind change will come from two sources: working Americans who are disenchanted with ever-rising costs and shrinking care, and U.S. corporations, which are increasingly refusing to pick up the added costs. They can't afford to, because America's privately funded system puts U.S. companies at a disadvantage with their competitors in the industrialized world, where universal health care is funded by government. General Motors says the cost of providing health care to its workers and retirees now totals $1,400 for each vehicle sold in the United States, more than the cost of steel. William Clay Ford Jr., the chairman and chief executive of Ford, says, "employers in this country, and particularly manufacturing employers, can't compete internationally with this burden around our collective necks."

This is why companies are cutting back, trimming, or eliminating health care for their retirees, and reneging on promises made to encourage workers to leave early. They are imposing higher co-pays and requiring employees to pick up an increasing share of annual premiums. In fact, many companies will require workers to pay for all future cost increases.

America's health care system is in critical condition, and we find ourselves at a turning point. But this crisis represents an exceptional opportunity to reconsider our values, our priorities, our budget, and our options. We can continue to hold garage sales to finance health care, or we can do what every other civilized nation on earth does— take care of our citizens.

Medicine in the Media

Most of us find out about the latest advances in medical tests, new drugs, treatments, clinical trials, and surgical procedures from television news programs, newspapers, or magazines. Unfortunately, routine daily or weekly health care reporting in all three media ranges from uncritical to exuberant. Usually, each new development is presented as a medical breakthrough with little or no attention paid to the potential harmful consequences or whether the supposed benefits outweigh the costs.

Such was the case in 2000 when TV and newspapers described the full-body scan as a cutting-edge test that "can reveal diseases and heart problems before they can become deadly." The torrent of publicity led to the building of more clinics where the scans could be performed. A representative of one clinic called the scan "a revolutionary way to detect early disease and assess the current state of your health." Left unsaid is that the scans often detect "problems" where there are none. They also show seeming irregularities that lead to recommendations for more testing, which ultimately shows no significant problems at all. Also left unsaid: If everyone were to have the scan, as was suggested, the costs would bankrupt

Medicare and Medicaid and drive the price of private insurance out of reach for many—all for the possibility of saving relatively few lives when many more lives could be saved by spending a lot less money elsewhere.

Too often, context is missing from daily medical reporting, especially in the hype over treatment of specific conditions. The full-body scan was pitched as a new tool to detect heart disease, which, we are reminded daily, is the leading killer of Americans. It has been so for decades. But missing is the context. Two-thirds of the people who died from heart disease in 2000 were seventy-five or older; more than four-fifths were over sixty-five. Only 7 percent were younger than fifty-five. Separate the age groups, and suddenly heart disease is not so significant for the population at large. That's not to say we ignore it. But it's worth remembering that with age comes an increasing likelihood of disease and the certainty of death.

A dollar spent to prevent disease will go much further than a dollar spent to treat it. But under the market system, treatment—not prevention—is where the money is. After all, there is no money to be made if a disease does not exist. No drug company is reporting annual sales increases; no physician's office is jammed with patients.

In 1997, Parke-Davis, a division of Warner-Lambert Company, introduced a drug called Rezulin to treat diabetes. The news media gave the new drug an enthusiastic reception, complete with favorable reviews from professionals in the health care field as well as comments from hopeful patients looking forward to using it. CNBC, the cable financial news channel, was typical:

"Well, here's some good news for millions of people who have diabetes," declared anchor Janice Lieberman. "The Food and Drug Administration has approved the first drug which helps some diabetics better control their insulin, and Sheila Stainback is here with those exciting details."

Stainback introduced an endocrinologist who hailed Rezulin as "a unique drug . . . the first in its class" and a patient who took daily insulin injections and other drugs to control her diabetes. The patient, said Stainback, "plans to try Rezulin and may no longer need any other drugs."

Lastly, the best news of all, Stainback said the endocrinologist was "beginning a study at New York's Albert Einstein College of Medicine where he's looking into whether Rezulin may even stop diabetes before it occurs in high-risk patients. Janice, very exciting."

Lieberman: "Wouldn't that be amazing."

Stainback: "Yes, absolutely."

USA Today told readers that Rezulin "may reduce or eliminate the need for insulin shots for nearly 1 million diabetics . . . The drug is taken orally and will help some Type II diabetics control blood sugar levels. Of the patients who can take Rezulin, 15% might be able stop insulin shots, officials said."

When potential side effects were even mentioned, they were dismissed as inconsequential. The Copley News Service called them "quite mild." The *New York Times* quoted an FDA official as saying that adverse effects "appeared to be rare and relatively mild, including infection, pain and headache." The only cautionary note was that "animal studies suggest that the drug should be prescribed with caution for patients with advanced heart failure or liver disease."

Three years later, Rezulin was pulled from the market after many patients died and others required liver transplants.

Such outcomes go beyond prescription drugs. Millions of patients have undergone angioplasty or bypass operations to clear arteries clogged with plaque. They were assured this would reduce or eliminate the risk of heart attacks. Now it turns out that many such operations are unnecessary, news that comes too late for all those who suffered heart attacks or died as a result of the treatment rather than the underlying disease. New studies and research show that cleaning out a couple of clogged arteries does little to improve heart health. In fact, diet and exercise alone yield better results than invasive procedures, whose primary benefits flow to surgeons and Wall Street investors in drug-coated stents.

Over time, surgical procedures often prove to be ineffective, unwarranted, or worse. In the 1940s parents were advised to have their children's tonsils removed to improve their health. During that same era newspapers reported on a new surgical procedure for curing the mentally ill: a lobotomy. In December 1943, the *New York Times* summarized a report on the operation published by the *Journal of the American Medical Association.* The operation consisted of "removing a lobe of the brain with a tube inserted through a hole drilled in the skull." According to the *JAMA* authors, "What is called prefrontal lobotomy has been successfully performed in about two hundred cases of depression, suicidal tendencies, persecution mania, and intense worry." The physician who came up with it in time would win the Nobel Prize for his efforts.

The surgical technique was refined into the 1950s, and a headline over a *New York Times* article in January 1951 declared: "BIG ADVANCE SEEN IN BRAIN SURGERY; New Means Relieve Hopeless Mental Ills and Victims of Intractable Pain." During that period, West Virginia instituted mass surgery using the procedure on the mentally ill. The new approach, according to the *Times*, involved inserting an instrument that resembled an ice pick "under the eyelid and twisted so as to sever the nerves that transmit fear, anxiety, and apprehensiveness." This method was popularized by Dr. Walter Freeman, a member of the Neurology Department at George Washington University in Washington, D.C., and head of the American Medical Association's certification board for neurology and psychiatry. In 1952, the *Times* noted that Dr. Freeman "has performed eleven hundred lobotomies at thirty state hospitals in fifteen states . . . Patients' ages ranged from seven to seventy." Technically, the procedure was called a "transorbital lobotomy." More commonly, it was the "the ice pick operation." The practice fell out of favor after that bastion of modern medical science, the Soviet Union, outlawed it as "inhumane."

If daily and weekly journalism contains reporting that is superficial at best and harmful to your health at worst, the good news is that in-depth reporting on health care issues has never been better, more perceptive, and more relevant. Thoughtful, detailed accounts of health care issues appear in newspapers large and small, magazines, books, and on investigative TV programs like NBC's *Dateline*. Compared with the barrage of announcements about new drugs, procedures, and treatment, these in-depth reports are like a stream of reality against a Niagara of hyperbole. For those who have an interest in health care, these reports are most instructive.

The following sampling is drawn largely from the library of the Investigative Reporters and Editors (IRE) organization whose members work for print and broadcast media.

LOS ANGELES TIMES. The reporting of a persistent *Los Angeles Times* writer, David Willman, beginning in 1998 and continuing to 2000, eventually goaded the FDA into withdrawing Rezulin, the lethal diabetes drug. Without Willman's work, many more people would have died. Willman and another *Los Angeles Times* reporter, Janet Lundblad, disclosed widespread conflicts of interest within the National Institutes of Health (NIH) in December 2003. Once, the NIH was known for "independent scientific inquiry on behalf of a single client: the public." But no more. Today, the *Los Angeles Times* disclosed, its senior scientists collect paychecks and stock options from biomedical companies and "take side jobs as consultants for drug companies." The articles showed how the conflicts taint the NIH's work and are detrimental to the nation's health.

ORANGE COUNTY REGISTER. This Santa Ana, California–based newspaper published a groundbreaking series April 16–20, 2000, called "The Body Brokers." It's must reading for anyone who plans to donate organs, or receive an organ, and for everyone who has an interest in how the medical-industrial complex works. The articles revealed that "American businesses make hundreds of millions of dollars selling products crafted from human bodies, even though it is illegal to profit from cadaver parts." The project was the work of Mark Katches, William Heisel, Ronald Campbell, Sharon Henry, and Michael Goulding. An extended report by Heisel and Mayrav Saar on April 7, 2002, "Doctors Without Discipline," catalogued the failure of California's Medical Board to discipline doctors "with a history of causing patients' injury or death."

FORT LAUDERDALE SUN-SENTINEL. Using information gleaned from multiple databases, including autopsy data and Medicaid physician billings, reporter Fred Schulte documented how a "small group of doctors have prescribed huge quantities of narcotic painkillers and other addictive drugs to low-income people on Medicaid, costing taxpayers hundreds of millions of dollars and adding a torrent of overdose deaths in the state." The series, "Drugging the Poor," was published November 30–December 3, 2003. In an earlier series in November and December 1998, "Cosmetic Surgery: The Hidden Dangers," Schulte and another reporter, Jenni Bergal, uncovered the deaths of thirty-four people "following seemingly routine plastic surgery in Florida."

CHICAGO TRIBUNE. In September 2000, Michael J. Berens wrote a three-part series, "Dangerous Care: Nurses' Hidden Role in Medical Error." Berens described how "overwhelmed and inadequately trained nurses kill and injure hundreds of patients every year as hospitals sacrifice safety for an improved bottom line." In another three-part series in July 2002, "Unhealthy Hospital," Berens tracked a "hidden epidemic of life-threatening infections that is contaminating America's hospitals, needlessly killing tens of thousands of patients each year." The *Tribune* found "serious violations of infection-control standards" in nearly three-quarters of the nation's hospitals.

NEW YORK TIMES. In "Medicine's Middlemen," a report published on March 4, 2002, Walt Bogdanich, Barry Meier, and Mary Williams Walsh disclosed how "just two companies could determine which life-saving drugs and other medical products most of the nation's hospitals bought and at what price. As national gatekeepers for billions of dollars in hospital supply contracts, these two companies used their unregulated power to enrich themselves through pervasive conflicts of interest and self dealing . . . Executives collected millions in personal stock options from the very manufacturers whose company products they were supposed to evaluate objectively. The buying companies steered thousands of hospitals to manufacturers in which the buying companies themselves had a financial interest."

WASHINGTON POST. A team of *Post* reporters led by Joe Stephens, Deborah Nelson, and Mary Pat Flaherty traveled the world for eleven months to research the pharmaceutical industry's testing of experimental drugs on the sick and the poor of other countries. In their December 2000 series, "The Body Hunters: Exporting Human Experiments," the *Post* reporters described "a booming, poorly regulated testing system that is dominated by private interests and that far too often betrays its promises to patients and consumers. Experiments involving risky drugs proceed with little independent oversight. Impoverished, poorly educated patients are sometimes tested without understanding that they are guinea pigs. And pledges of quality medical care sometimes prove fatally hollow . . . Drugmakers hop borders with scant government review . . . paying doctors to test thousands of human subjects in the Third World and Eastern Europe."

NEWSDAY. In a six-part report, "Managed Care and Doctors: The Broken Promise," *New York Newsday*'s Thomas Maier disclosed that the state's "biggest managed health care networks offered their customers dozens of doctors disciplined for serious—even fatal—wrong doing." This even though the insurers were "fully aware that the state had punished these doctors for such offenses as botched surgery, sexual misconduct, drug abuse or cheating government insurance plans." The series was published in November 1999.

FORTUNE. In a March 2004 article, *Fortune* magazine's executive editor, Clifton Leaf, demolished the widely repeated assertion that we are winning the war on cancer. Notwithstanding all the heralded new cancer medicines, Leaf wrote that "while there have been substantial achievements since the crusade began with the National Cancer Act in 1971, we are far from winning the war. So far away, in fact, that it looks like losing . . . Decades of breakthroughs have raised hopes again and again for people with cancer—but have failed to deliver on expectations." His story was all the more compelling because Leaf is a cancer survivor himself, having been diagnosed at age fifteen with Hodgkin's disease.

WALL STREET JOURNAL. Staff writers at the *Journal* routinely publish detailed reports on all phases of the health care industry. On January 13, 1998, Jonathan Kaufman recounted the plight of home health aide workers who toil in a thriving field for long hours, little money, and few benefits. On July 19, 2000, Scott Hensley and Shailagh Murray wrote about pharmaceutical companies raising their prices on prescription drugs while "at the same also giving away more free samples in an attempt to entice doctors to prescribe their medication." On June 6, 2001, Ann Davis recounted how thousands of middle-class and affluent retirees have milked the Medicaid program for the poor by sheltering their wealth in so-called "Medicaid annuities." The scheme allows the seniors to stay in nursing homes, with Medicaid picking up the tab, while they preserve their assets.

Brief summaries of more than one thousand health care–related project stories can be viewed on the IRE Web site (www.ire.org). Copies may be ordered. Copies also may be obtained at public libraries with access to newspaper databases, newspaper archives on microfilm, or through interlibrary loans.

Notes

CHAPTER 1: A SECOND-RATE SYSTEM

Descriptions of fund-raisers and benefits to pay medical expenses for uninsured or underinsured Americans were gathered from interviews and newspaper accounts.

Statistics on per capita health care spending, life expectancy, infant mortality rates, and healthy living were taken from the Centers for Disease Control (CDC), the World Health Organization (WHO), and the *Dartmouth Atlas of Health Care.*

Cases of patients gouged by inflated hospital charges came from reports, data, and documents compiled by the Consejo de Latinos Unidos, Los Angeles, and through interviews with its director, K. B. Forbes.

Data on the uninsured are drawn from many sources, including "Uninsured in America," the Kaiser Commission on Medicaid and the Uninsured, testimony of Diane Rowland, Director, before the U.S. House Ways and Means Committee, March 9, 2004; "Access to Health Care for the Uninsured in Rural and Frontier America," Issue Paper, National Rural Health Association, May 1999; "The Affordability Crisis in U.S. Healthcare," Commonwealth Fund, March 2004; *Public Papers of the Presidents, Dwight D. Eisenhower, 1954*; and authors' interviews.

The story of Lynn Oldham came almost exclusively from interviews with Lynn Oldham and her husband, Michael Granucci, and with her colleague at Manasquan High School, Pete Pappas.

Information about the high cost of prescription drugs in this country and the U.S. Food and Drug Administration's (FDA) efforts to discourage Americans from buying prescription drugs from Canada was collected from numerous sources, including the FDA's Web site; HealthCanada; Office of the Inspector General, U.S. Department of Health and Human Services; Congressional Research Service; the National Institutes of Health (NIH); and the U.S. Securities and Exchange Commission (SEC).

Sources for "Emergency in the ER" were numerous federal, state, and local records, including investigations by the Massachusetts Department of Public Health; data compiled by the Greater Cincinnati Health Council; reports by the General Accounting Office (GAO); congressional investigations such as "National Preparedness: Ambulance Diversions Impede Access to Emergency Rooms," by the Minority Staff, Special Investigations Division, of the Committee on Governmental Reform, U.S. House of Representatives, October 16, 2001; "Insured Americans Drive Surge in Emergency Department Visits," Issue Brief, No. 70, October 2003, Center for Studying Health System Change (HSC). Other sources for this section include author interviews and articles in newspapers and magazines.

Statistics used in the section on deaths caused by mistakes were drawn from the CDC and numerous studies in medical journals. The stories of Douglas Axen, Briana Baehman, Charles Cullen, Willie F. King, Kenneth Krutz, Edward Kyllonen, and Jennifer Rufer came from court records, state health department investigations, congressional hearings, hospital and state Web sites, and newspaper accounts. The *Chicago Tribune* published an extensive article on Kenneth Krutz's experience with the drug Cordarone.

Information in "Favors and Fraud" came from numerous court records. Among them: *U.S. vs. TAP Pharmaceutical Products Inc.* (No. 01-CR-10354-WGY), U.S. District Court for Massachusetts, Boston; *Congress of California Seniors vs. Pfizer Inc. and Parke-Davis,* Los Angeles County Superior Court; and *U.S., ex rel David Franklin vs. Pfizer Inc.* (Civil Action No. 96-11651-PBS), U.S. District Court for Massachusetts, Boston.

Details about the Medicare drug bill were gathered from hearings by congressional committees; data of the Center for Responsive Politics; documents of the U.S. Department of Health and Human Services; and public filings in the Senate Office of Public Records.

Information on HCA was obtained from SEC reports, U.S. Department of Justice releases, and court filings.

CHAPTER 2: WALL STREET MEDICINE

Material on Benjamin Lorello, Richard Scrushy, and HealthSouth came from various legal actions arising from the HealthSouth accounting litigation, as well as brokerage house reports, congressional hearings, newspaper articles, magazine stories, SEC filings, and professional journals. The litigation includes complaints by investors against HealthSouth and SEC civil and criminal proceedings against HealthSouth and its corporate officers. Among these actions: *In Re HealthSouth Corporation Securities Litigation*, CV-03-BE-1500-S, U.S. District Court, Northern District of Alabama; *United States of America vs. Richard M. Scrushy*, 03-CR-530-ALL, U.S. District Court, Northern District of Alabama, October 29, 2003; *Securities and Exchange Commission vs. HealthSouth Corporation and Richard M. Scrushy*, U.S. District Court, Northern District of Alabama, CV-03-J-0615-S; *United States of America vs. Emery Harris*, U.S. District Court Northern District of Alabama, CR-03-J-157-S; and Federal News Service, hearing before U.S. House Subcommittee on Oversight and Investigations of the House Committee on Energy and Commerce, November 5, 2003. Lorello's attire and fondness for strip clubs were described in a *New York Times* profile of April 8, 2003.

The campaign in Washington to promote for-profit, market-driven medicine beginning in the 1980s is documented in numerous contemporary sources, including reports by investment firms, professional journals, magazines, and newspapers. Part of the background on Alain Enthoven was found in *Promise and Power*, Deborah Shapley's biography of Robert S. McNamara. Information on the "body count" doctrine also came from *A Will to Measure: An Examination of Military Measures of Effectiveness*, published in *Parameters*, a publication of the U.S. Army War College.

The history of Tenet and information about other hospital chains were obtained from interviews, SEC filings, litigation, regulatory proceedings, brokerage house reports, and magazine and newspaper articles. The most complete rundown of legal actions against the company is found in 10-K and 8-Q reports filed with the SEC. Details of cardiac procedures at Tenet's Redding Medical Center are set forth in an October 29, 2002, affidavit of FBI agent Michael Skeen filed in U.S. District Court, Sacramento, California, as part of an investigation of Tenet's Redding Medical Center by the U.S. Department of Justice. The story of Lorraine Lydon is contained largely in her lawsuit against Palm Beach Gardens Community Hospital, Circuit Court of Palm Beach County, Florida, and in newspaper accounts. The *Orange County Register* is the source of material about Garden Grove Hospital. Details about corporate perks at Tenet came from SEC filings and newspaper articles.

The account of the disastrous attempt to build big physician practice management businesses (PPMs) was drawn from Wall Street investment house reports, SEC filings, professional journals such as *Modern Healthcare* and *Medical Economics*, and newspaper and magazine stories.

The analysis of changes that have swept hospitals in the era of free-market medicine was based on interviews with nurses and health care professionals as well as published studies. Numerous reports have documented these changes, but information provided by the Institute for Health & Socio-Economic Policy in Orinda, California, and its executive director, Don DeMoro, was especially helpful, as were the three nurses interviewed and quoted in this chapter, Sharon Penrod, Karen Higgins, and Trande Phillips.

CHAPTER 3: ANATOMY OF A SYSTEMS FAILURE

The story of KPC Medical Management and Dr. Kali P. Chaudhuri is documented in a series of bankruptcy cases and related civil lawsuits filed in U.S. Bankruptcy Court, Central District of California, Riverside Division; U.S. District Court in Riverside; and California Superior Courts in Riverside, San Bernardino, Orange, and Los Angeles Counties. These voluminous proceedings, which run to tens of thousands of pages, include the sworn declarations of doctors and patients, as well as depositions by many of the principals. These first-person accounts describe the daily operations of the Chaudhuri empire. Among the primary legal proceedings: *In re Chaudhuri Medical Corporation* (Case No. RS-00-26995-JB; jointly administered with Case Nos. RS-00-26996-JB through RS-00-27010-JB) in U.S. Bankruptcy Court in Riverside, and such adversary proceedings as *KPC Medical Management et al. vs. Pioneer Medical Group Inc. et al.*

Other sources include numerous related civil lawsuits, such as *Mary Hudson vs. KPC* (Case No. RCV-057423) at San Bernardino County Superior Court; interviews with health care officials in Hemet, Marcia Marcinko, and Iron Mountain officials; SEC filings; professional journals; and newspaper articles, notably from the *Press Enterprise* in Riverside and the *Orange County Register* in Santa Ana.

CHAPTER 4: THE LABYRINTH OF CARE

The case of Margaret Utterback is detailed in an investigative report by the California Department of Corporations after her death, which led to the fine of $1.1 million against the Kaiser Foundation Health Plan. The action is entitled *In the Matter of the Accusation and Notice of Intent to Assess Administrative Penalties Against Kaiser Foundation Health Plan, Inc.*, File No. 933-0055, May 12, 2000.

Data on health plans in the United States came from trade associations, professional journals, newspapers, and magazines. The statistic on the number of Seattle-area plans was in "Measuring the 'Managedness' and Covered Benefits of Health Plans," David E. Grembowski et al., *Health Service Research*, August 2000.

The limited ability of the U.S. health care industry to share computerized information is outlined in studies such as those of the Massachusetts Health Data Consortium, which was found at: www.mahealthdata.org/hipaa/resources/general/benefits.html.

Details and background about Milliman USA's length-of-stay guidelines were gathered from multiple sources: court actions, Web sites, newspaper and magazine stories, and interviews. Among the legal proceedings are *Musette Batas et al. vs. The Prudential Insurance Company of America*, Supreme Court of the State of New York, County of New York, Index No. 97/107881; *Thomas G. Cleary et al. vs. Milliman & Robertson Inc.*, District Court of Harris County, Texas, 99-56719; and *Charles B. Shane, M.D., et al. vs. Humana Inc. et al.*, MDL Litigation, 00-1334-MD-Moreno, U.S. District Court for the Southern District of Florida. Two articles that provided insights into the Milliman controversy were "Guidelines or Physician's Judgment?" *Texas Medicine*, July 2001, and "Coverage Denied? Why Your Insurance Company May Refuse to Pay for Your Child's Hospital Stay—And How You Can Protect Your Family," *Parenting*, April 2003.

Data on the costs of administering the U.S. health care system was drawn from "Costs of Health Care Administration in the United States and Canada," Steffie Woolhandler, M.D., M.P.H.; Terry Campbell, M.H.A.; and David U. Himmelstein, M.D., *New England Journal of Medicine*, August 21, 2003 (49:768–775). Data on projected savings from a single-payer system in Maine is from "Feasibility of a Single-Payer Health Plan Model for the State of Maine," Mathematica Policy Research, Inc., Princeton, NJ, December 24, 2002.

Many of the accounts by individual physicians of their experiences with downcoding and bundling are quoted from litigation that physicians and medical societies have filed against major insurers, as well as from professional journals. A number of these court actions have been consolidated as multidistrict litigation in Miami in *Charles B. Shane, M.D., et al. vs. Humana Inc. et al.*, MDL Litigation, 00-1334-MD-Moreno, U.S. District Court for the Southern District of Florida. Additional material came from the American Medical Association: "AMA Model Managed Care Contract, 2000, Description of Downcoding and Bundling," www.ama-assn.org/ama1/pub/upload/mm/368/supplement6.pdf. Background on ClaimCheck was found in both SEC filings and Wall Street analyst reports.

Interviews with call-center employees and industry consultants were a primary source for information about the call-center industry in the United States and abroad. The description of Kaiser's call center in Vallejo, California, came from interviews with nurses employed there. Details about U.S. health care call centers in India came from interviews with consultants and employees in the United States and India, and with voice trainers and call-center personnel in India. A series of papers by New Horizons Consulting, a Madison, Wisconsin–based consultant that assists American corporations in establishing operations in India, was especially helpful. Among New Horizons' reports: "The Offshore Outsourcing Opportunity in Healthcare Insurance" (2003); "State of the Industry & Market Dynamics for 2003 in Offshore Healthcare Business Process Outsourcing (BPO)"; "A Thought Leadership White Paper on Offshore Healthcare Business Process Outsourcing (BPO)." Other sources for this section included articles from newspapers, magazines, and Web sites both in India and the United States. The case of the Pakistani transcriber who threatened to post private patient records on the Internet was detailed in a *San Francisco Chronicle* story of October 22, 2003.

CHAPTER 5: MADISON AVENUE MEDICINE

Statistics on prescription-drug sales and hospital expenditures were drawn from a variety of sources, including the CDC, the Kaiser Family Foundation (*Prescription Drug Trends: A Chartbook Update,* November 2001), IMS Health Inc., and SEC filings.

The Listerine story is based on material from SEC filings; corporate histories; books (notably *The Medical Messiahs: A Social History of Health Quackery in Twentieth-Century America* by James Harvey Young, Princeton University Press, 1967); newspaper and magazine articles, such as "Pseudo Scientific Arguments in Advertising," *Advertising and Selling*, Feb. 23, 1937, p. 85; newspaper and magazine advertisements from the first half of the twentieth century; the Medicine and Madison Avenue Collection, a project of the National Humanities Center, the Digital Scriptorium, and the John W. Hartman Center for Sales, Advertising & Marketing History, Rare Book, Manuscript, and Special Collections Library at Duke University (http://scriptorium. lib.duke.edu/mma/ad-images).

The DES story is based on material from the *American Journal of Obstetrics & Gynecology* (June 1957); a report from the European Environment Agency, "The DES Story: Long-Term Consequences of Prenatal Exposure" by Dolores Ibarreta and Shanna H. Swan, Earthscan Publications, Ltd., May 1, 2002; *AMNews* (Aug. 4, 2003); Case No. 90,001, Supreme Court of Florida, *Susan F. Wood et al. vs. Eli Lilly and Co. and Upjohn Company Inc.;* and various newspaper and magazine articles.

Information on the fen-phen craze came from medical journals, including the *New England Journal of Medicine, Clinical Pharmacology and Therapeutics,* and *Journal of the American Medical Association*; the FDA; SEC filings; and newspaper and magazine articles. For the definitive word on this issue, there is one book: *Dispensing*

With the Truth: The Victims, the Drug Companies, and the Dramatic Story Behind the Battle over Fen-Phen, by Alicia Mundy.

The Lauren Hutton section is based on public relations releases, transcripts of TV programs, and newspaper and magazine articles. Information about Dr. Robert A. Wilson is drawn from his book, *Feminine Forever,* published in 1966 by M. Evans and Company Inc.

The discussion of Madison Avenue's move into the prescription-drug industry is based on information from SEC filings, Wall Street investment house reports, corporate Web sites, corporate public relations releases, newspaper and magazine articles, and television advertising transcripts.

Information on drug withdrawals from the market came from the FDA and SEC filings. Harry Loynd's quote about gullible doctors is from the book *Adverse Reactions* by Thomas Maeder, published in 1994 by William Morrow and Company Inc.

CHAPTER 6: THE REMEDY

The idea of a single-payer system in health care has been proposed for years by many different organizations and authorities, but the concept of a Federal Reserve System–style agency to administer such a system is our own. Medicare's low administrative costs have been documented in numerous studies, and the projected savings under a single-payer system have likewise been calculated in many reports, including "Feasibility of a Single-Payer Health Plan Model for the State of Maine," December 24, 2002, Mathematica Policy Research Inc.

Data on drug company earnings was derived from SEC filings and Wall Street analyst reports. Material on drug innovation came from "Changing Patterns of Pharmaceutical Innovation," National Institute for Health Care Management, May 2002. The study tracking the waning belief in market-based medicine to deal with health care's woes, "Are Market Forces Strong Enough to Deliver Efficient Health Care Systems? Confidence Is Waning," by the Center for Studying Health System Change, Washington, D.C., was published in *Health Affairs,* Vol. 23, Issue 2, March/April 2004.

Note on Internet Web sites: Given the ever-changing nature of the World Wide Web, some of the addresses in the text or in Notes may have changed or disappeared.

Acknowledgments

For the last fifteen years, many of the people we interviewed for stories on a broad range of subjects, from factory closings to corporate welfare, urged us to write about health care. Originally, we kept a mental record of the pleas. When they grew too numerous, we began jotting down notes. As time passed, we noticed that the subject came up constantly. No matter the issue at hand, the person being questioned, men and women, repeated the refrain: "When are you going to write about health care?" It is to these people, whose personal stories and frustrations were so poignant, that we feel especially indebted. Although some probably lost hope years ago of seeing anything in print, we hope this book will acknowledge our debt to them.

We also are indebted to countless health care workers—physicians, nurses, administrators, and technicians—for their observations and insights. We would like to thank all of them and others, from academicians to medical researchers, who gave so generously of their time to explain the intricacies of this immensely complex field. Most of these people must remain nameless, as the interviews with them were, for the most part, conducted on a background basis.

We owe thanks to many employees of federal, state, and local agencies who were helpful in locating and retrieving documents and reports. In particular, we would like to thank employees of the Massachusetts Department of Public Health, the Greater Cincinnati Health Council, the Minnesota Department of Health, and the American Medical Association.

Anyone who writes about health care benefits from the research of many specialized nonprofit organizations. So, too, did we, especially the work of the Henry J. Kaiser Family Foundation. We also benefited from the work of health care groups at the national and state level, among them Physicians for a National Health Program, the Institute for Health & Socio-Economic Policy, Public Citizen Health Research Group, Foundation for Taxpayer and Consumer Rights, Consumers Union, the Maryland Citizens' Health Initiative, the Center for Studying Health System Change, and from the work of numerous local medical groups, such as the Yuba-Sutter-Colusa County Medical Society in California. We owe special thanks to the staff and members of the California Nurses Association.

As has been the case for more than three decades, we are grateful for all the assistance provided by that unsung group, librarians everywhere, in towns and cities too numerous to mention, but especially the staffs of the government documents room at the Philadelphia Free Library and the Jenkins Law Library in Philadelphia.

At Doubleday, we have been very fortunate to have the support of Bill Thomas, editor in chief, who believed in this book from the start and made many valuable suggestions, and of Jason Kaufman, our editor, whose intellectual curiosity and edits made this a better book.

To Andrew Wylie, our agent, who urged us to examine the subject of health care, and to everyone at the Wylie Agency, especially Jeff Posternak, we are very grateful.

And finally, we are especially beholden to our most critical editors, Eileen Reynolds and Nancy Steele, our wives, whose thoughtful contributions are found on every page.

As always, whatever errors there may be, and we hope there are few, are attributable solely to us.

Index